Foreign Language Films
and the Oscar

Foreign Language Films and the Oscar

The Nominees and Winners, 1948–2017

MICHAEL S. BARRETT

McFarland & Company, Inc., Publishers
Jefferson, North Carolina

ISBN (print) 978-1-4766-7420-9
ISBN (ebook) 978-1-4766-3275-9

LIBRARY OF CONGRESS CATALOGUING DATA ARE AVAILABLE

BRITISH LIBRARY CATALOGUING DATA ARE AVAILABLE

Front cover: David Bennent in the 1979 German film *The Tin Drum*
(New World Pictures/Photofest)

Printed in the United States of America

*McFarland & Company, Inc., Publishers
Box 611, Jefferson, North Carolina 28640
www.mcfarlandpub.com*

For Roger, Julijs, Leo, Nancy
and a score of other true cinephiles

Table of Contents

Acknowledgments

Rather than using this space to thank the usual suspects—editors, family members, research assistants, volunteer readers—I wish to acknowledge a handful of people without whom this book would be, if not impossible, at least unlikely.

First, Stephanie Ogle, former proprietor of Cinema Books below the iconic Seven Gables Theatre in Seattle's University District, whose advice in 2010 led me to write this book. She coincidentally directed me to McFarland Publishers, for which I am most grateful.

Next, going back to the beginning, I'd like to acknowledge the late manager of the Varsity Theatre in Seattle, Lawrence J. McGinley, a dapper gentleman who had once worked for J. Arthur Rank and whose famous Connecticut family helped nurture the playwright Eugene O'Neill. Regardless of the infamous Seattle winter weather, McGinley would emerge from his theater attired in an usher's tux to regale those of us waiting patiently on line to buy tickets to the latest foreign blockbuster of the early 1960s. He was an inspiration and an abiding, dedicated cinephile. He died in 1968, age 74.

Third, the staff of the Whatcom Library System, Bellingham, Washington—in particular Beth Farley and Faye Fenske—for their remarkable assistance in dredging up hard-to-find films from library collections across the country, as well as those on local shelves. I would include the young staffs at the Seattle and Bothell campuses of the University of Washington and the Knight Library, University of Oregon, Eugene.

Another person who deserves acknowledgment is Jean Hersholt, the inimitable board member of the Academy of Motion Picture Arts and Sciences in Hollywood who suggested, when the Oscars were inaugurated in 1929, that they establish a category just for foreign films, although that didn't happen for another nineteen years.

Let me put in a kind word for the late, great Roger Ebert, whose insightful and detailed reviews for print and broadcast media since 1961 helped shape my own perspectives on the films I've catalogued. There were many excellent critics and reviewers, but in my opinion, Ebert was the best.

Here's a brief list of directors, living and dead, whom I would honor perfunctorily for making my movie watching so enjoyable over the years: Pedro Almodóvar, Gabriel Axel, Ingmar Bergman, Luis Buñuel, Vittorio De Sica, Federico Fellini, Miloš Forman, Marleen Gorris, Akira Kurasawa, Ang Lee, Caroline Link, Jiří Menzel, Istaván Szabó, Jacques Tati, Jan Troell, François Truffaut, Andrzej Wajda, just to name a few.

Today's wealth of online research materials and availability of films from libraries, streaming services and video outlets—not to mention the multitude of marvelous movie houses and cable channels I have exploited—make writing a book like this relatively easy, if labor and time intensive. Reviews, synopses, analyses and general discussions about foreign films are out there for anyone willing to hunt them down and study them, and I would encourage true cinephiles to do so.

Finally, I will honor my many film-going compatriots who encouraged me to complete this exercise from day one. I'll single out Rolin Miller, who participated from the beginning, who I'm sure would have broken my arm had I given up the project.

Introduction

When asked why I wanted to write a book about all the films nominated for a foreign-language Oscar during the past seventy years, I really didn't have a tidy answer. The subjective nature of the selection process and, indeed, partiality and occasional controversy created by politics or corrupt influences make the exercise a bit dodgy at best, or so some believe. Even so, it seemed the right thing to do when the idea first struck me in 2010.

Since 1960, I have been perfecting my ability to read subtitles quickly, or to understand the sometimes-incomprehensible parlance of Britain's Geordie, Black Country or Bow Bell dialects, by attending the latest film offerings at local art theaters. Starting with the English comedies of Ian Carmichael, Terry-Thomas, Alec Guinness and the Carry On gang, as well as darker, counterculture productions from working-class Britain, such as *Saturday Night and Sunday Morning* and *The Loneliness of the Long Distance Runner*, and moving on to West Germany's children-at-war tale *The Bridge*, Satyajit Ray's *Apu Trilogy* from India and the latest perplexing New Wave films of France and Italy, my teenage mind began to develop a particular and dedicated taste for cinema from abroad.

This is not to say I didn't enjoy noteworthy, old-fashioned American movies. If anything, my interest in the celluloid world was keen and voracious. I saw my share of dramas, comedies and musicals, whether in color or black and white, long or short, good or bad. But I couldn't help gravitating to the foreign fare whenever the urge grabbed me, and that was often. It should be mentioned that I wasn't alone in this; several others—notably a triumvirate of film buffs of similar age and mindset—were quick to seize on what was playing at the Varsity, Guild 45th, Edgemont, Ridgemont and other Seattle movie houses specializing in *auteur* films, or, a little later, to those films playing at university-sponsored cinematic series or "film festivals" with common themes, often national in nature. Thus were we introduced to swashbuckling Akira Kurosawa samurai movies, slice-of-life Federico Fellini flicks, introspective Truffaut features and inventive monochromatic melodramas from remote and reclusive places like Czechoslovakia, Poland and the Soviet Union. And I tried to go to all of them.

When I moved to New York City in the mid–1960s, I quickly discovered the Thalia and Elgin theaters, both of which often changed imported double bills every two or three days. You could see a heck of a lot of films in a matter of a few weeks just by following the highly graphic and informative fliers that appeared regularly around town.

Once overseas, I would carry on this obsession, but there—like here, with a mind-numbing overabundance of American movies to choose from—knowing what was good or mediocre without the sage advice of respected film critics or the enthusiastic word of mouth from peers was impossible. Two careers later, I would pick up where I left off with the advent of home video machines and independent film rental dealers, especially those specializing in offbeat and foreign flicks. The same applied when DVDs supplanted VHS tapes. Eventually, the local libraries began stocking up on imports, which were easily obtainable with a card, and they were *free*. Today, even the Internet can be a good source of hard-to-find foreign features, if you know where to look, and there's always Netflix, Amazon Prime, YouTube.com and similar sites doling out classic films for a nominal fee.

In short, viewing motion pictures from abroad has always been a passion of mine, and as this book attests, it continues to be. It's also a great time for film buffs, given the number of sources available nowadays.

So I've arrived at documenting sixty years of film-going, and what better place to begin but with the number-one movie promoter in the world, the Academy of Motion Picture Arts and Sciences (AMPAS).

This book concentrates solely on foreign-language films and their casts and directors whom AMPAS recognized for achievement in the cinematic art form between 1948 and 2017. They do not include nearly 2,000 motion pictures submitted for consideration, but only the 312 that have garnered nominations. How this worked is easily explained. From 1948 through 1956, the Board of Governors randomly chose a foreign-language film to honor. The rules changed in 1957 to allow any recognized nation to submit a feature for deliberation. Five selections were made annually by the Foreign Language Film Award Committee and these were turned over to the membership for a vote. Only those willing to view all contenders equally were given ballots.

Such is the subjective nature of the selection process—whether by committee or individual—and in a way, this is understandable, since it took the Academy two decades to get around to honoring foreign-language films at all.

In this book, we are excluding great, well-respected films that might normally have qualified under AMPAS rules except that they were never submitted for whatever reason. Examples include Federico Fellini's *La Dolce Vita* from Italy and François Truffaut's *Jules et Jim* from France, but there are dozens more. Contrariwise, a few films submitted but discounted by the judges enjoyed critical and public acclaim later. For instance, Sweden's *The Seventh Seal* was ignored in 1958, as was India's *The World of Apu* in 1960 and Italy's *La Notte* in 1962. More recently, *Wadjda*, a delightful feature from Saudi Arabia (one of only two submitted by that country to date) did not make it to the finals in 2014. Nor did France's *Elle*—a Golden Globe winner in 2017—despite the fact the star, Isabelle Huppert, was nominated for a Best Actress Oscar and had earlier won a Golden Globe in that category. *Elle*, itself, didn't even make the Academy's January shortlist.

"Foreign" movies were often ignored by Hollywood, and no specific category to cover the genre existed until 1948. So, such outstanding pre–World War II films as *M*, *The Blue Angel*, *Alexander Nevsky*, *Day of Wrath* and *Rules of the Game* were never nominated, nor even considered. One French feature, *Grand Illusion*—an antiwar and humanistic drama—was, however, and for Best Picture no less; it became in 1939 the first foreign-language flick to be so honored in the history of the event. Indeed, to date, nine foreign-language films have been tapped for Best Picture without winning. After *Grand Illusion*, they were *Z* (1970), *The Emigrants* (1972), *Cries and Whispers* (1974), *The Postman: Il Postino* (1994), *Life Is Beautiful* (1999), *Crouching Tiger, Hidden Dragon* (2001), *Letters from Iwo Jima* (2007) and *Amour* (2013); three of those—*Cries and Whispers*, *The Postman* and *Letters*—were never submitted for a Best Foreign Language Film award, while the others were.

Four other foreign-language films have been selected for other Academy Awards since the initial Oscar ceremony of May 16, 1929. *À Nous la Liberté* from France became the first honoree when it was a runner-up for a 1932 statuette in the Art Direction category. Three more received nominations in the Original Screenplay subgroup. They were *Marie-Louise* from Switzerland in 1946 and *Open City* from Italy and *Children of Paradise* from France, both in 1947—the year before a specific classification for Best Foreign Language Film was declared.

Then things changed. In its twentieth year of presentations, AMPAS decided to proffer an "Honorary Award" to the non–American producers of a movie deemed by the Academy's Board of Governors to be the best foreign film in a language other than English. After that first honorary award, the Oscar was conferred on the country of origin by way of the filmmaker. This went on every year except one until the twenty-ninth ceremony in 1957 when, for the first time, five foreign films were selected to vie for the annual honor.

The competition itself was highly regulated. Firm rules were established in which any recognized nation could submit a film, but it had to arrive at AMPAS in Los Angeles by a certain date and in a structured manner, the movie could not have dialogue with more than 49 percent English, and so forth. Richard Shale's *The Academy Awards Index* put it this way: "To be eligible, a film must have a soundtrack in the original language and carry English subtitles. Each country decides what film to submit to the Academy, and only one film is accepted annually from each country." Over the years, rules were tightened as more countries entered the submission process, sometimes finding themselves disqualified for infractions large or small. Rules were changed slightly now and then to accommodate ongoing controversial political and social circumstances. Today, under the title *Rule Thirteen*, AMPAS defines a foreign-language category submission as a "feature-length motion picture produced outside the United States of America with a predominantly non–English dialogue track." In order for it to be eligible, it "must be first released in the country submitting it" over one year up to September 30 and be shown for "at least seven consecutive days in a commercial" theater. The rule goes on:

1. Foreign Language Film nominations will be determined in two phases: a. The Phase I Foreign Language Film Award Committee will screen the original submissions in the category and vote by secret ballot. The group's top six choices, augmented by three additional selections voted by the Academy's Foreign Language Film Award Executive Committee, will constitute the

shortlist of nine films. b. The Phase II Foreign Language Film Award Committee will screen the nine shortlisted films in New York, Los Angeles and London and vote by secret ballot to determine the category's five nominees.

2. Final voting for the Foreign Language Film award shall be restricted to active and life Academy members who have viewed all five motion pictures nominated for the award.

3. The Academy statuette (Oscar) will be awarded to the motion picture and accepted by the director on behalf of the picture's creative talents. For Academy Awards purposes, the country will be credited as the nominee. The director's name will be listed on the statuette plaque after the country and film title.

Many films submitted did not measure up, were late, or the script just failed to appear; or it was found that the picture was not a product of the country submitting it or used too many actors and crew members from a neighboring nation; the script contained too little "foreign" language and therefore did not qualify; or even that the submitting country simply did not exist in the minds of the Academy members. But these were rare cases, and they are well documented by various source materials.

Since the first eight films were submitted for consideration in 1957, 118 nations have participated in the process by proffering 1,996 accepted feature motion pictures including a few odd documentaries. As said, five were selected each year for nomination with one exception: Uruguay's contribution in 1992 was first approved and then deemed in violation of a rule regarding origination (it belonged more to Argentina, which already had submitted a film) and could not be replaced in time; therefore, only four films were nominated that singular year. There has never been a case where a nation sent in two or more films in a single year, which would be in violation of the rules, and only one case in which a film was tendered and then disqualified because the country of origin didn't exist—this was the strange occasion when "Palestine" offered a movie before the territory was recognized as a legitimate government. Even so, Greenland, an autonomous territory of Denmark, and Puerto Rico, a protectorate of the United States, have had films admitted, and a feature was accepted from "the Palestinian Territories" a few years later. As mentioned at the outset, much of the Oscar process is highly subjective—in these cases, some might conclude, to a fault.

Every year, a new collection of outstanding foreign-language movies arrives on the AMPAS doorstep, and in recent years especially, countries that rarely, if ever, produced quality pictures have been presenting top-tier films for consideration. War-torn Yemen that some believe is a "failed state" came up with a submission for 2017. Paraguay made its debut in 2016, and the year before, four countries filed for the first time: Malta, Panama, Kosovo and Mauritania, the latter making it through to the nomination process with *Timbuktu*. In fact, there has been at least one inaugural submission each year since 2010.

There was a time when media gurus predicted an end to the celluloid industry, owing in part to the advent of television in the '40s and '50s. The end never came, of course, for a long list of reasons, but organizations such as AMPAS and a multitude of others, from Cannes to Canada, gave impetus to a host of movie makers to offer their best products for prizes. As political entities became nations and developed film industries of their own, the list of submissions grew until, out of 196 countries and a few territories and possessions in the world, a total of 118 have submitted at least one film since the 1948 ceremony. Leading the list was France, with sixty-four submissions, thirty-nine nominations and twelve wins; Italy with sixty-four submissions, thirty-one nominations and fourteen wins; and Japan, also with sixty-four submissions, but only fifteen nominations and four wins. Spain is next with sixty submissions, nineteen nominations and four wins, followed by Sweden with fifty-six, sixteen and three; Denmark with fifty-five, thirteen and three; Hungary with fifty-three, nine and two; and the Netherlands with fifty, seven and three. Three other countries—Israel, Mexico and India—have fifty submissions but no wins, although Israel has ten nominations. There are sixty-four countries (more than half) that have turned in films over the years without achieving even one nomination.

For my own amusement, and I hope yours, I have imposed a subjective "grade," based on a survey of each film viewed, and ranked it among its annual competitors, as appropriate. Of the 312, there were nine I could not position, since they were, as of this writing, virtually unobtainable for personal analysis. There is, however, enough information available to paint summaries, and if and when they should be found, future editions of this volume will correct the omissions.

Finally, it is worth mentioning that, unless otherwise noted, dates attached to films found in this book correspond to the years in which the titles *received their awards*, not in which they were made, released or nominated.

I am always open for comment, criticism, correction or communication and would love to hear from you. You can reach me at bestforeignfilm@gmail.com.

The Honorable Years:
1948–1956

(Unless otherwise noted, film dates correspond to the years in which the titles
were up for awards.)

The Iowan-born performer Conrad Nagel established himself as a matinee idol
and character actor during moviedom's crossover years between silent and sound,
appearing in 111 films. In 1927, he and thirty-five giants in motion pictures—including the likes of Douglas Fairbanks, Jr., Harold Lloyd and Mary Pickford—joined
forces to found a nonprofit, professional honorary organization to promote both creative and technical achievements of the industry. Nagel wanted to call it the Academy of Motion Picture Arts and Sciences *International*, recognizing all aspects
of worldwide moviemaking. For whatever reason, however, he was persuaded to drop
the "International," and for many years AMPAS appeared specifically dedicated to American films, with very few exceptions. Nagel served as AMPAS's president 1932–33
and hosted or cohosted the annual awards ceremony three times before his death in
1970.

Although a few foreign-language films were cited by the Academy in its first
nineteen years—notably *Grand Illusion*, nominated for Best Picture in 1939—nothing
much was put forward to honor non–English-speaking films at the Hollywood Oscar
ceremony. Other award festivals had been doling out prizes to global filmmakers since
the late '30s, and influential cinema organizations and media representatives were promoting the idea of an international Oscar award by the end of World War II, but to no
avail.

Then, for the twentieth ceremony February 15, 1948, the AMPAS Board of Governors decided to bestow a new Best Foreign Language Film Award on the Italian Neorealistic picture *Shoeshine*. This arbitrary process would carry on for eight of the next
nine years.

Dominating the early stages of the foreign-language category were two countries
practically destroyed during World War II: Italy and Japan, with war-ravaged France
close behind. One could argue that these three countries developed their damaged film
industries as quickly as possible in order to offer comfort and support to their belea-
guered populations. It's also true that out of the ashes of war came a crop of innovative
filmmakers champing at the bit to do something creative and useful, and this was shown

in the new styles of moviemaking under which they labored, fervently promoted and eventually attained undying fame.

In Italy, the movement was known as Neorealism (*Neorealismo*). Films were made on location—often with the scars of war as backdrops—and concentrated on the plight of the poor and working classes. Indeed, most directors used novice actors. In part, the purpose was to illustrate how World War II had affected the way people had to live and work in a devastated Italy.

In Japan, a slew of motion pictures was created against a background of economic deprivation and loss of face in war, but the three films gaining international recognition during this period harkened back to another age, the proud era of the samurai—the feudal warrior or vassal—steeped in supreme *Bushido* loyalty and valor, which buoyed the shamed population and salved their damaged egos. These *jidaigeki*, or period dramas, were the creations of overtly talented and equipped directors, screenwriters and producers who had lived through the war honing their skills as artists and entrepreneurs.

In France, a group of *auteurs*, meaning directors who controlled all aspects of their creative output, stylized what was called the French New Wave. They were social and political iconoclasts who experimented with new ways to shoot movies, again on location using handheld cameras, unusual lighting, innovative editing and loose, even improvised, dialogue.

Such were the global honorees for the first eight statuettes given out specifically to foreign-language films by the Academy from 1948 to 1956. (There was no honorary Oscar in 1953.) Although late in coming, the award probably made Conrad Nagel proud.

1948

B+   *Shoeshine*   Italy

We begin our journey of official Oscar recognition of non–English-speaking international films in 1948 with **Shoeshine**, an early directorial product of Italy's Vittorio De Sica. This edgy, black-and-white feature is one of the more respected Italian Neorealism films to follow the chaos and destruction of World War II and centers on two inseparable *ragazzi*, boys, who make a living shining shoes on the dusty, gritty streets of postwar Rome. Their aim is to buy a horse on the illegal black market, which they do, but a subsequent scam results in their arrest and incarceration in a draconian boys' reformatory, where they have a falling out. The hour-and-thirty-three-minute film, which De Sica said cost him a million lire ($4,000) to make, was released April 28, 1946, and came to the United States August 26, 1947, qualifying it under newly crafted rules for a "Special Award" Oscar at the awards ceremony, held in the Los Angeles Shrine Civic Auditorium March 20, 1948. The Academy was quoted as saying, "The high quality of this Italian-made motion picture, brought to eloquent life in a country scarred by war, is proof to the world that the creative spirit can triumph over adversity." Pauline Kael, the doyenne of mid-century movie critics, called *Shoeshine* "a social protest film that rises above its purpose." No other foreign film was proposed in this new category, a practice that continued for seven of the following eight years. Coincidentally,

Boys will be boys in Italy's postwar Neorealistic *Shoeshine* (1948), starring Rinaldo Smordoni (*left*) and Franco Interlenghi and directed by Vittorio De Sica.

Shoeshine (*Sciuscià* in Italian, and sometimes written in English with a hyphen) was nominated for a writing award, as was the French film *Case of the Nightingales*—the former for Original Screenplay and the latter for Motion Picture Story. De Sica, as will be highlighted elsewhere in this guide, was a major force in the world of motion pictures. Not only did his films receive two of the first three specifically foreign-language film honors, including *The Bicycle Thief* (1950), but two others—*Yesterday, Today and Tomorrow* (1965) and *The Garden of the Finzi-Continis* (1972)—won Oscars during the competitive, nominative days starting in 1957, and one other film, *Marriage Italian Style* (1966) was nominated but did not win. This film deserved a B+ in the research survey conducted for this book.

1949

B–   *Monsieur Vincent*   **France**

Monsieur Vincent from France was "voted by the Academy Board of Governors as the most outstanding foreign-language film released in the United States during 1948," which is the way the Academy of Motion Pictures Arts and Sciences (AMPAS) characterized approval of its official Special Award presentation at the brand-new Academy Award Theater in Hollywood during the twenty-first ceremony on March 24, 1949. The biopic, subtitled on the VHS version: "The Moving Story of Saint Vincent de Paul," tells the tale of the compassionate priest, "father of the poor," who was born in 1581, spent two years as a slave and went on to comfort thousands during a plague and perform numerous charitable works. The hour-and-fifty-one-minute, black-and-white film has marvelous acting and sets and was co-written by future playwright Jean Anouilh; Claude Renoir, Jean's nephew and artist Pierre-Auguste's grandson, served as cinematographer. It was directed by Maurice Cloche, his only contribution to the Academy. The picture opened November 5, 1947, and came to the United States in distribution December 20, 1948, an important element to qualify it for the 1949 honor and a B– rating in this study.

1950

A–   *The Bicycle Thief*   Italy

Vittorio De Sica, already an established actor, writer and director (*Shoeshine* 1948), graduated to producer for the 1950 honorary Special Award Oscar winner, **The Bicycle Thief** (*Ladri di biciclette*), which he also wrote and directed in the Italian Neorealism vein. Set also in war-torn Rome immediately after the armistice, the simple, humanistic film depicts a man's frantic attempt to retrieve a bicycle stolen from him just as he is about to start a new job that requires it. The stark street scenes, with their sweeping esplanades and byways filled with Romans trying to get along in desperate times, is a masterpiece marked by Carlo Montuori's cinematography and considered not only one of De Sica's best but, by many standards, among the greatest films ever made. Also known as *Bicycle Thieves*, the hour-and-twenty-nine-minute movie was released November 11, 1948, and in the United States December 13, 1949. The film was also nominated for writing in the Screenplay category along with another Italian film, *Paisan*, for its Story and Screenplay. The picture was made for an estimated $133,000, or nearly $1.5 million in today's currency. Graded here with an A–, the film is readily available in stores and libraries that feature classic movies.

1951

B+   *Walls of Malapaga*   France-Italy

Italy and France partnered to produce **The Walls of Malapaga** (*Au-delà des grilles* or *Le mura di Malapaga*), the 1951 selection by the AMPAS Board of Governors as the most outstanding foreign-language film released during the previous year. René Clément's hour-and-twenty-nine-minute tour de force, which thrust him into the global spotlight, starred Jean Gabin, France's answer to Clark Gable, as a murderer who escapes to Italy only to run into one difficulty after another, not the least of which is a romantic tryst with a waitress that affects her charming, but headstrong, daughter. The movie— which opened in Italy September 19, 1949, in France November 16, 1949, and in the United States March 26, 1950—was seen first in black and white without subtitles over a streaming website but made more sense when viewed again in a complete French-Italian version, and was given a B+. Clément would go on to receive the board's honor again in 1953 for *Forbidden Games* and later, in the first competitive season, garner a nomination for *Gervaise* (1957). Gabin starred in the 1939 drama The *Grand Illusion*, the first foreign-language film ever nominated by the Academy—but for "Best Picture."

1952

A+ *Rashomon* **Japan**

Truly one of the great films of all times, ***Rashomon*** was the first Japanese film to receive an Oscar, and deservedly so. Among director Akira Kurosawa's many splendid period masterpieces, this 1950 chef-d'œuvre is based on two short stories by the Japanese father of that genre, Ryonosuke Akutagawa, and takes place in the Heian period (8th-12th century) at Kyoto's main gate, *Rasho-mon*, during a time of civil strife. The city portal is significant as a refuge for thieves and cutthroats, a place to stash corpses or to leave unwanted babies—all of which figure into the film—and represents the moral and physical decay of Japanese civilization and culture of the era. The storyline is complex and the script well crafted; much has been written about this film, and imitations abound, but basically, it's about a rape and murder seen from four completely different perspectives and the unethical attempt to reconcile the surprise moral of the ending. Highlighting the acting as the bandit was a young Toshiro Mifune, whom Kurosawa would use over again in his swashbucklers, as well as modern-day features. Machiko Kyo was the ravaged woman and Takashi Shimura, perhaps best known as the leader of the famous (but not nominated) *Seven Samurai*, played the voyeur woodcutter. This was a movie one never tires of viewing. Indeed, even the lesser-known American version, *The Outrage*, with Paul Newman and Edward G. Robinson, is worth a gander. One of the few foreign films given

Toshiro Mifune and Machiko Kyo are problematic lovers in Akira Kurosawa's episodic Japanese classic *Rashomon* (1950).

an A+ in the research survey, *Rashomon* is definitely a must-see on any moviegoer's list. It runs an hour and twenty-eight minutes and cost about $250,000 to make. The motion picture—which opened in Japan August 25, 1950, and was first introduced in the United States December 26, 1951—also was nominated in the Art Direction-Set Decoration category for black-and-white films in the 1953 Academy Awards ceremony, as occasionally happened with foreign films—getting through the first review process and being nominated in other Oscar categories during different years. Kurosawa was responsible for five submitted films; two of them—*Dode'ka-den* (1972) and *Kagemusha* (1981)—received nominations. He also garnered a Lifetime Achievement Award in 1990. Kyo was in *Gate of Hell* (1955) and Shimura starred in *Kwaidan* (1965) and many of Kurosawa's long list of films, including *Kagemusha*.

1953

B+   *Forbidden Games*   France

Forbidden Games (*Jeux interdits*) garnered René Clément an "Honorary Foreign Language Film Award," as the Academy was calling it then, and was the French master's second Oscar in three years (*Walls of Malapaga* won in 1951 and *Gervaise* would receive a nomination in 1957). Made in France, it opened May 9, 1952, and was first seen in America December 8, 1952. The feature is about a young girl, orphaned by Nazi bullets, who gravitates into the lives of a poor urban family. It's tender, poignant and a little unnerving at times—especially scenes involving a dying and dead puppy—but thoroughly engaging nonetheless; a lot of love expressed in the family. Clément began a craze among pre–New Wave French *auteurs* for successfully using children in films, leading to Truffaut's unsubmitted *400 Blows* and beyond. The young boy was played by Georges Poujouly, who starred in the nominated film *Paix sur les Champs* (1971). The black-and-white motion picture, deserving of a B+, opened May 9, 1952, and in the States December 8, 1952, and it also received a nomination for Writing in the Story category the following year. It runs an hour and twenty-six minutes.

1954

—   None   —

No foreign-language film was selected for an honorary award 1954. No explanation was given, and it was the only year between 1948 and 1957 that no foreign feature was so designated.

1955

B   *Gate of Hell*   Japan

The Japanese know how to put on a costume drama, one with intrigue, death, deep emotions and lots of melodrama—read that: soap. ***Gate of Hell*** (*Jigokumon*) is all of that, and also the six-times-nominated *Fatal Attraction* (1987) in reverse. The protagonist Morito, whom we dislike from the start when he kicks a dog, is a high-level samurai, the Glenn Close character; Kesa, who is married to one of the emperor's guards, Wataru, is in the Michael Douglas role. The film, one of the earlier post–World War II *jidaigeki*, or "period drama," samurai films and an Oscar honoree in 1955, is set in very olden times (Heiji Rebellion of AD 1160). Thugs claiming to be revolutionaries raid the Kyoto fortress to kidnap the emperor and empress. The chaos of the attack is demonstrated by fluttering curtains as the palace staff races to escape. Kesa volunteers to pose as the empress and leave in the royal carriage, thus drawing the renegades away, a move that succeeds after a flurry of intense sword fighting. She eventually arrives at Morito's secluded home where, overwhelmed by the battle, she promptly faints. While trying to wake her, Morito becomes hopelessly smitten by her. The rest of the story is about his unabashed and oft-cruel means of winning her over, down to an agreement to help him murder her husband. To say more would give the ending away, but let it be said that it falls into the realm of Shakespearean, as so many Japanese movies of this ilk did. *Gate of Hell* was directed by Teinosuke Kinugasa in his only submission to the Academy. The film was in color, the first non-black-and-white offering of the honored foreign films, and it garnered a B in the survey. Incidentally, Kesa was played by Machiko Kyo, the woman in *Rashomon* (1952).

1956

A–   *Samurai I*   **Japan**

The Zen/Noh samurai films of the 1950s were hardly known or respected outside of Japan until director Akira Kurosawa and actor Toshiro Mifune became international stars in the 1952 honorary Oscar selection *Rashomon*, revered today as one of the more important and innovative flicks of the post–World War II period. But for American and other *gaijin* moviegoers, the point was well taken. Four years later, the first of three separate *jidaigeki* samurai films by Hiroshi Inagaki, **Samurai I: Musashi Miyamoto**, won an honorary Oscar, this being the last before the "Foreign Language Film Award" (aka "Best Foreign Film" or BFF) was introduced as an Oscar category with a strict nomination process through an AMPAS committee. All three Inagaki motion pictures starred Mifune as Miyamoto, an orphaned small-village brute bent on becoming a respected samurai sans credentials, but also a superman in his well-tested abilities to win battles despite impossible odds. What's more, he shunned women, even though they begged him and his muscular frame to—as one character exclaims—"take me, do whatever you want with me." There's nothing particularly remarkable about *Samurai I* except its vibrant color; lush, summery, rural landscapes; *in situ tableaux* post-battle scenes; and the macho *Bushido* conduct of the warrior class—read that: the good guys. The hour-and-thirty-three-minute picture, which earned an A–, opened September 26, 1954, and came to the United States November 18, 1955. Besides Mifune—also cast in *Rashomon* and the 1962-nominated Mexican entry *Ánimas Trujano: El hombre importante*—the movie starred Rentaro Mikuni; he was also in *The Burmese Harp* (1957) and *Kwaidan* (1966). By the way, television's Turner Classic Movie (TCM) channel has shown this film along with the second and third movies in the trilogy, *Samurai II: Duel at Ichijoji Temple* and *Samurai III: Duel at Ganryu Island*, neither of which received an Oscar nomination nor was submitted for one. It's interesting to note that of the eight films that garnered honors as best foreign films between 1947 and 1957, three of them were from a war-battered and struggling Japan—that's saying something.

Making Waves:
1957–1967

International films entered a new era in the late 1950s, and the Academy of Motion Picture Arts and Sciences moved to acknowledge this by making as a permanent fixture at the annual awards ceremony a new category called the Best Foreign Language Film. Up through 1956, Academy members chose one foreign film to honor, and that was it. By 1957, however, countries other than the United States and Britain were committing more time and resources to their fledgling film industries—some of them state-sponsored propaganda machines, it's true, but others devoted to making art for art's sake.

The Academy decided to receive one submission a year from any legitimate nation other than the United States as long as the film was in a language other than English, or at least with limited English, and predominately produced by the country of origin. It had to have subtitles and arrive by a certain date for the Board of Governors or Foreign Language Film Committee to view and grade it. From the motion pictures that met all criteria the Academy selected five contenders for the Oscar and members voted by secret ballot for a winner.

In this next section, and subsequent chapters, we'll take a look at the five films per annum that received Best Foreign Film (BFF) nominations. Every year there was only one winner, but to make it more interesting, the author begs to interpose his own ranking to each of the five, and it will be discovered that the Academy and writer do not always agree; indeed, some films to which the Academy members gave Oscars might find themselves here mere also-rans. In this regard, the motion pictures reviewed in this book will be rated from A to D and, taken together annually, be ranked in grade order. It would be nice if we could count the ballots of all of the voting Academy members to see just how diverse, let alone subjective, the evaluations were.

At the 29th annual Academy Awards—held March 27, 1957, in the RKO Pantages Theatre, Hollywood, California—the first foreign-language winner was announced by Academy President George Seaton. A total of eight countries submitted features for consideration in this first competitive year. Chosen were the pictures from Denmark, France, Germany, Italy and Japan. The other three films came from the Philippines, Spain and Sweden.

1957

A	*La Strada* (winner)	**Italy**
A–	*The Burmese Harp*	Japan
A–	*Gervaise*	France
B	*The Captain from Köpenick*	West Germany
—	*Qivitoq*	Denmark

Federico Fellini, undoubtedly one of the most revered movie makers in history, must have felt highly optimistic about the fifth film he made as a director, *La Strada*, when he submitted it to the Venice Film Festival a full three weeks before its public premiere on September 22, 1954. Even though it had not yet appeared in a theater, it garnered the Silver Lion Award. But he didn't stop there; Fellini presented it to a multitude of prize screenings to huge acclaim and success, culminating in the first-ever competition for Best Foreign Film in Hollywood. At the heart of the black-and-white film is Gelsomina, played by Fellini's wife Giulietta Masina, who is sold by her mother to a traveling strongman (Anthony Quinn), who treats her as his property. The two perform in town squares for donations until they join a small circus, where a tightrope walker (Richard Basehart) opens the simple girl's eyes to her sorry fate. Things go badly

Giulietta Masina, wife of director Federico Fellini, plays the wayward Gelsomina in his 1957 winning foreign film *La Strada* (1954).

from there. The author has seen the film numerous times, and followed suit with the ranking of a solid A. It also received a nod for Writing–Original Screenplay, which the wonderful French film *The Red Balloon* won. It should be noted two other foreign films that year were considered for Writing–Motion Picture Story: *The Proud and the Beautiful* (Jean-Paul Sartre, France) and *Umberto D.* (Cesare Zavattini, Italy). The marvelous Japanese film *Seven Samurai* was nominated for Costume Design–Black and White. Oddly none of these other non–English-speaking features was considered in the Best Foreign Film (BFF) category. This first competitive Oscar was presented to the *La Strada* production company headed by producers Agostino "Dino" De Laurentiis and Carlo Ponti. When called up to receive the two statuettes, De Laurentiis made a point to acknowledge Fellini for his work. It would be the only time the production company was so honored; henceforth, the Oscar would be presented to the film's country of origin with the statuette going to the director. Fellini, himself, won a Lifetime Achievement Award in 1993.

Foreign movies began turning up weekly in urban art theaters at the start of the '60s and it didn't take long for us to pick up on anything British, French, Swedish or Italian. Among our favorites as adolescents, however, were the Japanese samurai flicks; we looked forward to the swashbuckling movies starring Toshiro Mifune, Takashi Shimura, Bokuzen Hidari (Bokuzen Hidari?), et al. However, we weren't expecting what Kon Ichikawa served up when we first viewed **The Burmese Harp** (*Biruma no tategoto*) or, three years later, his *Fires on the Plain*. These were antiwar films of the first caliber: raw, contrite and without a hint of romance. It was, after all, less than a dozen years since the end of World War II. *The Burmese Harp* (aka *Harp of Burma*) involves two platoons of soldiers. One, when told the war is over, lays down its arms to Anglo-Australian forces. The other holes up in a cave, refusing to surrender as per the *Bushido* Code of "honor unto death." Mizushima is the harpist for the musical first group, and he's dispatched by his victors to try to convince the recalcitrant cave-dwellers to surrender. Using the harp (it figures in the movie not only as a musical instrument but also as a signal of danger or safety), he fails in his attempt and is actually shot at by his desperate countrymen. Eventually he makes it to the cave, but when he tries to launch a white-flag surrender, he is beaten. The platoon fights on and is devastated; only Mizushima survives. He steals a monk's robe and becomes a sort of self-guided holy man and dedicates the rest of his existence burying as many corpses as he can as a means of spiritual healing. His platoon learns of this through a long letter read by the captain aboard a ship headed back to Japan. As Ichikawa himself proclaimed: "The film is about hope in the best sense, hope for mankind." Ichikawa—one of the Four Horsemen of Japanese cinema that included Akira Kurosawa, Keisuke Kinoshita and Masaki Kobayashi—had three of his films submitted for consideration by the Academy, but this was his only nomination. The first part of the hour-and-forty-eight-minute picture opened January 27, 1956, and the second part twenty-two days later, but the stark black-and-white film as a whole, garnering an A– here, was not distributed in the United States until April 28, 1967. Starring was Rentaro Mikuni, also cast in *Samurai I* (1956) and *Kwaidan* (1966).

To say **Gervaise**, France's entry in the 1957 Oscar race, is a downer is like calling *Star Wars* a movie about space—there's more to digest here than meets the eye. The focus of the drama is on the title's heroine, Gervaise Marquart, a club-footed washerwoman played by the incomparable Austrian actress (and sister to Max) Maria Schell and her many emotional ups and downs in a sordid, late-19th-century Montmartre slum. In a nutshell (no pun intended), she marries and has two children by a philanderer who leaves her for another; she remarries and has a little girl, this time by a weak, accident-prone alcoholic, who happens later to invite her first husband—recently jilted by the floozy for whom he'd left Gervaise—to come live with them; her second husband soon goes on a binge, wrecks her laundry business and dies in hospital. Her future prospects shattered, Gervaise turns to drink herself and begins to neglect her children.

Title character Gervaise, played by Maria Schell, collects laundry for her business in a scene from René Clément's third honored foreign film *Gervaise* (1956).

Yes, a shame, but even so.... Owing primarily to excellent directing and acting, this hour-and-fifty-six-minute, black-and-white film by Réne Clément—his third-consecutive honor after *The Walls of Malapaga* 1951) and *Forbidden Games* (1953)—rates an A–. As the longtime *New York Times* late film critic Bosley Crowther pointed out, "'Gervaise' [is] a deeply moving flow of human revelation." This is true. Based on Émile Zola's novel *L'Assommoir*, the picture opened August 3, 1956, and came to the United States November 11, 1957. The cast included François Périer from *Nights of Cabiria* (1958).

The Captain from Köpenick (*Der Hauptmann von Köpenick*), a hard-to-find foreign film nominee from West Germany, is a thoroughly pleasant, often hilarious and sometimes sad tale of a hapless shoemaker who finds a reluctant home in prison because bureaucracy and prejudice won't allow him to obtain a residency permit, passport or job—and even issues him an expulsion order—in late 19th-century Germany. The militaristic element is evident here, a mere decade after the fall of the Third Reich. But that's not the point. Willem is innovative, ambitious and conniving to the point that he buys a less-than-perfect captain's uniform, hijacks two units of soldiers returning to barracks and invades the town of Köpenick to arrest the mayor and all who made him a virtual man without a country or town. There are marvelous scenes: In one, the real captain desperately goes to the tailor for a new uniform he needs, but it doesn't show up on time; he tries on his old, ill-fitting uniform and it is ripped, so he discards it (is it the one Willem buys on the streets?) just as the tailor shows up. In another scene, Willem is welcomed by his brother-in-law, even though his sister seems cold and uncertain. Among the best segments are those involving his command of the weary troops and marching them to City Hall. The film, which justifies a B, was based on a play performed in 1931 as Hitler's Nazi party was coming into power, and it showed. The first question a soldier asks a civilian is whether they served in the military, because only if they have are they acceptable. The VCR tape came from Augustana College in Rock Island, Illinois, and was on its last legs: the color washed out, the white subtitles difficult to read and full of streaky scratches throughout. VCR tape is proving as fleeting as real cellulose acetate; after all, it runs over rollers and heads. There can only be so many times this can happen before the tape goes bad. It is only hoped these films/tapes are sooner than later converted to laser-read DVDs. The hour-and-thirty-three-minute film was made by Helmut Käutner, his only submitted entry, and opened August 16, 1956, and in America July 25, 1958.

Qivitoq translates from the Inuit Kalaallisut language to "wandering spirit" and refers to a person humiliated enough by his peers to seek solace among the icy peaks of Greenland. It is also the name of a rare Danish-language film that received a 1957 nomination. Completely filmed on location, it's the story of a young Danish teacher named Eva who comes to Greenland to surprise her physician fiancé only to discover he's marrying his attending nurse instead. Mortified, the woman heads for another small fishing village where she's taken in by a grouchy outpost trader named Jen to await the arrival of a ship to take her home. During the wait, the two fall in love. Meanwhile, a true *qivittoq* (proper spelling), a hopeful fisherman who is bullied by villagers, heads out on a glacier where he finds and saves Jen from certain death. That makes the young man an instant hero. But when Jen returns to his outpost, he finds that the rescue boat has sailed and Eva with it. Or so he fears. *Qivitoq* celebrated its fiftieth anniversary with a newly restored print on DVD. Those lucky enough to find a copy raved at the color and how beautiful the Greenlandic scenery was, and how the story diplomatically balanced Danish colonization with the Greenlanders' acceptance of it (Greenland is an autonomous region of Denmark). The film is unrated here; it is one of the few unseen films on the entire list, although a good portion of it was once viewable on YouTube.com. In addition, copies were available at the University of Michigan and Gordon College in Massachusetts, both in European format. The film itself runs a minute short of two hours and opened in Denmark November 6, 1956, but never reached distribution in the United States. Erik Balling was the director, and he had one other film submitted but not nominated.

1958

A	*Nights of Cabiria*	**Italy**
B	*Gates of Paris*	France
B–	*Nine Lives*	Norway
C–	*Mother India*	India
C–	*The Devil Strikes at Night*	West Germany

Giulietta Masina's doe eyes and fragile demeanor are on full display in her director-husband Federico Fellini's masterpiece and 1958 Best Foreign Film *Nights of Cabiria* (*Le notti di Cabiria*). Fellini's second win in a row (*La Strada* was the first of all *nominated* winners in this category), *Nights of Cabiria* is about a Chaplinesque prostitute seeking true love on the seedier side of Rome during the gritty, desperate postwar period in Italy. Cabiria may be a hooker, but—quoting Fellini via Charlotte Chandler in *I, Fellini*—"her basic

Federico Fellini's *Nights of Cabiria* (1957) won a second statuette for the Italian director, in great part because of the acting of his real-life wife, pixie-like Giulietta Masina (shown here).

instinct is to search for happiness as best she can," surviving on the streets and the little hovel of a home she occupies. "She wants to change, but she has been typecast in life as a loser. Yet she is a loser who always goes on to look again for some happiness." The hour-and-fifty-minute movie, in stark neorealistic black and white, was scripted by Pier Paolo Pasolini with music by Nina Rota. It was later adapted to the 1966 Broadway stage under the title *Sweet Charity*. Also in the film cast was François Périer, known for *Gervaise* (1957) and *Z* (1970). This film, which opened first in France October 16, 1957, and in the United States twelve days later, definitely deserved its Oscar and an A. Fellini films would go on to win two more Oscars: *8½* (1964) and *Amarcord* (1975). He was also nominated for Best Director for *La Dolce Vita* (1962), a film oddly never submitted in the foreign category. Masina, of course, was also in *La Strada*.

Gates of Paris (*Porte des Lilas*) featured an ensemble cast, including balladeer Georges Brassens, acclaimed actors Pierre Brasseur and Henri Vidal and pixielike Dany Carrel as the love interest and was directed by René Clair in his only submitted foreign film. Telling a simple story that takes place on a street in the farthest Right Bank arrondissement, the last of twenty, the black-and-white film is about a drunkard nicknamed Juju who lives in a ramshackle house with The Artist (Brassens), a guitar player who plays to the scant regulars in the community bar where Carrel works. The ne'er-do-well Brasseur fancies the girl, who happens to be the proprietor's daughter. (Carrel reminds one of Giulietta Masina who starred in Fellini's winning films for 1957 and 1958, *La Strada* and *Nights of Cabiria*.) The barmaid teases Brasseur but offers no more than pecks on both cheeks. Meanwhile, a murderer escapes the police by hiding in the hovel's cellar, where he inveigles the oaf and The Artist into taking care of him. When the girl discovers him, this "Don Juan" seduces her. The bum finds out and, in a surprise twist by Clair, he turns on his guest with vengeance and walks away none the worse for wear. There are some excellent set pieces in the hour-and-thirty-five-minute film: for example, the street urchins mimicking a slapstick police search and Brasseur attempting to climb over a rickety fence; in addition, the editing keeps the story moving linearly without a bump and uses well-positioned fade-outs and fade-ins. This was one of the hard-to-find films that just popped up one day on YouTube.com. A B film, it opened in Italy September 20, 1957, in France five days later, and in the United States January 14, 1958.

Norwegian Arne Skouen was no stranger to the film-award circuit by the time his black-and-white heroic drama **Nine Lives (Ni Liv)** was nominated for an Oscar. It's the true story about resistance fighter Jan Baalsrud and his 1943 escape through Nazi lines and over cold, icy mountains to neutral Sweden after a failed attempt to blow up a German air traffic control tower. The film—seen over an online site in oddly disordered but good-quality segments and, yes, English subtitles—is considered by Norsemen as the best film Skouen, and perhaps any Norwegian, has ever made, according to author John Sundholm. The director began his career in 1949 and was famous for anti–Nazi movies he churned out year after year, many such as *Nine Lives* qualified to be shown at the famous French film festival at Cannes. Some of the outdoor photography resembled at times the set-up chase shots of American Westerns. Repeated shots detected by unique cloud formations appear to have been filmed at different locations and times. Struggling in deep snow high above tree line, the actors abruptly make their way through a forest of scraggly trees. But photography aside, this is one hell of a rah-rah film that celebrates man's ability to endure the ravages of severe weather and war and still survive. It merits a B–. Skouen had another feature submitted the following year but it was not nominated. *Nine Lives* opened in Norway October 3, 1957, and in New York City January 5, 1959. It runs an hour and thirty-six minutes.

Mother India, the *Gone with the Wind* of the Subcontinent, was tagged for a possible Oscar in 1958 and can usually be found online free, as are so many Indian films from that era. The story is about a village woman named Radha who, with her disabled husband, is rearing two sons, one bad and the other good. She inherits debt and falls victim to the vile moneylender, and it's only by her strength, courage and connection that she's able to succeed. Call it an allegory about India struggling for independence from Great Britain. The epic drama, laced with comedy and Bollywood music, is five minutes short of three hours long and in Gevacolor, an unstable process favored by Bombay's film industry at the time. It was directed by Mehgoob Khan, his only submission, and premiered in India February 14, 1957; it wasn't until August 23, 2002—forty-five years later—that it found distribution in the States. It warranted a C–.

It took the postwar German film industry a long time to catch up with the rest of Western Europe. Nevertheless, when a notable release got attention, the West Germans were quick to place it on the Oscar list, and 1958's strange pairing of Nazis and a serial killer was no exception. **The Devil Strikes at Night** (*Nachts, wenn der Teufel kam*), directed by Robert Siodmak, is set in Hamburg and resembles the British television series *Foyle's War* in that a police chief inspector attempts to solve a civil crime while surrounded by the Gestapo. The two-hour-and-twenty-two-minute, black-and-white film is rough and pretentious, with obvious fake scenery, poor lighting, odd angles and gorgeous actors; one might dispute Bruno, a central character who in another time and

A sinister Mario Adorf plays serial killer Bruno Lüdke in the West Germany thriller *The Devil Strikes at Night* (1957).

country might have been played by William Bendix, of being anything but beautiful, but in his way, he might be the best of the bunch, with his muscular physique, broad shoulders and laborer's features. He also serves as the comic relief, notoriety notwithstanding, and there's a comedic element in this otherwise deadly serious film—subtle as it is. One example would be when a prim and perfect Gestapo *gruppenführer* snakes into the room full of Nazis and cops and everyone gives the "Heil Hitler!" sign, including Bruno even though his hands are manacled in front of him. *Devil* is not worth more than a C–. It was difficult to find but eventually located, complete and solely in German, off one of the computer streaming services. West Germany, until united with East Germany in 1990, put out nominees every year from 1957, when the five-a-year system went into effect, to 1960. Of those four contenders, only *The Bridge* was a credible offering. It would be 1974 before another West German film made it to the Academy Awards, and there was no Oscar winner until 1980 with *Tin Drum*. Siodmak had no other foreign film submissions to the Academy, although his directorial credits included U.S.-made pictures *The Killers* (Best Director nomination) and *The Spiral Staircase*, both up for awards in 1947. *Devil* opened September 19, 1957, and came to New York City January 29, 1959.

1959

A+	*Mon Oncle*	France
A	*Big Deal on Madonna Street*	Italy
B–	*Arms and the Man*	West Germany
C–	*Road a Year Long*	Yugoslavia
—	*La Venganza*	Spain

There's no getting around it: **Mon Oncle** may be the author's favorite comedy of all time. The French winner for 1959 is one of only a handful of films made by comic genius Jacques Tati. Its predecessor, *Mr. Hulot's Holiday*, released in 1953 *before* foreign competition for Oscar began, may arguably be funnier over all, but *Mon Oncle* has the best sight gags. Tati, himself a visual gag with his fedora, long-stemmed pipe, bowtie, ankle-length raincoat and hiked-up pants, relied heavily on sidesplitting humor and limited dialogue for his laughs. It's the punchy japes in *Mon Oncle* that stand out: the wacky fish fountain that squirts a pathetic jet of water into the air whenever turned on for guests; the ultra-materialistic but sterile home with all its ludicrous contraptions; the house's upstairs porthole windows in which silhouetted heads become searching eyeballs; the plastic tubing, extruded from its Rube Goldberg–like machine, looking like white wiener links; the juvenile joke of whistling at people and causing them to bump into a telephone pole. One never tires of the carefully orchestrated silliness. It's one of only three films in this book to garner an A+. It cost Tati roughly $60,000 ($500,000 in today's money) to make

French comedian Jacques Tati pedals his onscreen nephew, played by Alain Bécourt, around town in *Mon Oncle* (1958), arguably one of the funniest movies ever made.

the hour-and-fifty-seven-minute picture, which opened May 10, 1958, and later, November 3, 1956, in the United States.

Nothing goes right in the Italian caper movie **Big Deal on Madonna Street** (*I soliti ignoti* or *The Usual Suspects*). It's a real slapstick farce, which might have done better among Academy voters had it not been up against Jacques Tati's wonderful comedy (see above). In the liner notes, film historian Bruce Eder wrote, *Madonna* "is that genuine rarity in popular culture" that includes Italian Neorealism and French and American *film noir*, but it is consistently hilarious in both dialogue and action. A group of petty thieves in economically tough postwar Rome searches for someone willing to take the place of their failed car-thief friend, now in prison, so he can complete an elaborate plan to rob a pawnshop safe by tunneling from the vacant apartment next door. The element of political satire is rife, since the pawnshop is supposedly operated by the government. Each of the characters—two of them played by Marcello Mastroianni and Vittorio Gassman—has a quirk that makes him stand out and it's this ensemble acting that moves the story along. While the conclusion of the film is arguably one of the funniest scenes in all of cinema, the boggled planning and misfit behavior leading up to the caper will keep the viewer in stitches. This hour-and-forty-six-minute film rates a solid

A. It first opened September 19, 1958, and had a run in New York City starting November 22, 1960. The director, Mario Monicelli, was also nominated the next year for *The Great War*, later for *The Girl with the Pistol* (1969), and later still for part of the multistoried, anthology film *Viva Italia!* (1979). Mastroianni starred in *8½* (1964), *Yesterday, Today and Tomorrow* (1965), *Marriage Italian Style* (1966) and *A Special Day* (1978). Gassman, with 128 acting credits to his name, was also in *The Great War*, *Scent of a Woman* (1976), *Viva Italia!* and *The Family* (1988).

A rare find online well into the film research project put one in touch with *Helden*, a film play based on George Bernard Shaw's **Arms and the Man**, and the West Germany entry. Raina, played by Jane Wyatt-lookalike Liselotte Pulver, and Captain Hauptmann Bluntschli, sort of a Ronald Colemanish Otto Fischer, stand out as would-be lovers during and immediately after the Bulgarian-Serbian war of 1885. Shaw's humor, along with farce and horseplay, hold sway, and cross-functional characterizations are typical of his later stuff. Indeed, staging and dialogue were Shaw through and through. The scene is set in 19th-century Bulgaria with sweeping moustaches on Raina's father, the soldiers and the portrait of the reigning Bulgarian Orthodox Archbishop on the family-room wall. The film is a B− nominee, in part because of the long stationary shots as fixed as a stage-play film and fact it was produced with no close-ups, minimalist settings and unconventional music. Directed by Franz Peter Wirth in his only submitted foreign film, the hour-and-thirty-six-minute picture opened in West Germany November 20, 1958, and in New York City February 23, 1962, more than three years later.

One of the founders of Italian Neorealism in film, Giuseppi De Santis over four years put together a script and cadre of mostly Italian actors and traveled to Istria in today's Croatia to film the Yugoslavia entry **Road a Year Long,** one of the harder-to-find films in the nearly seventy years of foreign submissions. The story is simple: Inhabitants of the isolated fictional village of Chiaravalle request that the government build a connecting road to the main highway that leads to the city, but no funds are available. So Emil, pickaxe in hand, takes it upon himself to begin construction. Despite official interference and chronic cynicism, the villagers join in until quite a crowd is heaving and hoeing along the barren mountainside. The cast includes all the usual characters: the righteous officials, the macho leaders, the dubious but submissive wives, the village prostitute, the naïve young bucks, the town drunks (which appear to include them all). The two-hour-and-forty-two-minute, black-and-white film, in Italian, could be viewed as an antigovernment production, but De Santis, while characteristically nonconformist when it came to making turgid, overdramatized propaganda flicks, was also a Communist dedicated to making populist films. He fought against Nazi censorship during the war. There's a bit of flag-waving in this effort, but it's considered neither mainstream nor leftist. The acting appears barely sufficient, the cinematography is not too inspiring, and at times it's difficult to empathize with the people's plight. And that may be some of the reasons this is a film you have to go far out of your way to see. It received a C−. Obscure as this film is, it's worth noting how many working titles it has; originally titled *Chiaravalle Goes to the Valley*, it is also known as *Cesta duga godinu dana* in Croatian, *La Strada lunga un anno* in De Santis' native Italian, and *The Year-long Road* wherever the others don't fit. It opened in Yugoslavia July 12, 1958, but did not include general distribution in America; indeed, it only appeared in Argentina and Hungary over three years. Oh, and one last thing: For what it's worth, it did *win* the Golden Globe in 1959 for Best Foreign Film, tied with *Das Mädchen Rosemarie* and *L'Eau vive*, so some people must've liked it. In the cast was Branko Tatic from *The Ninth Circle* (1961).

Another *Romeo and Juliet*? one asks about an obscure Spanish movie set in rural La Mancha. It's called **La Venganza** (Vengeance) and the film itself has a story more interesting than what's written on the script. It was directed by Juan Antonio Bardem—Javier's uncle—who fought the censors all the way to the box office because, after all, Spain was still under the dictatorship of Francisco Franco. It seems the Nationalist strongman and his henchmen did not like the movie's theme, basically about a clash of cultures just as potent as Catalonia's continued attempts to gain autonomy from the rest of Spain. In *La Venganza*, a man is imprisoned for ten years for a murder he didn't commit. When he gets out, he joins his sister in a plot to wreak vengeance on his informer, but before that can happen, the sibling falls in love with the accuser and the plan goes awry. The script was rewritten several times to appease the censors—even the original title, *Los Segadores*, was changed because those in charge thought it a reference to the anti–Fascist anthem of repressed Catalonians—and the final release date was delayed a year. Where to see it? According to WorldCat.org (a website dedicated to listing titles of books, films and other media and where to find them), DVDs are available at the University of Wisconsin–Madison and Dickenson University in Carlisle, Pennsylvania; a VHS tape is in the Dartmouth College library in New Hampshire; and copies are available in Europe. The author declined to rate it, since it was not viewed in full before this book was published; only a six-minute trailer and a couple of one-minute clips were found online to give a gist of the story. The film, which opened first in the Netherlands January 8, 1959, in Spain February 16, 1959, but not in the United States in regular distribution, runs two hours and two minutes in length. Bardem made Spain's second, third and fourth submitted films, but only this one in the middle made it to nomination. In the cast was Italian actor Raf Vallone, who appeared in a number of Western Oscar nominees, including *El Cid*, *The Cardinal* and *The Godfather: Part III*, among others.

1960

A–	*Black Orpheus*	**France**
A–	*The Bridge*	West Germany
B+	*The Village on the River*	Netherlands
B	*The Great War*	Italy
C	*Paw (Boy from Two Worlds)*	Denmark

Bossa Nova, that irresistible, rhythmic music imported from Brazil in the early '60s, largely emerged on the back of the brilliant Marcel Camus' film **Black Orpheus** (*Orfeu Negro*), the winner of the 1960 foreign Oscar. The color film was shot entirely in Rio de Janeiro in Portuguese but was entered by France, Camus' home base. It was not received well by all critics, many of whom were entrenched in the French New Wave at the time and viewed this film as too metaphysical and fantastical, laced with false humanism. In other words, it wasn't *400 Blows* or *Breathless*, but a rather naïve,

Surrounded by unidentified passengers, trolley conductor Orfeo (Breno Mello) appears happy as a lark during Carnival time in the Brazilian musical drama *Black Orpheus* (1959).

mythological representation based around the gaiety, color and supposed apprehensions generated by Rio's famous Carnival. Music is key, and the consistent samba beat and "new trend" *bossa nova* that made composers Antonio Carlos Jobim and Luiz Bonfá famous outside Brazil can almost be considered the stars. The real leads are Breno Mello playing Orpheus and, as Eurydice, Marpessa Dawn, a beauty from Pittsburgh, Pennsylvania, whom Camus discovered acting in a small film in Paris. Both are black, and most scenes were shots in the slums, or *favela*, high above the city, the first time that was done successfully. The hour-and-forty-minute picture. It opened in France June 12, 1959, and in the States December 21, 1959, and was assessed an A– in the survey.

Heartbreaking! A word that describes the West German Oscar entry ***Die Brücke*** (*The Bridge*), about a coterie of high school-age boys conscripted into the Hitler Youth and ordered to hold an obscure bridge in their own village at the very close of World War II. Released only thirteen years after the purportedly actual event, the film's war sequences are surprisingly realistic and the characters—played by amateur actors—so well sculpted, so three-dimensional, that when each meets his ultimate doom, it's like a kick in the ribs. There's a point in the film when the lads are neatly clustered in the center of the small humpback bridge shrouded in fog. Moments later, one by one they fall out in disarray and each goes off to ponder his situation. Shellfire is heard in the distance; the Americans are coming. "We'd better go home," cries one. "Are you crazy?"

bellows another. "We're soldiers! We have orders to hold the bridge!" "This little bridge can't win the war," remonstrates yet another. They all know they must stay and fight, despite the futility of what's to come—knowledge most Germans realized at the time. Defeat was their destiny. Bernard Wicki, the director, who also co-directed the German sequences in the award-winning *The Longest Day* a few years later, used compelling visual imagery and brutal realism to convey the brutality of war most effectively. *Die Brücke*, his only submission, is considered important as one of the first antiwar films produced by Germany after the fall of fascism. (Some might wish to compare it to the Danish film *Land of Mine* [2017]). An A– movie, it opened October 22, 1959, and in the States May 1, 1961. Wicki, by the way, *acted* in two significant films, neither an Oscar contender: *La Notte* (1961) and *Paris, Texas* (1984).

The first of a few but highly competitive Dutch films to reach the BFF nomination stage is the spice-of-life **Village on the River** (*Dorp aan de rivier*). A premier directorial effort by Fons Rademakers—who had five films submitted and two nominated, the other being *The Assault* (1987)—this black-and-white motion picture is a season-by-season series of snapshots of how rural townspeople live, grieve, work and worry. Central to the story is the stern but wise Tjerk van Taeke, played by Max Croiset, who is about to celebrate his twenty-fifth anniversary as the town's only doctor. Over the years this outlander (a native Frieslander) has delivered babies, treated unspecified and sometimes mysterious illnesses including STDs, and dealt with a slew of ailments, and always with stoicism and a seeming lack of a physician's compassion. Yet, except for a few, the townspeople cannot do without this "peculiar" doctor. Deaf Cis, a poacher who resides with his dog in a houseboat on the Maas (Meuse) River, is van Taeke's friend and confident; it's from his perspective the story is told. Cis, played by Bernard Droog who was also in *Character* (winner 1998), features in two important comedic scenes: One when he is inveigled by a hefty, dark and starving gypsy who, after a night on the houseboat with him, takes an apple to her husband who's been waiting patiently all night by their donkey cart on the dike. The other takes place after a frenetic chase scene when the constable and his deputy find Cis hiding in the outhouse cesspool. When he tells his story to the judge, the courtroom erupts in gales of laughter. Tension in the film revolves around the relationship between the doctor and the burgomaster, who conspires to rid the town of his adversary by "paying him off" and then firing him at an elaborate jubilee celebration. The scene is the climax to the hour-and-thirty-two-minute dramedy. *Dorp aan de Rivier* is not easy to find, but the author happened to be in the Netherlands on vacation and located a copy at the university library in Utrecht in 2014. It was assigned a B+, if for no other reason than the delightful courtroom scenes. It opened August 19, 1958, and at the San Francisco film festival, its only known American venue, December 1, 1959, and cost an estimated $110,000 to make, nearly a million dollars in today's money.

The Italians pulled off a coup when they came up with the epic seriocomedy **The Great War** (*La grande guerra*). Its balanced mixture of satire, irony and drama and the remarkable pairing of Alberto Sordi and Vittorio Gassman, as well as documentarian-style battle scenes featuring thousands of extras, gave the black-and-white motion picture a flair that's hard to beat in early Best Foreign Film nominations. Midway through the First World War, two cowardly conscripts are sent to the frontline to fight against

Austro-Hungarian troops. They try everything to get out of combat and succeed to the extent they somehow are entrusted to deliver a vital message to Italian headquarters, but the plan backfires. The comedic interplay between Sordi and Gassman in itself is worth watching, but there are exceptional scenes of battle and resultant death and destruction. Ultimately, however, this is a picture about friendship, life in the trenches and the realities of war as witnessed and experienced by the hoi polloi. It deserved a B. A couple of notes: The motion picture was the work of Mario Monicelli, who also directed *Big Deal on Madonna Street* with Gassman (1959), *The Girl with the Pistol* (1969) and the anthology film *Viva Italia!* with both Gassman and Sordi acting in separate episodes (1979). The highly productive actors partnered in a total of five Italian films from 1959 to 1970, this one being the only nomination. The two-hour-and-seventeen-minute film opened October 27, 1959, and in New York City August 30, 1061.

Denmark's contribution in 1960, **Paw** or *Boy from Two Worlds*, touches on the question of racial discrimination, but from a child's perspective. Adapted from a 1918 children's book, the movie is about a brown-skinned preteen who is sent to live with his white father's sister in Denmark when his dad and West Indian mother have passed. He befriends a hunter, a Swede named Anders, and when his aunt dies leaving the townspeople baffled about what to do with him, Anders steps in. But Anders is arrested for poaching and the kid is sent to a work camp for boys. Things don't go well for him there, so he escapes—twice, as it turns out. The second time, he befriends an orphaned fox kit and both flee to a small island where they hide out in the woods. When he's eventually found, he's taken in by a squire and his daughter, who have hired Anders to be their gamekeeper, and everybody lives happily ever after. This is one of those films that's almost impossible to find. The only copies listed on Amazon or eBay are from Europe under the title *Heimweh nach dem Silberwald* (Homesick for Silverwood), and are no doubt Region 2 P.A.L. format. G.G. Communications released a shortened video in 1970 under the title *Boy from Two Worlds*. A difficult film to locate, unless you're willing to visit the Danish Film Institute in Copenhagen, it was eventually discovered on the website rarefilmm.com in a free streaming format. The hour-and-thirty-three-minute drama garnered a C. Directed by Astrid Henning-Jensen, her only submission, the film opened December 18, 1959, and in the States for a short run in April 1970.

1961

B+	*La Vérité*	France
B	***The Virgin Spring***	**Sweden**
B–	*Kapò*	Italy
B–	*Macario*	Mexico
C+	*The Ninth Circle*	Yugoslavia

La Vérité (The Truth) by Henri-Georges Clouzot, France's entry to the 1961 running, is a remarkable film for many reasons: It is harsh, blunt and uncontrived as truth should be; it is a courtroom drama not unlike *Judgment in Nuremberg* or *Anatomy of a Murder*, with well-placed flashbacks that tell the story as presented by the litigants;

it is a well-acted drama, a character study, with fits of passion, remorse and anger; and it stars one of the most mystifying and fetching actresses of the 1950s, Brigitte Bardot. And yet few outside France have seen it. The court is trying to determine the guilt of a young "loose" woman—as one review put it, "a sort of rebel without a cause"—who allegedly murdered her musician lover in a fit of jealousy. The film begins with a prison scene and, for much of its two hours and two minutes, swings back and forth between the crowded, sometimes boisterous French courtroom and the flashbacks that include street scenes, nightclub interiors, a musician's rehearsal hall and a number of apartment flats and hallways where the protagonists live, all of this in stark black and white. These diverse scenes are crammed full of people or things to the point of claustrophobia. Said one critique about the film: "...on its own, it's a magnificent exploration of the human soul, a masterfully written courtroom drama, and still a Clouzot film with its dark and pessimistic undertones, and the eternal cloud of ambiguity that envelopes the characters' personalities." We concurred and gave it a B+. Despite his renown for pioneering the French New Wave cinema, it was Clouzot's only submission to the Academy (think unsubmitted films *The Wages of Fear* and *Les Diaboliques*). *The Truth* first opened November 2, 1960, and later in New York City June 26, 1961.

Between 1957 and 1968, Sweden submitted seven Ingmar Bergman films to the Academy for Best Foreign Film consideration. Four of them (*The Seventh Seal*, *The Magician*, *Silence* and *Shame*) were disregarded, but the other three were winners, including the third, **The Virgin Spring** (*Jungfrukällan*). Like *The Seventh Seal*, the film

Max von Sydow, star of several nominated foreign films, consoles his doomed daughter, played by Birgitta Pettersson, in *The Virgin Spring* (1960), the dark Ingmar Bergman winner for 1961.

takes place in medieval times when Sweden was struggling to adapt to Christianity after centuries of paganism, and this is one of several themes that run through this simple morality play Bergman crafted in black and white with help from his favorite cinematographer, Sven Nykvist. The young, naïve daughter of an upstanding farming family is brutally murdered on her way to deliver candles to a church. Ironically, the three felons show up at the family's door trying to sell the girl's garments. The father, played marvelously by Max von Sydow, takes matters into his own hand and wreaks revenge. This results in a crisis of conscience for the farmer as he waivers between grief over his daughter's death and the reality of his un–Christian crime of passion. The film was well received throughout the world, despite the violence that included a rape scene not witnessed before in such a mainstream international feature. Despite its Oscar and reputation as a classic, the hour-and-twenty-nine-minute movie was dark and heavy-handed and merited only a B, tumbling it to second on the year's list. It opened February 8, 1960, and in the United States November 14, 1960, and also was nominated for Best Costume Design-Black and White. Bergman's other two winners were *Through a Glass Darkly* (1962) and *Fanny and Alexander* (1984). Von Sydow, with 156 acting credits according to the International Movie Database (IMDb.com), received two nominations himself but not for Best Foreign Language Film nominees. Nykvist later directed his own 1992-nominated *The Ox*.

Italian director Gillo Pontecorvo, an accomplished documentarian better known for his 1966 Oscar-nominated film *The Battle of Algiers*, produced one of the first fictional accounts of life in a Nazi death camp in **Kapò**, the nominee from Italy (with French help). The main character, played by American actress Susan Strasberg of *Picnic* fame and Broadway's play *The Diary of Anne Frank*, is a teenage Jewess who is sent to Auschwitz with her parents. She escapes death by offering her virginity, which leads her to becoming a *kapò*, an inmate who guards other prisoners, often with little or no impunity. She partners with a Russian prisoner, her lover, to lead an escape, but it fails and both are martyred. The hour-and-fifty-six-minute, black-and-white film collected a B–. It first opened September 29, 1960, and in New York City June 1, 1964, nearly four years later. Among the cast was Emmanuelle Riva, who fifty-three years later, in 2013, was a nominee for Best Actress in *Amour*. Sad but true, this picture would partner well with another death-camp Holocaust film, *Son of Saul* (winner 2016).

Macario, as the peasant protagonist in this first nominee from Mexico is called, has an encounter with the dead during Día de los Muertos, a national holiday akin to Halloween. This is supposed to be a happy occasion, but the woodcutter is transfixed by the death symbols, in particular skulls and skeletons, which are served up as marionettes. Macario has a family of a pretty and devoted wife and a passel of children, all hungry and eager to gobble up the special treats sold at booths during the celebration. He dreams a lot, both of the dead and of the traditional roast turkey, which he is offered—even one cooked by his wife. In one scene, a candlemaker exhorts Macario: "We must be nicer with the dead, because we spend more time dead than alive. Anyway, we are all born to die." The author viewed this DVD at the University of Washington's Odegaard Media Center in Seattle. The images were clear and looked restored, although the subtitles at times were too bright. But it was like watching a 1950s television show, with TV music and cheap sets. The male lead, Ignacio López Tarso, a tall, skinny

Death, played by Enrique Lucero, stalks living souls by candlelight during the Day of the Dead in *Macario* **(1960), Mexico's first Oscar nomination.**

campesino, is naïve and not all too intelligent. At the end, his wife says, "You were like a child"—a whimsical child—"[who] couldn't even finish his turkey." It was an intriguing film, worthy of a B–. The hour-and-thirty-one-minute drama, Roberto Gavaldón's only submitted foreign film, opened in June 9, 1960, but was apparently never distributed in the United States.

The Yugoslav entry to the Oscar race, **The Ninth Circle** (*Deveti krug*), took a prevalent theme in Eastern Europe, the Holocaust, and developed a touching story about Ivo, 19, a Christian, marrying Ruth, a mature, Jewish teenager, to protect her from the Nazis after her family is carried off to a concentration camp. Ivo's father has an obligation to Ruth's dad and promotes the marriage, despite Ivo's reluctance. All of that is melted away as the film goes on, however. Particularly inventive is director France Štiglic's use of lighting through arched portals and along walls during night scenes and expressly when Ruth, not so keen on this union herself, tries to run away. The textures and shadows are exquisite, reminiscent of *The Third Man* and similar stark, black-and-white films of the era. The hour-and-forty-seven-minute film was viewed online in Croatian with no subtitles. A C+ does it justice. It was Štiglic's only submitted film and starred Branko Tatic, who appeared in *Road a Year Long* (1959). It opened April 21, 1960, and in New York City September 14, 1961.

1962

B+	***Through a Glass Darkly***	**Sweden**
B+	*Harry and the Butler*	Denmark

B	*Plácido*	Spain
B–	*The Important Man*	Mexico
C	*Immortal Love*	Japan

An exponent of the minimalist "chamber play" (or film), Swedish master-director Ingmar Bergman wrote and directed **Through a Glass Darkly** (*Såsom i en spegel*) employing just four characters, ensconced on a remote island at the height of summer, to tell the story over a 24-hour period. One is a female suffering from schizophrenia and played brilliantly by Harriet Andersson, who appeared in Berman's 1974 multi-nominee *Cries and Whispers*, which was not submitted for a foreign award. The other actors, all male, include her worried and sexually frustrated husband, Martin; her frightened, confused and also sexually frustrated 17-year-old brother, Minus; and her writer-father, David, who studies her with morbid fascination as a potential subject for a novel he is writing. The black-and-white picture is considered by many critics to be one of the finest ever filmed and, according to Criterion film writer David Blakeslee, "one of the most powerful depictions of a mind coming unhinged." It won the 1962 Oscar for Best Foreign Film. Bergman made it as the first of a trilogy, the others being *Winter Light* the following year and *The Silence*, which was submitted but not nominated for 1963. In fact, Bergman had won the foreign Oscar the year before with *The Virgin Spring* and would win again for *Fanny and Alexander* (1984). *Through a Glass Darkly* (the title comes from 1 Corinthians 13) applies to a mirror through which we see one another. Former *Chicago Sun-Times* film critic Roger Ebert, referring to all the movies in the trilogy, said, "...we're struck by Bergman's deep concern that humans see the world as *Through a Glass Darkly*, and are unable to perceive its meaning." Maybe. And what about God as a spider?—a minor theme in the film. The feature was also nominated for Writing—Directly to Screen and perhaps should have been considered for Sven Nykvist's lighting and cinematography as well, but was not. The hour-and-twenty-nine-minute, B+ picture opened October 16, 1961, and in the States March 13, 1962.

Delightful and clever: an apt description for **Harry and the Butler** (*Harry og Kammertjeneren*) the Danish entry. With strong similarities to Jacque Tati films, Bent Christensen's black-and-white comedy is stacked with eccentric characters, cunning dialogue and fun set pieces. In a nutshell, an indigent man, Harry Adams, who works and lives in a scrapyard, inherits a small sum of money from a cousin he has never met and decides to invest it all on a butler for as long as it lasts. "The only thing I miss is someone to pamper me awhile," he states. Enter Fabricius, former valet to an assortment of highborn people, who takes the job on a lark but quickly falls into step with Harry and his pals, the Bishop and Prince Igor, Magdalena, Trine and Krause, as well as a collection of young raggamuffins who hang out in the junkyard including ten-year-old Poul, forever trying to build a functioning scrap-built rocket. Why does the refined Fabricius take the job? He tells a colleague: "It's hard to understand, but I long for something to do. I guess I can last for a couple of weeks." Indeed, the ending twist is something to behold and well worth the hour-and-forty-five-minute wait. "Life is a card game," says the ever-quoting Bishop. "Even the bad cards must be played." Another Danish film that's hard to locate, it was viewed in full over rarefilmm.com before the site went to subscription, and received a B+. The picture opened September 8, 1961, but not in the United States. It was Christensen's only submission.

At first glance, the Spanish film ***Plácido*** appears to be a spoof along the lines of Italy's *Big Deal on Madonna Street* (1959), some of Federico Fellini's work, or even a Marx Brothers comedy. But behind the frenetic comedic scenes lies a more sinister motive of director Luis García Berlanga. Like the post–Neorealistic *Madonna*, this is a dramedy-satire of the highest level. Once voted by critics and members of the film industry the fourth-best Spanish-made film, *Plácido* is a black comedy dealing with poverty and how the rich react to it—a veritable diatribe against the then-heavy-handed dictatorship of Generalissimo Francisco Franco, who ruled the country from 1939 until his death in 1975. Plotlines are woven together in such a way as to keep the viewer interested the whole time. It was viewed in black and white, online and without the help of subtitles, but not too difficult to follow, helped along by a smattering of the language and four Spanish-language synopses and reviews. It deserved a B. The hour-and-twenty-five-minute movie opened in Barcelona October 20, 1961, but was not distributed in the United States. Berlanga had one other submission, but no other nomination. His main actor, José Luis López Vázquez, also starred in *My Dearest Señorita* (1973).

Why Mexican director Ismael Rodríguez chose Japanese actor Toshiro Mifune to star as a drunken peasant lusting after the title of *Important Man,* or *Majordomo,* in ***Ánimas Trujano: El hombre importante*** is obvious: watching Mifune's face run through many emotions à la method acting is worth the price of admission. The truth that he's almost constantly holding onto and swigging from a liquor bottle gives credence to a boozy demeanor that, one, is a Mifune signature role (e.g. *Yojimbo* when he drinks in the sake bar); two, provides exaggerated facial contortions like few other actors could; and three, masks the fact Toshiro never learned to speak Spanish, although proved obviously good at faking it. As a Siskel and Ebert show *At the Movies* disclosed years ago, his stand-in would speak the lines for him and he would mimic them without knowing their meaning, one or two lines at a time. The remarkably clear DVD came from the Mansfield Library at the University of Montana, where according to World-Cat.com many oddball foreign films reside. It warranted a B–, despite Mifune—great actor that he was—because watching the carryings-on of the drunken lout got to be rather tiresome. Rodríguez had one more submitted film, but without nomination, two years later. Mifune appeared in two other foreign films honored by the Academy—*Rashomon* (1952) and *Samurai I: Musashi Miyamoto* (1956)—although there were many that should have been submitted, notably *Seven Samurai.*

Eien no Hito (*Immortal Love*) is a black-and-white Japanese film incorporating dissimilar tales of love, or lack thereof, involving infidelity. But it was tough to watch, especially when it came to such images as volcanic flames accentuated by out-of-place flamenco music—sometimes utilizing incongruous Japanese lyrics—and close-ups of feet and sandals. Long views of people running against a backdrop of Mt. Fuji were intriguing. But it was no more than a C film. The director, Keisuke Kinoshita, had one other movie submitted but no other nominations. The film, an hour and forty-three minutes long, opened September 16, 1961; it made it to the United States that same year.

1963

B+	*Sundays and Cybèle*	France
B	*The Four Days of Naples*	Italy
B	*Keeper of Promises*	Brazil
B	*Tlayucan*	Mexico
B−	*Electra*	Greece

The poetic black-and-white winning film for 1963, **Sundays and Cybèle** (*Les dimanches de Ville d'Avray*), considered by many the antithesis of the pedophilic *Lolita* of the same year, is about a 30-year-old pilot who crashes during the Indochina War, killing a young Vietnamese child, but survives with amnesia and the mind of a 15-year-old. He befriends an 11-year-old girl abandoned by her father and the two have an idyllic "love affair" that never develops into the sordid subject of the Nabokov story. Hardy Krüger, who plays Pierre the man-child, has said of the film: "There is poetry in every shot." The love story is there, but it could be interpreted as the love between a little girl, Cybèle, and her adopted father, or that of a girl and a boy who enjoy each other's company and like to play together in the woods outside her orphanage on the outskirts of Paris every Sunday. In any event, the first-time director-writer Serge Bourguignon paints a serene and sublime tale that garnered an Oscar win and a B+. What makes this film so special is the chemistry between Krüger and the girl, played brilliantly by Patricia

Manchild Pierre frolics with youngster Cebèle in Serge Bourgiugnon's *Sundays and Cybèle* **(1962), starring Hardy Krüger and Patricia Gozzi.**

Gozzi. The hour-and-fifty-minute picture was also nominated for Best Writing–Screenplay from Another Medium and Musical Score Adaption by Maurice Jarre. It opened first in New York City November 12, 1962, and in France nine days later. Bourguignon made only three full-length motion pictures and no other submissions to AMPAS. Krüger, who appeared in *The Battle of Nerevta* (1970), was also in a number of American films that came into Oscar prominence, including *Hatari!* (1963), *The Flight of the Phoenix* (1966) and Best Picture nominee *Barry Lyndon* (1976).

The Four Days of Naples (*Le quattro giornate di Napoli*), from Italy, was a rare documentary submission in this category, although it is really a historical reenactment. It's about the popular uprising against the Nazis September 27–30, 1943, a calculated risk that succeeded just before the first Allied forces, members of Britain's 1st King's Dragoon Guards, arrived on October 1. The film's direction by Nanni Loy evokes the Neorealistic films—such as Oscar-honored pictures *Shoeshine* (1948) and *The Bicycle Thief* (1950). There are no real stars in this contender, but the feeling Loy attained was that of using documentary footage to convey a tale. The Neapolitans overcame a much larger force of Germans despite overwhelming firepower and siege tactics and drove the Nazis out of Italy's fourth-largest city, leaving behind chaos, destruction but relatively few deaths. The city eventually received a Gold Medal of Military Valor for all the heroics. The picture, which opened November 16, 1962, but got little attention in the United States, did garner another Oscar nomination in 1962 for Best Writing–Story and Screenplay Written Directly for the Screen. Meriting a B, it runs an hour and fifty-six minutes long and was Loy's only nominee, although he did have another submission in the 1980s.

Brazil's entry to the 1963 Academy Award's ceremony, **Keeper of Promises**, is a passionate display of religiosity at a time when cultural change was rife in parts of South America. You might even say it is Buñuel with a Samba beat. Stark black and white and in Portuguese with no subtitles describes the rare print found online. Although it won the Palme d'Or at Cannes and was an Oscar nominee, the film is still not obtainable in the mainstream media—unfortunately the case of many excellent films from the '50s and '60s. There has been much written about *O Pagador de Promessas*, also known as *The Given Word*, including one Brazilian critique who called it the best film that country ever produced. One could contend *Black Orpheus* (1960) stands head and shoulders above this film, but there is great merit in *Pagador* that cannot be denied. It's about a peasant, Zé do Burro (Joe Ass?) who promises to carry a full-sized Christian cross to a church to honor Santa Barbara for curing his horse, the victim of a lightning bolt that nearly killed it. His efforts, thwarted by the church, draw more and more supporters, including the media. Near the end, he is given quasi-sainthood by numerous people who line up for his blessings and possible cures to various ailments. For the final fifteen minutes or so, the atmosphere is Carnival-like as the people celebrate the spiritual cross-bearer. There's a sidebar that concerns the man's wife, Rosa—played by Glória Menezes—who is groomed by a pimp and causes a jealous reaction among the women. One submitted review called it the "complex social dynamic" of Brazil at the time and how the play, written by filmmaker Dias Gomes, "is implicit history of the northeastern people, buffeted by the hinterland, the Colonels, naïve religious beliefs, the rural and urban crisis, the media manipulator that anything was due to the tabloid press today...."

The world produces its martyrs and they open the doors to the crowds, strengthening the hopes of the weak." The reviewer went on to call the movie "a landmark of national cinema and a testimony of competence." The motion picture premiered in Portugal April 17, 1962, and in New York City March 24, 1964, and runs an hour and thirty-eight minutes. It was director Anselmo Duarte's only submitted film and earned a solid B.

Tlayucan—some call it *The Pearl of Tlayucan*—is about justice and miracles in a small village, Oaxtepec, Morelos, Mexico (at least that's where it was filmed). The Oscar candidate has a cast of veteran Mexican actors, but it feels like a movie shot on a shoe-string budget: there are few sets and just as few locations; some of the seasoned actors resorted at times to reading cue cards, or so their wandering eyes would suggest; and it was in black and white, although that doesn't matter much. Director Luis Alcoriza, who had two other submissions but no other nominations, employed hundreds of extras to sing and celebrate their patron Santa Lucia, whose statue in the sizable church wears a halo mounted with several pearls. The loving, peasant couple who dominates the action, played by Julio Aldama and Norma Angélica, have a son, Nico, who becomes ill from slurping ice made from polluted water. His father, a swineherd, steals the biggest pearl to buy the medicine needed to heal his beloved *hijo*, but he's found out. Worse, he loses the pearl in a pig trough at feeding time. The townspeople are up in arms and try to wait out the porkers' digestive cycle to no avail. The wife serendipitously finds the pearl and it's clandestinely replaced in the statue, which kicks off another devout

Mexican peasants, played by Julio Aldama and Norma Angélica, ponder the fate of their poisoned child in *Tlayucan* (1962), an Oscar candidate in 1963.

celebration, this time proclaiming a miracle. This hour-and-forty-five-minute dramedy (classified as a comedy, however) was viewed in Spanish on a DVD from the Aurora (Illinois) Public Library, via the local system. It was clean and clear and garnered a B. It opened December 27, 1962, but apparently was not distributed in the United States.

International film star Irene Papas buttressed two of Michael Cacoyannis' Greek tragedies, both nominated for BFF awards, and played opposite Katharine Hepburn in the middle film of his trilogy. *Electra* was the first one, shot in the stark countryside of the northeastern Peloponnese in ancient Greek costumes. The dialogue was adopted from Euripides' famous play written in 413 BCE. Cited as outstanding were Papas' performance, Cacoyannis' use of the land and sky, the cinematography and the music by Mikis Theodorakis. The director is known also for his Oscar-nominated Best Picture *Zorba the Greek* (1965). One is put off by the expansive bleakness of the filming location for the hour-and-fifty-minute, black-and-white film, as well as the slow-developing plotlines involving uxoricide and matricide. Even so, it received a B–. It originally opened in France October 24, 1962, and in New York City December 17, 1962, The middle installment of Cacoyannis' trilogy was *The Trojan Women* and the last *Iphigenia*, nominated in 1977. Papas also appeared in a number of honored films, including *Z* (winner 1970), *The Guns of Navarone* (1965) and *Zorba the Greek*. Those three films alone garnered nineteen Oscar nominations and six wins.

1964

A	*8½*	**Italy**
A	*Knife in the Water*	Poland
B	*Los Tarantos*	Spain
B	*The Red Lanterns*	Greece
—	*Twin Sisters of Kyoto*	Japan

The opening sequence of the iconic Federico Fellini film from 1964, *8½*, sets the dual theme for this oft perplexing, black-and-white motion picture that won the Oscar for Best Foreign Film against some terrific competition. Guido Anselmi, a celebrated film director underplayed brilliantly by Marcello Mastroianni, is trapped in his gridlocked car dying of asphyxiation while those in vehicles nearby gawk at the macabre sight. Anselmi is suffocating from the unrelenting attention he is receiving. Throughout this murky film, he's the victim of his own dreams of being pressured by his producers and a string of actresses fresh and beautiful or washed up and desperate, or later his relentlessly suspicious wife. He's expected to start filming an epic movie that he cannot come to grips with, has little or no idea what the plot will be aside from the fact the great climax has something to do with a space launch for which a massive and expensive scaffold has been prepared, and cannot even decide who will be his star. All of this is making him sick and tired *to death*. And the dreams: involving women from his childhood, mother figures and nuns and La Saraghina, the imposingly fat sexpot of the beach who will dance for him and his pals if offered a few lire. Tomes have been written about this film, which Fellini himself admitted was autobiographical, and few people can explain it, or really want to. But it garnered an A just because of what it is and how it is put together, and of course because of Mastroianni and his costars Claudia Cardinale, Barbara Steele and Anouk Aimée, who received a Best Actress nomination for *A Man and a Woman* (1967) and also appeared in BFF nomination *Live for Life* (1968). The two-hour-and-eighteen-minute picture opened in Rome February 13, 1963, and in the U.S.A. June 25, 1963. It garnered an Oscar also for Best Costume Design—Black and White and was nominated as well for Director, Writing (Story and Screenplay Written Directly for the Screen) and Art Direction-Set Decoration: a tidy bundle. Mastroianni appeared in 144 films in his career and was singled out three times to compete unsuccessfully for Best Actor. Among the films selected for Best Foreign Film competition in which he appeared were *Big Deal on Madonna Street* (1959), *Yesterday, Today and Tomorrow* (1965), *Marriage Italian Style* (1966) and *A Special Day* (1978) for which he received one of his personal nominations. Cardinale also starred in *Big Deal on Madonna Street*. Fellini, like De Sica, deserves a chapter all his own, going back to the first competitive honors: *La Strada* (1957) and *Nights of Cabiria* (1958), and there was one more to come, *Amarcord* (1975).

Had *8½* not been nominated in 1964, ***Knife in the Water*** (*Nóz w wodzie*) likely would have been the winner, a marvelous achievement for Roman Polanski, a 20-something Polish director fresh out of school. The minimalist, black-and-white film used

In Roman Polanski's first feature-length film, *Knife in the Water* (1962), Zygmunt Malanowicz (*left*) and Leon Niemczyk (*right*) vie for the attention of the beautiful Jolanta Umecka.

only three actors—an established, middle-aged bourgeois man of supposed authority, his dutiful but cowed wife, and a 19-year-old hitchhiker they pick up on their way to a Sunday overnight outing on their small sailboat. The film is rife with sexual tension between the woman and each of the two men, but more apparent is the subtle competition the men engage in to impress the oft-disinterested female. In the beginning, the woman, played by Jolanta Umecka, wears strange '50s-style spectacles, making her appear rather plain and unappealing; but as the hour-and-thirty-four-minute film progresses, she transforms into a curvaceous beauty in a bikini or, in two carefully framed scenes, nothing at all. By the end of the film, she has transformed again, back to the bespectacled wife. An overlay theme is how the couple negotiates a deteriorating relationship. (Spoiler alert!) This is especially apparent at the very end, when their vehicle reaches a crossroads on the way home: five kilometers to the right is the police station where the man believes he must confess to killing the drifter, while to the left is home. He does not believe his wife when she tells him the teenager is alive and well on the road to nowhere. This is a strong A picture. It opened March 9, 1962, and in the United States October 28, 1963, and was Polanski's only foreign film submission, but his filmography is chockablock with honored and honorable films: *Rosemary's Baby* (1968), two Oscar nominations and a win; *Chinatown* (1975), eleven nominations (including Best Picture and Director) and a win; *Tess* (1979), six nominations (including Best Picture and Director) and three wins; *Pirates* (1987), one nomination; and *The Pianist* (2003), seven nominations (including Best Picture) and three wins (including Best Director).

Following up on a host of good reviews, the author went to the 8th Street Cinema in New York City one fall day in 1964 and saw a screening of Francisco Rovira Beleta's **Los Tarantos** from Spain. Like Carlos Saura's award-winning Flamenco Trilogy (*Carmen* was a nominee in 1984 and *Tango* in 1999), *Los Tarantos* centers around dance. It also follows Shakespeare's *Romeo and Juliet* but in modern Catalonia style involving two rival gypsy families in Barcelona. Juana and Rafael fall in love but are forbidden to marry. The star-crossed lovers are murdered by a jealous brute—the girl's betrothed and a shady colleague of her irate father. The thug is confronted by Rafael's brother who then murders him. In the end, Juana's father and mother grieve and the two families reconcile. All the while, dancing abounds—mainly the gritty, languid style of flamenco. Many of the contemporary Gitano artists perform in this movie, including the superb Carmen Amaya, who died shortly after her brief but stunning part was filmed. The difficult-to-locate, hour-and-twenty-three-minute picture opened November 5, 1963, and in America June 29, 1964, and deserved a B. Rovira Beleta also directed the 1968 contender *El Amor Brujo*, also known as *Bewitched Love*—one of the more difficult BFF films to find—based on Manuel de Falla's ballet, which was recreated by Saura in 1986 as one of *his* Trilogy films.

The Greek film **The Red Lanterns** (*Ta kokkina fanaria*) is the antithesis of an earlier, Jules Dassin classic, *Never on Sunday*, which was nominated in 1960 for several Oscars including Best Director but not in the foreign-language film category. In the later film, directed by Vasilis Georgiadis, who did *Blood on the Land* (1966), three prostitutes experience different encounters while their pimp, who desires one of them, tries in vain to keep them all in line. This film, like Dassin's movie, has a lot of Greek "Opa!" music and even a party scene in which several men do the Sirtaki (the *Zorba the Greek* dance) around some of the brothel women. There's also a line in which one of the women says, "Oh, we're even open on Sundays." The dialogue on the black-and-white, grainy, VHS tape was difficult to interpret at times, often for an entire conversation, because of the white-on-white subtitles. But the gist was always there and never too hard to figure out. The two-hour-and-twelve-minute film was judged a B, in great part because of the acting of the three women: Anna, Mary and Eleni and their respective outside love interests. The tape arrived from the Yocum Library at the Reading Area Community College in Pennsylvania, thanks to an interlibrary loan. *The Red Lanterns* opened in 1963 but didn't come to the United States until March 31, 1965.

Twin Sisters of Kyoto is a Japanese contribution now out of print and no longer found except in a very few places. Chieko and Naeko were separated at birth because of a superstition in rural Japan that twins brought bad luck to the family. Now 20, the young women (both played by Shima Iwashita, also star of *Portrait of Chieko* in 1968), meet by chance and decide to pursue a friendship. Chieko grew up happily in the home of a humble kimono designer and merchant; her sister's upbringing was less fortunate. To add to the conflict, Chieko is dating an educated man who suddenly takes an interest in Naeko. Directed by Noboru Nakamura who also made *Portrait of Chieko*, the romantic drama, filmed in sumptuous color, was also known as *Koto* and remade under that title in 1980 by Kon Ichikawa, celebrated for his nominated features *The Burmese Harp* (1957) and the submitted but not nominated *Fires on the Plain* (1960). WorldCat.org, the catalog of media in worldwide libraries, lists *Twin Sisters of Kyoto* as existing in three places: As a fast-fading celluloid film at the University of California, Berkeley; as a VHS print at Cornell University in New York; and as a tape at Waseda University in Japan. Some streaming websites list it but do not actually have it, and besides, one risks contracting serious computer viruses by logging in. A trailer without subtitles was found at wildgrounds.com. Surely there are more copies of the film somewhere. It runs an hour and forty-seven minutes and first opened January 13, 1963, with limited distribution in the United States starting March 1964. Argentina was the only other country mentioned on the distribution list.

1965

A–	*Woman in the Dunes*	✓	Japan
B+	*The Umbrellas of Cherbourg*		France
B	*Sallah*		Israel
B–	***Yesterday, Today and Tomorrow***		**Italy**
C+	*Raven's End*		Sweden

Woman in the Dunes (*Suna no Onna*), Japan's 1965 entry, was not particularly groundbreaking, but American filmgoers loved it. In his 1971 book, authority-on-all-things-Japanese Donald Richie summed up the plot this way: "...it is about a school teacher on an outing imprisoned by the local folk in a large sand pit with a recently widowed woman. His attempts to escape are all unsuccessful, and he eventually discovers a way to make potable the water which seeps from the sand. In this way he discovers himself, his purpose, his life, and when the chance finally comes to escape, he refuses it." Hiroshi Teshi-gahara made the film, from a script by novelist Kobo Abe, and though he considered himself more of a cinematographer, he ironically was also nominated (in 1966) for a director's Oscar for *Woman OF the Dunes* (the proper translation). He filmed it in black and white with *noir*-like lighting and shadowing; the final result was considered a technical magna opus. It has also been tagged as an example of Japan's "New Wave." Another aspect of the picture: it featured nudity and sex scenes—perhaps a rea-

Entomologist Niki Jumpei, played by Eiji Okada, stumbles into a hole occupied by the "Woman in the Dunes," but the sifting sand makes escape an insurmountable challenge (1964).

son for its American popularity, only fourteen months after the release of Jayne Mansfield's risqué performance in the farce *Promises! Promises!*, a first among mainstream U.S. films. A comment from a 1971 Screen Series book states: "Teshigahara's exercise in the absurd is a discussion of freedom, of disillusion, of man's invincible urge to stay alive. The frequent use of extreme close-ups with bodies like landscapes gives a compelling feeling of presence to this elemental drama. The human skin and the dazzling sand are the main elements in its extraordinary visual style." First viewed at a University of Washington Japanese Film Series in 1967, and again over the years, the movie garnered an A–, eclipsing the winning picture as did two other nominated films. It was Teshigahara's only submitted film and runs two hours and three minutes long. It premiered February 15, 1964, and opened in the United States October 25, 1964.

Occasionally a unique foreign contender comes along that begs to be watched. The animated *Waltz with Bashir*, seven-hour *War and Peace* and anthology films such as *Yesterday, Today and Tomorrow* and *Wild Tales* are unconventional examples that have vied for Oscar recognition. Another is France's **The Umbrellas of Cherbourg** (*Les Parapluies de Cherbourg*), an operetta with no spoken words. It starred Catherine Deneuve, only 20 during filming, who sang up a storm to a delightful score by Michel Legrand, along with costar Nino Castelnuovo. The film did not win during its Oscar year, owing to competition from Italy; yet, it scores higher than the actual winner with a B+. In any event, *Umbrellas* is a delightful change-of-pace motion picture, directed by Jacques Demy in his only submitted feature, and deemed "one of the most beloved romantic movies of all time," according to its DVD liner notes. As occasionally transpired with Best Foreign Film (BFF) contenders, the feature received an additional four nominations from the Academy a year later, in 1966: Best Story and Screenplay Written

Directly for the Screen, Best Original Song ("I Will Wait for You," the theme), Best Original Score and Best Musical Treatment. It opened in France February 19, 1964, and in America December 16, 1964, and runs an hour and thirty-one minutes. Deneuve was nominated for Best Actress for foreign film winner *Indochine* (1993); appeared in BFFs *Tristana* (1971), *The Last Metro* (1981) and *East/West* (2000); and participated in *Persepolis*, nominated in 2008 for Best Animated Film.

The Israeli actor Chaim Topol is a delight to watch. In the nominated Israeli film **Sallah** (*Sallah Shabati*), a Bourekas comedy with minor dramatic overtones and a message, the actor better known as Tevye in *Fiddler on the Roof* (Best Actor nomination 1972) is a boorish Ashkenazi immigrant who, with his extended family of five boys and two girls, wife and an older woman he has trouble identifying is sent to a muddy transit camp where residents have been waiting for Israeli government housing for at least six years. Although ignorant of civil law, yet a natural conniver, Sallah Shabati schemes every which way, right down to the sale of his eldest daughter for marriage, to come up with the cash required to get the house he wants. This is a particularly fun film, a firm B, with memorable characters and hilarious scenes and dialogue. It was directed by Ephraim Kishon, who also made *The Policeman* (1972). The hour-and-fifty-minute picture opened June 2, 1964, and in the States March 10, 1965. Cast member Zaharira Harifai was also in *The Policeman* (1972) and Gila Almagor was in *The House on Chelouche Street* (1974).

Chaim Topol, title star of *Sallah* (1964), is a conniver and a schemer, bent on obtaining enough money to move his family out of a squalid transit camp.

A trilogy of sex-centered short farces, **Yesterday, Today and Tomorrow** (*Ieri, oggi, domani*) the actual winner of the 1965 Best Foreign Film, brought together two of Italy's most famous actors, Marcello Mastroianni and Sophia Loren, and director Vittorio De Sica. Each story featured Loren in a title role—Adelina of Naples, Anna of Milan and Mara of Rome—and Mastroianni as her foil. In the first segment, Adelina, a cigarette-seller in trouble with the law, stays pregnant to avoid incarceration, that is until she wears out her poor husband. Anna, a high-flying socialite, takes her lover out for a spin in her husband's Rolls-Royce, has a slight accident and finds solace in a passing motorist who helps her out, giving her lover the air as she drives off with her new beau. Mara shirks one of her clients for a postulant priest, who is willing to chuck church for her amours. Despite the Oscar, the anthology film of three comic tales deserved only a B–, allowing three other films to pull ahead in the rankings. The feature, a minute short of two hours, opened December 21, 1963, and in the United States March 17, 1964. For the record, Loren appeared in BFF nominees *Marriage Italian Style* (1966) and *A Special Day* (1978), received Best Actress for *Two Women* in 1962, and won a Lifetime Achievement Award in 1991. Mastroianni also starred in *Big Deal on Madonna Street* (1959), *8½* (1964), *Marriage Italian Style* and *A Special Day*. De Sica was honored as director of the first two pictures given Oscars specifically to foreign films, *Shoeshine* (1948) and *The Bicycle Thief* (1949), and a few others along the way.

Raven's End (*Kvarteret Korpen*) has been seen little in the States, although a brief appearance in Chicago was enough for one reviewer, none other than the late Roger Ebert, formerly of the *Chicago Sun-Times*, to screen and comment on it. The Swedish film is about a writer's coming of age in a poor section of Mälmo and was written and directed by Bo Widerberg, who claimed it to be fiction although it supposedly closely resembled his own adult beginnings. It drags at times and lacks drama, which may be a factor in its lack of attention outside Sweden. Even so, one viewer called it—rather disingenuously—better than anything Ingmar Bergman ever produced. The black-and-white feature was a C+ in the view of the author, who on first view in 1976 wrote: "too soap-operatic ... but great drunk scene." It opened December 26, 1963, and in America May 21, 1970. Widerberg had four films submitted with three nominations, including *Adalen 31* (1970) and *All Things Fair* (1996).

1966

A	*Marriage Italian Style*	Italy
A–	**The Shop on Main Street**	**Czechoslovakia**
A–	*Kwaidan*	Japan
C+	*Dear John*	Sweden
C–	*Blood on the Land*	Greece

Marcello Mastroianni might not have been the first international male star, but he definitely made his mark in the 1960s with Federico Fellini's *La Dolce Vita* and *8½*, Neorealism at its best. Then came **Marriage Italian Style** (*Matrimonio all'italiana*), directed by one of the most prolific Oscar contenders as actor, writer and director, Vittorio De Sica (*Shoeshine* in 1948, *The Bicycle Thief* 1949, *Yesterday, Today and Tomorrow*

1965, and *The Garden of the Finzi-Continis* 1972). This film, Italy's 1966 nominee for Best Foreign Film, did not measure up to previous Fellini pictures or Pietro Germi's unsubmitted *Divorce Italian Style* (1961), but it was a formidable entry nonetheless. Playing opposite Mastroianni as the prostitute Filumena was Sophia Loren, who appeared with him in several De Sica and Fellini films and received a nomination in the Best Actress category in 1965 for this film; she won that category with *Two Women* in 1962. *Marriage Italian Style* is an hour-and-forty-two-minute romp in color, a "fluffy farce," as one critic labeled it, alternating between humor and sadness. Lothario Domenico (Mastroianni) is in and out of bed with Filumena and other women but later promises his hand to another. When he learns Loren's character is dying, he decides to leave his betrothed to marry the hooker. His fiancée naturally is furious, but he tells her he will return to her when Filumena dies. Of course, what happens next is one of the better turns in this twisty comedy, which should be left for the viewer to see. This picture opened December 19, 1964, and in America the next day. It warranted an A, placing it ahead of the winner for the year. Mastroianni, as aforementioned, was in a slew of excellent foreign productions, five of which were nominated for Best Foreign Language Film.

One of the better Holocaust films, ***The Shop on Main Street*** (*Obchod na korze*), deals with forced Aryanization of Jewish businesses. Co-directed by Ján Kadár and Elmar Klos, this second-ever Czechoslovakian entry to the Academy (and first of four

A Nazi commander (František Zvarík), accompanied by Tóno (Jozef Kroner), a hapless carpenter, is intent on ferreting out Jews hiding in the main-street town he oversees in *The Shop on Main Street* (1965).

consecutively nominated films) is about a good-guy carpenter, Tóno, who is selected by his bad-guy brother-in-law to take over a doddering old Jewish woman's notions store in 1942. The woodworker learns that the shopkeeper, oblivious of Nazi persecution, has failed in business but that patrons continue to support her financially by pretending to buy her buttons. Tóno goes along with the scheme and becomes quite attached to the aged woman, played by Ida Kamińska, who also was nominated for a Best Actress award, but in 1967. The Gestapo catches up with the Jewish population of the town, however, and the carpenter tries to keep her safe with tragic results. The Czechoslovak "New Wave" picture, worth an A–, was released October 8, 1965, and in the United States January 24, 1966, and was the only submission by either Kadár or Klos. The New Wave was a near tsunami in Prague at this time; the three nominations that immediately followed included Miloš Forman's *Loves of a Blonde* (1967) and *The Firemen's Ball* (1969), with Jiří Menzel's winning *Closely Watched Trains* tucked in between.

Kwaidan, Japan's 1966 entry, is an anthology film consisting of four parts. *Kwaidan* means "ghost stories," and for the most part it's a sort of Japanese version of *Tales from the Crypt*, only much better. Directed by Masaki Kobayashi and based on stories by Yakumo Koizumi (the Greek-Irish American born Lafcadio Hearn, who became a Japanese citizen in 1895), *Kwaidan* is considered by David Ehrenstein, writing for The Criterion Collection, as "one of the most meticulously crafted supernatural fantasy films ever made." Each chapter is quite different in an impressionistic way. The first is a true horror film built on guilt and repression; the second revolves around weirdness and betrayal; the third may be the most terrifying and gruesome; and the final, purposely left unfinished both in original form and by Kobayashi, is more along the lines of anticipation and paranoia and is considered the least satisfying story of the four. The picture was shot on giant sets in color and employed innovative lighting techniques to enhance the ghostly images. The movie was first seen at a Japanese film festival in the 1960s, reviewed in 2007 and given an A–. Kobayashi had one other film submitted but not chosen for Oscar. The filmed cost ¥350 million (about $970,000), and was three minutes over three hours in length. It starred Rentaro Mikuni of *The Burmese Harp* (1957) and opened at home January 6, 1965, and in America November 22, 1965.

A "date movie" of the time, *Käre John* (*Dear John*), was made in 1964 but not nominated for an Oscar until 1966, well into the so-called "sexual revolution." At the time, three years before *I Am Curious (Yellow)* featured full-frontal nudity, *Dear John*, with its subtle and tasteful nude scenes, would not rate a Richter point as anything salacious today. But enough of that. This simple, black-and-white Swedish romance, almost impossible to find, is now more trite than stirring. It's about a lonely seaman, whose wife left him some time ago, who slowly, ploddingly seduces a young single mother, Anita, a café waitress. The 20-something woman, who's been to bed with only two previous men—her 4-year-old daughter's father and another seducer who said all the right things, had his way with her and then up and left—is cautious, fearing the affair will develop into another one-night stand. But she's as lonely as John; they are both in need of a good hug; and both of them prefer that hug to be done stark naked. Lars-Magnus Lindgren, the director, used a technique throughout of showing the two together for a few minutes in real time and then snapping back to the chronology of their daylong courtship that included a car, bus and plane journey across the Oresund Strait to nearby Copenhagen to show Anita's daughter the zoo. Jurgen Schildt, a Swedish film critic, wrote: "To get through the story requires the same patience as attaching socks on an octopus." Well, it wasn't that bad, but borderlining the banal, it's easy to see why this film is now so obscure. Nothing was available at the time of this notation on either Amazon.com or eBay.com and any critical commentary and synopses found were relegated to one or two lines. Even so, the writer was able to find it on the dandy website rarefilmm.com; the free streaming picture (at the time) had a vivid HD image and English subtitles, albeit a bit ragged at times. Unfortunately, one must subscribe to watch it today. The hour-and-fifty-five-minute film, which rated a C+, opened November 23, 1964, and in New York City March 8, 1966. The two leads were Jarl Kulle, who played the General in *Babette's Feast* (1988) and was also in *Fanny and Alexander* (1984), and Christina Schollin, who was in *Fanny and Alexander* as well.

Sergio Leone's "Spaghetti Westerns" set the tone for a new genre of film in the mid–1960s. **Blood on the Land** (*To Homa vaftike kokkino*), Greece's nominee for Best Foreign Film, comes as close as any feature of that period to duplicating that subgenre. Even one of the posters advertising it—showing a man kneeling next to a body through the splayed legs of an adversary, a horse in the background—smacks of Leone. A symbolic piece of rivalries between peasants and landowners, the film depicts two conflicted brothers who happen to be after the same girl. There is violence and death (what Greek play would be without them?), nudity (a rarity for the period) and a raw, outdoor setting (replete with pinnacles of rock reminiscent of the American West). It was apparently filmed in the Metéora region on the Plain of Thessaly. There is faint little available on this motion picture. One needs to see it, but it's difficult to find. In the writer's case, it was discovered online and downloaded to view in black and white on a forty-five-inch TV screen, but in Greek (no subtitles). Vasilis Georgiadis directed two Greek films to Academy Award nominations, the other being *The Red Lanterns* in (1963). One cannot help but wonder if he didn't take a page from Leone to make this one. It garnered a C–. The two-hour-and-twenty-minute film premiered January 11, 1966, but was not distributed in the USA.

1967

A–	*A Man and a Woman*	France
A–	*The Battle of Algiers*	Italy
B	*Three*	Yugoslavia
B–	*Loves of a Blonde* ✓	Czechoslovakia
C–	*Pharaoh*	Poland

Driving a rental car into the Normandy Riviera city of Deauville during the summer of 1998, the author inserted a cassette of Francis Lai's marvelous music from France's 1967 winning entry for Best Foreign Film, **A Man and a Woman** (*Un homme et une femme*), and turned up the volume. It was August and the French were enjoying their month-long holiday, and the traffic was stop-and-go all the way through the resort town, allowing enough time to hear all of the music on the tape twice through. The music alone is enjoyable. Claude Lelouch's hour-and-forty-two-minute-long, mostly black-and-white masterpiece merited an A–. It entwines two lonely people, whose spouses have recently died, in a love relationship "as only the French know how to do it," according to one critic. While a simple love story, the motion picture is considered to have been influenced by the French New Wave films of Jean-Luc Godard, François Truffaut, Alain Resnais and others. But it's arguably the Lai music, nominated as well for Best Song and Best Film Score, that gets to you. Lelouch, who also created *Live for Life* (1968), received a nomination for Best Director and the film garnered one for Best Writing–Story and Screenplay Written Directly for the Screen. Anouk Aimée was nominated for Best Actress; she also starred in *8½* (1964) and *Live for Life*. Another cast member, Jean-Louis Trintignant, appeared in *Z* (1970), *My Night at Maud's* (1970) and *Amour* (2013). The film opened May 27, 1966, and in America July 12, 1966.

It takes a moment to realize that ***The Battle of Algiers*** (*La battaglia di Algeri* or *La bataille d'Alger*) is not a French film, nor wholly Algerian; it may be in French and Arabic, but it's definitely Italian-made. Director Gillo Pontecorvo strived for gritty authenticity and assured us he employed no newsreel footage in piecing together the story of the eight-year war, pitting colonialists against nationalists, that ended only three years before he began filming in 1965. There's a direct correlation, however, to the Italian Neorealism of the late '40s and '50s. (There is much about this film that reminds one of the urban guerrilla warfare of today, including the bombing of civilians

In its documentary-like style, Italian-made historical drama *The Battle of Algiers* (1966) draws Algerian nationalists into direct confrontation with French colonialists.

by both sides.) It's no surprise to learn that, even though he remained somewhat impartial in making the quasi-documentary, Pontecorvo obviously sided with the rebel National Liberation Front (FLN). It was first released in Italy September 9, 1966, and when it came out in France five years later (October 21, 1971), reviewers who favored the film were roundly criticized by critics who condemned it. It has also served as a training film for guerrilla groups and Pentagon officials alike. A plot exists in the picture and basically it revolves around the FLN leader and a French colonel, as well as citizens serving either as victims or belligerents, or both. Pontecorvo, responsible for *Kapò* (1961), was nominated in 1969, two years later, for Best Director of *The Battle of Algiers*, which garnered, that same year, a Best Writing–Story and Screenplay Written Directly for the Screen nomination. This nominee, which runs a minute over two hours and cost an estimated $800,000 to make, received an A–. It first appeared in the United States September 20, 1967.

Death on three levels—ironic, heroic, and gratuitous—is the theme of the Yugoslav anthology film *Tri* (*Three*). This is a beautifully filmed black-and-white movie, with close shots on tense, rough faces, grand sweeps of countryside and swamplands, and tight setlike images of a peasant village. A difficult film to find, it was finally discovered online in six parts, but in Serbo-Croatian with no subtitles; even so, the dialogue is sparse and relatively easy to follow. As so often is the case with East European entries, director Aleksandar Petrović used the backdrop of World War II for his triptych: Part I shows hero Miloš Živojinović as a student who happens across a railroad station where he witnesses frightened refugees who are waiting in hope of escape by train. A detachment of reservists shows up and begins examining the citizens' papers. One of them cannot produce his and he is shot in cold blood just moments before his wife arrives to prove his innocence. The second part is more intense: Miloš, a member of the Resistance, is escaping the Nazis through mountains when he happens across another partisan. The two of them find themselves in open swampland where they are pursued by a small plane with an active mounted machine run, which despite an incredible number of bullets and a shooting-fish-in-the-barrel situation, manages not to kill or wound either of these two men. The follower eventually sacrifices himself to save Miloš, who watches as the Germans burn him alive in a straw shack. The third film is less poignant. Miloš now is a partisan commander and orders the execution of a group of Nazi collaborators, one of whom is a fetching woman in short skirt and low heels who attracts him. They must, however, be punished, and he issues his order with no apparent remorse. Death is the protagonist and witness in this film. As one reviewer put it: "It's a movie without rhetoric and schemes, achieved with the creative force born of passion and reason, and that often reaches poetic heights." The film deserved a solid B (and perhaps the camera work an easy A). One moment in the second part stands out: Miloš hides among a large flock of sheep to escape his pursuers when suddenly the sheep scatter in all directions, leaving him alone on a barren slab of dirt, the camera capturing all of this from 50 feet above. Petrović also made *I Even Met Happy Gypsies* (1968) and had one other film submitted but not nominated. *Three*, which runs an hour and twenty minutes, opened May 12, 1965, and in New York City June 29, 1967; two other countries, Argentina and Mexico, reportedly received distribution.

The bittersweet comedy **Loves of a Blonde** (*Lásky jedné plavovlásky*), Miloš Forman's early entry from the Czechoslovak New Wave movement about a blonde teen-ager's one-night stand and subsequent unrequited love, was a 1967 entry that critics today still regard as a classic. In some ways it takes on an awkward tone akin to that found in two of François Truffaut's French New Wave films, *Shoot the Piano Player* and *Jules and Jim*, released in France in 1960 and 1962 respectively and neither submitted to AMPAS for Oscar consideration. In all of their flawed wisdom, shoe factory governors decide to hold a mixer so their bored and companion-hungry working girls can mingle with a contingent of army soldiers brought to the provincial town for training. Nothing wrong with that; all will be supervised and remain innocent, or will it? The troops for the most part are humorously inept, but when they see the nubile young ladies they clumsily go about enticing them to their table. Meanwhile, a somewhat more worldly but damaged girl named Andula fends off the oafs and finds herself in bed with a young man named Milda, who was hired as the event piano player (Truffaut again?). She takes his endearments to heart and impulsively seeks him out at his family home only to learn he didn't really mean all that he said to her. David Blakeslee of Criterion called this a "simple tale of youthful lusts and emotions in full bloom." The film can be construed as sincere but a trifle forced. The mixer scenes, while hilarious at times, were drawn out and claustrophobic, while the bedroom vignette seemed overly long and then—bang!—it was over. Simon Abrams of *Slant* noted, "The cagey nature of Andula's tentative romance with Milda is also what gives the film a quietly stifled melancholic tone." Agreed. The B– film was available in pieces online but viewable. It's in black and white, runs an hour and twenty-eight minutes, and opened November 12, 1965, and in the States October 26, 1966. Forman's résumé is formidable. Two years later, he would see *The Firemen's Ball* nominated for Best Foreign Film, and he is also known for American Best Picture/Best Director films *One Flew Over the Cuckoo's Nest* (1976) and *Amadeus* (1985), as well as *Ragtime* (1982) with eight nominations and *The People vs. Larry Flint* (1997) with two nominations, including Best Director. Andula is played by Hana Brejchová, who was in *Amadeus*.

Faraon (*Pharaoh*) crossed the line into absurdity and garnered a C– when all was said and done. Naturally, it's about ancient Egypt and there is a lot of that. But to see pharaohs and advisers, priests and petitioners, wives and mistresses, and other patricians gallivanting around in period skirts and headdresses *speaking Polish* provided unintentional amusement. The three-hour color film, on DVD seen at the University of Washington library in Seattle, was in widescreen color, and there was adequate cinematography of desert scenes, some with hundreds of extras, and hypostyles with hieroglyphs and pyramids that were actually filmed at Giza, Egypt. The female nudity, mostly through diaphanous gowns, seemed a little out of place, and there really wasn't much to it; it had more of a modern feel than one of a culture 2,500 years old. No doubt about it, this was a strange film for an Oscar candidate. Directed by Jerzy Kawalerowicz, responsible for one other submitted, but not nominated, picture, *Pharaoh* opened March 11, 1966, and in New York City more than eleven years later, June 22, 1977.

New Realities: 1968–1973

France wasn't the only country with a New Wave film industry. Poland, Czechoslovakia, Spain, Japan—even America—had renaissances of sorts. *Bonnie and Clyde*, for example, was a Hollywood film that incorporated many "New Wave" techniques and garnered ten Oscar nominations including Best Picture in 1968. The next year, *Easy Rider*, another gritty counterculture drama, came to the silver screen and received two nominations. Particularly telling was *The French Connection*, with its location shooting during a harrowing car chase under the BMT subway line in Brooklyn, New York, which caused quite a sensation when the film came out. In 1972, it won five of the eight Academy Awards for which it was nominated including Best Picture. It also costarred the Spanish actor and Luis Buñuel favorite Fernando Rey, who would go on to appear in three Best Foreign Language Film nominees over the years.

Japan, meanwhile, was still churning out second-rate period pictures. Sweden caught on with long-winded but captivating historical dramas like *The Emigrants* and its follow-up *The New Land*. And France and Spain gave Buñuel a stage for his surrealist films.

But nowhere during this period were the new realities of movie production more apparent than behind the Iron Curtain in Czechoslovakia. Miloš Forman, who would go on to greatness directing prize-winning American films, had just produced *The Firemen's Ball* when the Prague Spring invasion by Russian tanks altered the lifestyles and attitudes of millions of Czech people that would last for decades. The Communist government banned the film, but the Academy gave it a definitive okay with a nomination.

Poland's output continued apace, with the likes of Andrzej Wajda churning out seven flicks of which only one was submitted but not nominated. Nonetheless, not since *Knife in the Water* (1964) by Roman Polanski—another Iron Curtain director who would go on to score big in Hollywood—and Jerzy Kawalerowicz's nominated *Pharaoh* (1967) had there been a Polish candidate.

The Soviet Union, never afraid of dramatizing a "better" side of communism through emotional puffery found in multiple reels of celluloid, came out with *War and Peace*. At seven hours plus it was as long and detailed as Tolstoy's book. Later came the sad tale of war without peace called *The Dawns Here Are Quiet*. Both films focused in different ways on reality writ large.

Meanwhile, François Truffaut's *Day for Night* made it through the nomination process—to a win in 1974—and is regarded today by cinephiles as the last product of the French New Wave Movement.

Here's a more detailed picture of the nominees of this period.

1968

A–	***Closely Watched Trains***	**Czechoslovakia**
B–	*I Even Met Happy Gypsies*	Yugoslavia
C–	*Live for Life*	France
C–	*El Amor Brujo—Bewitched Love*	Spain
—	*Portrait of Chieko*	Japan

The tenor of **Closely Watched Trains** (*Ostře sledované vlaky*) is established at the very outset when the main character, young Miloš, parades before the wall photos of his misfit ancestors, some in uniform, while his dowdy mother helps him don his own work outfit for a new job as a railroad station guard. "You must be careful not to have the trains crash," she says, rolling up a sleeve. "The whole town would envy us." Train crashes notwithstanding, this is a story of innocence, coming of age and destiny. While humor there is, it's not a comedy and the characters are understated. Critic Roger Ebert called it "a quiet, charming, very human film." It takes place during World War II when backwaters like Miloš' stood by waiting for the Nazis to arrive and shake up the tranquility of rural life. Miloš might fail in love, but he becomes a hero of sorts, or so we are to believe. Jiří Menzel directed the black-and-white film; he had three submissions and one other nomination, *My Sweet Little Village* (1987). The cast included Vlastimil Brodský, who was also in *Jacob the Liar* (1977). Menzel's picture deserved an A–. It debuted November 18, 1966, before arriving in New York City for a run starting October 15, 1967.

Who the "I" is in *I Even Met Happy Gypsies* is mystifying, since the whole film, the Yugoslav entry, is all about and acted by ethnic Steppe Romani who lived in rural Serbia. The original title in Serbo-Croatian is *Skupljači perja*, which translates to just "Happy Gypsies." This is a tribal affair, where principals who stray from clannish customs are banished, and centers on Bora, a goose-feather gatherer, and Tisa, still a young girl, both of whom have mismatched marriages and eventually link up only to find themselves in life-and-death struggles. It's well acted by a seasoned 34-year-old male actor and a 16-year-old in her first of only four roles, both speaking Romani. The hour-and-thirty-four-minute movie was made in farmland outside Belgrade, and one thing you come away with is that practically every outdoor scene involves mud—lots and lots of mud. The film, directed by Aleksandar Petrović who did *Tri* (1967), merited a B–. It opened March 27, 1967, and came to the States March 20, 1968.

Why **Live for Life** (*Vivre pour vivre*) was ever nominated for Best Foreign Film is beyond reason, and apparently other reviewers felt that way as well. Roger Ebert in 1968 describes 29-year-old director Claude Lelouch's opaquely colored motion picture as "a tawdry little domestic tragicomedy (which could have been a good tawdry little domestic tragicomedy)" but fails. Indeed. Citing Lelouch's other nominated film, Ebert

Beli Bora Perjar (*right*), played by Bekim Fehmiu, hears out an unidentified Steppe Romani cart driver in the Yugoslav drama *I Even Met Happy Gypsies* (1967), by director Aleksandar Petrović.

continues: "[It] has all of the faults of 'A Man and a Woman' [but] none of the virtues and is an ugly and corrupt film which pretends to be beautiful and ethical." Well, well, well. Fact is, Yves Montand, who was also in *Z* (1970), is a philanderer of the first order, with a gorgeous wife, a beautiful model for a mistress of whom he tires, and has eyes on Candice Bergen, performing in her third movie role. He smokes too much. He's 40. And he apparently likes to watch violence as part of his job. It received a C–. Oh, Francis Lai's music makes it worth watching, as it did for *A Man and a Woman* (1967). A difficult film to source, *Live for Life* was found online in French with, believe it or not, Portuguese subtitles; but the viewing was free. It opened September 14, 1967, and in New York City December 18, 1967, and runs two hours and ten minutes.

Manuel de Falla composed the ballet *El Amor Brujo* in 1914–15. The libretto is complicated, but basically it's about a gypsy girl called Carmelo whose husband, Diego, dies, freeing her to go after the man she has always loved named Candelas, only to have Diego return as a ghost with whom she is compelled to dance interminably. She and her lover believe that performing together de Falla's famous "Ritual Fire Dance" will break the spell, but it does not. Now speed ahead to 1968: A film version of the story, also called ***El Amor Brujo*** (but also *The Bewitched Love* and *Love, the Magician*), was on the docket for a BFF but unavailable. Directed by Francisco Rovira Beleta, who also did *Los Tarantos* (1964), the movie is said to follow the ballet closely enough, but with dialogue and without the ghost aspect. Instead, Carmelo is pursued by two men: one evil and one not. Beleta staged the colorful dance sequences, for the most part, in the aggressive Andalusian *flamenco* style. Jump ahead nineteen years more and we find that director, dancer and choreographer Carlos Saura has recreated *El Amor Brujo* once again. In this second adaptation in 1986—the final part of his *Flamenco Trilogy*, which included *Carmen*, an Academy Award foreign nominee in 1984—Saura employed Antonio Gades as his choreographer and lead. Gades also starred in Beleta's version. The real difference between the two pictures, reviewers said, was timing: The Beleta version was made when fascist dictator Francisco Franco was in power, while the Gades version came out after Spain became a free democracy. The only "critic" listed at IMDb.com was Dave Sindelar at *Fantastic Movie Musings and Ramblings*, who noted the visual content of the 1968 nominee. "Despite having been based on a ballet," he wrote, "the movie is not one, though it does use dance extensively, particularly in some rather striking and eerie dream sequences." It opened September 14, 1967, and for a short run in New York City five years later, starting September 15, 1972; only the Soviet Union, oddly enough, got a full distribution.

Within four years, director Noboru Nakamura and actress Shima Iwashita had teamed up to make two Japanese motion pictures that negotiated their way through the AMPAS nomination process—Iwashita coincidentally playing different characters with the name of Chieko. The second film, **Portrait of Chieko** (*Chieko-sho*), relates the story of two artists who fall in love, marry and share an equal life together, which was unconventional at such a place and time. Said to be a true story based on the writings of sculptor Kotaro Takamura who penned the *Chieko Poems*, the movie is said to be a subtle, beautifully filmed and colorful testament to the "new woman" of modern Japan, but told with less sentimentality than one might imagine, according to amateur reviewers. The score by Masaru Sato—found online—tends to be a bit schmaltzy. Like his earlier movie *Twin Sisters of Kyoto* (1964)—or *Koto*, as it was also known—Nakamura's *Portrait* is one of the most difficult to find films in the catalog. Nothing is available on Amazon, eBay or rare-video merchandising sites, and legitimate online locations are impossible to come by, unless in clips promoting Sato's music. At the time of this writing, there was a two-hour-and-four-minute print in seven reels available at the University of California, Berkeley and a film version at Waseda University in Japan, according to WorldCat.org. It was released June 5, 1967, and actually ran for a while in Los Angeles starting March 13, 1968; no other distribution has been noted.

1969

B	*War and Peace*	**Soviet Union**
B	*The Boys of Paul Street*	Hungary
B	*Stolen Kisses*	France
B–	*The Girl with the Pistol*	Italy
C+	*The Firemen's Ball*	Czechoslovakia

Sergei Bondarchuk's **War and Peace** (*Voyna i mir*) winner of the 1969 prize, has been compared in scope and grandeur to *Gone with the Wind*. It's understandable; the Soviet Union nominee cost $100 million (more than $660 million in today's dollars) and involved a cast of 120,000, including top-flight actors in starring roles. (Bondarchuk himself plays Pierre, the intellectual and illegitimate aristocrat who dominates much of the storyline.) Based faithfully on Leon Tolstoy's epic novel, the film stands out in another way: It is seven hours and seven minutes in length, produced and distributed initially in four parts, and stands as the longest film ever nominated for an Oscar. It would take another book to outline all of the plots, so suffice to say it is a remarkable motion picture, with excellent cinematography on the level of *Ben-Hur* and *GWTW*, and it also was nominated for an Oscar in the Best Art Direction-Set Decoration category. It deserved its win, but owing to its television-series length and overambitious goals, it merited only a B, tying it with two other BFFs of the year. The film opened March 14, 1966, and in the United States April 28, 1968. Bondarchuk had two films submitted, but this was the only nominee. Also in the cast was Irina Gubanova from *Private Life* (1983).

The Boys of Paul Street (*A Pál-utcai fiúk*), based on a 1906 children's book by Ferenc Molnár, was Hungary's entry, and although the story has been told a number of times on film—in 1919, 1934 (as *No Greater Glory*), 1935 and 2003—this Academy Award nominee is difficult to locate. It's the story of schoolboys in Budapest who fiercely defend their turf against the "Redshirts," the Slavs, another gang of older boys. The battleground is the *Grund*, a neighborhood square they inhabit and turn into a scene of

Anthony Kemp as young Nemecsek Ernõ figures into *The Boys of Paul Street*'s (1969) turf-war story of boy gangs in Budapest, based on a children's tale by Ferenc Molnár.

trench warfare. It could be a scene from *West Side Story* meets *The Lord of the Flies*, but less dramatic. And where are the adults? The "professor" in the beginning seems oblivious to classroom chaos; family members are equally unresponsive, except perhaps for one boy's parents; the adult *Grund* guard is important enough to have a speaking part; only a few mature people are seen strolling streets or riding horse-drawn carriages, and during the battle they become observers high above the fray. This is conflict from a child's perspective, an allegory for national war, and it gets nasty, if comical, at times. Seen as a widescreen print in excellent color but in Hungarian, the film warranted a B. The picture opened April 3, 1969, and in New York City June 23, 1969; a wider distribution in the United States came exactly forty-six years later in 2015. The director, Zoltán Fábri, had four submitted films and two nominations, including *Hungarian Rhapsody* (1979).

The third in the Antoine Doinel series of five films by François Truffaut, **Stolen Kisses** (*Baisers volés*) features Jean-Pierre Léaud as Doinel and Claude Jade as the enigmatic Christine. At 14, Léaud starred in Truffaut's critically acclaimed but not Academy-nominated *400 Blows*. This is not like the first of the series, now considered an icon of the French New Wave Cinema with a rare 100 percent rating from Rotten Tomatoes. But it has its moments. The mischievous and perpetually love-struck Doinel, now dishonorably discharged from the army, becomes a private eye. He pursues the vacillating, oft-indifferent Christine, has a brief fling with an older woman, is jilted by the former who believes he has a lot of growing up to do, which is true, and finally becomes engaged to the younger woman. Writing for Criterion, Jamie S. Rich reported, "The maturing Antoine Doinel is every bit as charming as he was when young, and there is a looseness and unpredictability to Truffaut's plotting that keeps us wanting to know what happens next." DVD liner notes called the film: "Whimsical, nostalgic, and irrepressibly romantic…. Truffaut's timeless ode to the passion and impetuosity of youth." So true. The survey gave it a B. It cost an estimated $350,000 to make and opened September 4, 1968, in France and in February the next year in the States. It also starred Delphine Seyrig, who appeared in Luis Buñuel's *The Discreet Charm of the Bourgeoisie* (1973). Truffaut had three films submitted and nominated, including *Day for Night* (winner 1974) and *The Last Metro* (1981).

Monica Vitti made some sixty films in her career—notably Michelangelo Antonioni's *L'Avventura*, *Red Desert* and *La Notte*, the latter of which Italy unsuccessfully submitted for an Oscar in 1962. Indeed, of her films, only Mario Monicelli's **The Girl with the Pistol** (*La ragazza con la pistola*) made it through the nomination process. Not many critics liked it—or, more to the point, few took the time to deconstruct it. IMDb.com listed only two external sources: one a short blurb and the other a Portuguese-language review by the name of "Rick's Cinema." Basically, it's about honor the Sicilian way—not in the *Godfather* sense but extracting revenge for stealing a woman's virtue, and doing so with enough levity to make the film less of a drama and more of a comedy (something Vitti was not particularly known for). In fact, Monicelli is actually satirizing *fuitina*, the Sicilian practice of elopement following seduction, only in this case the violated Vitti is jilted next morning by the "man with a moustache." In fact, he has absconded to Scotland and she, pistol at the ready, chases after him, intending to assuage her disgrace. Most of the movie, which garnered a B−, takes place in the U.K. and there is considerable

English spoken, but not enough to disqualify the picture in the running for Best Foreign Language Film (must be more than 50 percent). Monicelli was responsible wholly or in part for three other nominees: *Big Deal on Madonna Street* (1959), *The Great War* (1960) and *Viva Italia!* (1979). British actors Stanley Baker and Corin Redgrave also had parts in this film. It opened in Milan September 20, 1968, but was not distributed in the United States. It is in color and runs an hour and forty minutes.

Soviet tanks rumbled into Czechoslovakia's capital on August 21, 1968, in a successful attempt to quash the Prague Spring uprising that had started more than nine months before. About the same time, the communist government permanently banned ***The Firemen's Ball*** (*Hoří, má panenko*)—a film by Miloš Forman that had been released the previous December—because it was deemed critical of the regime. How right they were! It satirized Moscow's continuing theft of Czech products, which impoverished the satellite and its bourgeoisie. The fire chief is retiring at age 86 because he has suddenly developed cancer. His colleagues, after some deliberation, decide to hold a ball in his honor and give him the gift of a gun he'll never be able to use. The fete is attended by everyone because they know they must, but it's a disaster. Prizes, especially hard-to-get foodstuffs, go missing during power failures; an attempt at holding a beauty pageant goes awry because none of the young women want to participate; and the insult of all insults takes place: the venue burns down as the helpless and hapless firemen, many of them too drunk to fight or care, do nothing. Through these metaphoric

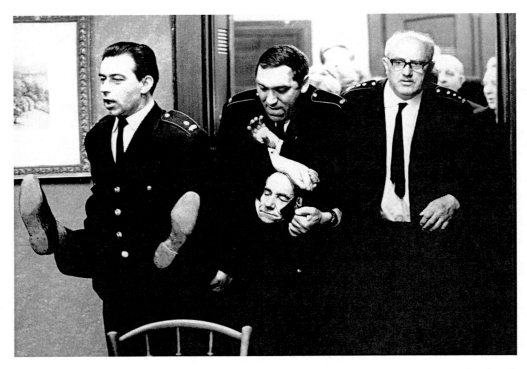

Chaos and drunken mayhem, as well as a heavy serving of thievery, mark the Czechoslovak New Wave film *The Firemen's Ball* (1967) by the late Miloš Forman. Jan Vostrčil (*left*) and two unidentified actors carry a drunken František Debelka.

vignettes, Forman's film, which ironically was funded by the Czech government, succeeds in dramatizing the country's unwieldy bureaucracy, political censorship, group procrastination, citizen insouciance and theft of goods by Russia—right down to the retirement gift! The short (one-hour-and-eleven-minute) color movie was entertaining enough but deserved only a C+. Forman's film *The Loves of a Blonde* (1967) was nominated earlier. He left Czechoslovakia not long after *Ball* was banned and became an institution in Hollywood with the likes of *One Flew Over the Cuckoo's Nest* (1976) and *Amadeus* (1985), both Best Picture winners. This film was released December 15, 1967, and in the United States September 29, 1968. It also starred Jan Vostrcil and Josef Sebánek of *Loves of a Blonde*.

1970

B	*Z*	**Algeria**
B	*Adalen 31*	Sweden
C	*My Night at Maud's*	France
C	*The Battle of Neretva*	Yugoslavia
C	*The Brothers Karamazov*	Soviet Union

An example of the international political intrigue of the '60s comes alive in *Z*, an intriguing color film by Costa-Gavras that not only was nominated and won for Best Foreign Film of 1970, but also garnered the Best Film Editing Award and received rare nominations for Best Picture, Best Director and Best Writing–Screenplay Based on Material from Another Medium, all for production host Algeria. It's a tightly woven storyline bolstered by brief, scattered flashbacks and repeated passages to maintain continuity and alleviate confusion. Members of the left-wing opposition party attempt to rally in support of their leader only to be thwarted by a conspiracy of right-wingers, police and junta bureaucrats. The leftist leader is assassinated, but police insist he's the unfortunate victim of a car-pedestrian accident, even though the incident takes place in a large square filled with club-totting thugs. A young photojournalist, taking on the airs of a paparazzo, manages to stir the pot by producing snapshots implicating hirelings, cops and high officials and substantiating flaws in their official report. With the help of a brave magistrate, they prove that the event wasn't an accident, nor a case of manslaughter, but an outright political murder. The affair takes place in Greece (the country is not as important as the theme, and it's in French anyway, as well as offered for consideration by Algeria) and is based on an identical occurrence six years earlier in the country's second city, Thessalonica. *Z* (which symbolically means "he lives" in Greek) had little competition for Best Foreign Language Film this particular year, but it stands out nonetheless as an exceptional film by dint of its other win and nominations, the first time a foreign submission had garnered both Best Foreign Film and Best Picture nominations; previously, only French-made *Grand Illusion* received a Best Picture nomination, but that was in 1938, long before a BFF category was instituted. *Z* opened in France February 26, 1960, and in the United States December 8, 1969, and brought in $7.1 million in U.S. rentals during its initial distribution. A B film, it was Costa-Gavras' only contender for the foreign prize, although he was prolific as a director and an actor.

Among his cast, however, were Yves Montand, Irene Papas and Jean-Louis Trintignant, all three appearing in nominated foreign films, including for Trintignant a competitor for this year, *My Night at Maud's*. Montand was in *Live for Life* (1968), while Papas starred in *Electra* (1963) and *Iphigenia* (1978) from Greece.

A Shakespearean theme exists in **Adalen 31**, a nominated Swedish film about a famous riot in the north-central pulp-mill district around Lunde near Kamfors on May 14, 1931. Kjell Andersson, elder son of a blue-collar family so poor his father and mother cannot afford sex, impregnates teenager Anna Björklund, whose father is among the capitalist class. They are the Romeo and Juliet of this otherwise true tale. Workers in the region and beyond have been striking for more than three months—some for half a year—against people like Anna's father. He and his cohorts eventually summon military troops to quell the riot, and in the melee that ensues, five workers are killed and five wounded. The event triggered social change in Sweden that exists today. This is one of the hard-to-find films, discovered late in the game on the streaming service YouTube.com during a rare moment in which the copyright-protection mavens had not yet caught on. As good luck would have it, it also contained sparse English subtitles. It should be noted that the substantial set-piece protest trek through town, labor banners and a marching band leading a host of extras along the dirt road, and the subsequent ambush are dramatically photographed and could be found in YouTube clips of varying lengths. There are some touching fictional moments in the otherwise documentary-style film. The small child, Martin Andersson, played by director and screenwriter Bo Witerberg's son, Johan, is endearing. At the end, he chases transitory bubbles he blows, perhaps a symbol for life—also the grieving widow climbs into bed with her children, more for her own need of consolation than to comfort them. It's difficult to tell why this hour-and-fifty-minute film doesn't receive more exposure; it's well acted, well directed and well photographed, the first half in a bucolic, romantic, springlike setting (much of it was filmed in Adalen). Maybe politics played a hand. The movie rated a B. It opened May 1, 1969, and in the States October 22, 1969, and cost an estimated $600,000 to make. Witerberg had four films submitted of which three were nominated, among them *Raven's End* (1965) and *All Things Fair* (1996). Also in the cast was Kerstin Tidelius, who appeared in *Fanny and Alexander* (1984).

The third of Éric Rohmer's *Six Moral Tales*, the dialogue-driven French film **My Night at Maud's** (*Ma nuit chez Maud*) involves a man of religious principles who spends the night simply talking with a recent divorcee while she's in bed. It's heavy into philosophy, sexual tension and chance encounters. Starring a 30-something Jean-Louis Trintignant—*A Man and a Woman* (1967), *Z* (1970) and the more recent *Amour* (2013)—as Jean-Louis, a Catholic who spies a young blonde in his provincial church one Sunday and decides she will one day become his wife. He runs into a friend, a Marxist professor, who invites him along to visit his girlfriend, Maud, at her home, but after an evening discussion on religion, philosophy, love, morality and mathematics, the friend insists on leaving, despite a severe snowstorm. Jean-Louis's character, however, chooses to remain, and—spoiler alert!—for the rest of the night, he continues in deep conversation with the woman. At times, one expects that he'll end up sleeping with her, since she all this time is in her nightie in and out of her bed, but while intimacy is often close at hand, the man sits or stands near her and only occasionally comes touchingly close. *Film Comment*'s editor-at-large Kent Jones pointed out: "Believability and plausibility at the most minute level are key characteristics of Rohmer's films—in this case, how single people in their thirties, living in the provinces, behave when they're alone, how they move, what they talk about, how they draw each other out and defend themselves from self-exposure." "I like surprises," Jean-Louis says at one point. As another narrative-heavy French drama, and also an hour and forty-five minutes long, *My Night at Maud's* was a bit tedious. Online clips reinforced a C ranking for the film, which opened June 4, 1969, and in America March 22, 1970. It was Rohmer's only submission and was nominated again in 1971 for Best Writing–Story and Screenplay Based on Factual Material or Material Not Previously Published or Produced. Also in the cast was Marie-Christine Barrault, a contender for Best Actress in *Cousin Cousine* (1977).

Bombs, machine-gun fire, strafing aircraft, death, destruction—the mayhem of war—lead off the hour-and-forty-eight-minute "patriotic" film from Yugoslavia *The Battle of Neretva* (*Bitka na Neretvi*), which took place in 1943 between outmanned partisans and German, Italian and Chechen forces, ironically in the Bosnia and Herzegovina region. Cinematography displaying sweeping battle scenes in the rolling hills of western Bosnia was the highlight of the early part of the film, but later, sound-stage scenes and last-gasp battles in snow-clad hills reign supreme. Another plus for this, the "most expensive film ever made by Yugoslavia," is an international cast that includes Yul Brynner, Orson Welles, Curd (Curt) Jürgens, Hardy Krüger and Franco Nero, among others. Thanks goes to the Texarkana (Texas) Public Library for supplying the VCR tape. Patriotic films don't always succeed as works of art, and this is one that definitely fits the description—the acting was rather mediocre to boot. The picture warranted a C. It runs an hour and forty-five minutes long and was directed by Veljko Bulajić, prolific with seven submissions but only this one nomination. Among the cast, Krüger is known for *Sundays and Cybèle* (1963) and Nero for *Tristana* (1971). Brynner and Welles, of course, collectively have a couple of statuettes on their shelves. This film opened October 7, 1969, and arrived in America— oddly in Bismarck, North Dakota—on February 25, 1971. It was estimated it cost $12 million to make.

No longer the childlike Pierre of *Sundays and Cybéle,* Hardy Krüger joins an all-star cast as Colonel Kranzer in *The Battle of Neretva* (1969).

As of this writing, there has been scant discussion published about the three-hour-and-fifty-two-minute, triptych adaptation of Fyodor Dostoevsky's novel *The Brothers Karamazov*, which the Soviet Union entered as a nominee for the 1970 prize. Indeed, the film **Bratya Karamazovy**, seen online without subtitles in three separate parts, is said to be available on DVD at a few U.S. college libraries and, for a price, on at least one online film dealer. But the International Movie Database (IMDb.com) lists no reviews and little dialogue from readers. The film is in color and quite theatrical, with what has been described by Russian commentators as outstanding acting all around. But while viewing the film, one could not help but think of Russian teacher Constantin Stanislavski and his form of method acting in describing the stagy presence and bombast of the main characters. The set designs were nominal and often appeared as painted backdrops, although interiors tended to be realistic enough with considerable prop and property placement, rustic or decorative furniture, and ornate or minimal wall coverings; this apparently was fairly common in Soviet filming at the time. The film rated a C. It was co-directed by actors Kirill Lavrov, who appeared in *Tchaikovsky* (1972), and Mikhail Ulyanov from *Private Life* (1983), as well as Ivan Pyryev who died during filming. None had another submission. This film opened January 10, 1969, in the Soviet Union, and later in five other countries, but not America.

1971

B+	*Investigation of a Citizen Above Suspicion*	Italy
B+	*Tristana*	Spain
C	*First Love*	Switzerland
—	*Hoa-Binh*	France
—	*Paix sur les Champs*	Belgium

Getting away with murder has long been a theme of detective stories, and in Gian Maria Volontè's Machiavellian character in **Investigation of a Citizen Above Suspicion** (*Indagine su un cittadino al di sopra di ogni sospetto*), the newly appointed political director of Rome's police department believes he's found a novel way. He's so powerful in his job that no one dares suspect him of the crime, even when he confesses. The 1971 winner of the Best Foreign Film analyzes this phenomenon as part of a "Trilogy of Neurosis" by director Elio Petri, who uses psychology and suspense to carry the opaquely colorful dark comedy forward, replete with a memorable and playful score by the great Ennio Morricone of "Spaghetti Westerns," *The Good, the Bad, and the Ugly* and *Cinema Paradiso* (1990). Volontè's unnamed chief inspector murders his mistress and then throws the crime in the face of his subordinates, taunting them to get off their duffs and solve it. It's a "we-know-who-dunnit" with a lame police procedural that never makes the right connection. In a taped confession, Il Dottore, the inspector, says he has proven that investigations "sidetrack" inquiries when people in power—those like himself who are "above suspicion"—raise doubt: a rather callous and psychopathic reason to commit murder in the first place. His mistress goads him into staging and photographing her impersonating the victims in a number of grisly murders he has solved. In a flashback, one of many where we learn how this cop and his prey interacted, he prophetically tells her: "I could murder you with my bare hands." She replies, "How brave. You'd lead the investigation. Who'd solve the crime?" It's an opening he feels is worth putting to the test. Calling his neurosis an "occupational disease," Il Dottore points out, "In the end, we policemen aren't that different from criminals: Same way of speaking, same habits, sometimes even the same gestures." It's a time of student revolution in Italy and the inspector uses the anti-gay, communist, subversive, authoritarian nature of his fellow cops to his advantage until he decides to let the cat out of the bag, by which time his colleagues, from commissioner on down, refuse to believe he could ever have committed the crime. It's a Kafkaesque study in how to get away with murder on a cynical level, and it works excellently. It was evaluated as a B+ picture. Volontè was also in *Open Doors* (1991). The hour-and-fifty-five-minute film, Petri's only submission, opened in Milan February 12, 1970, and in New York City December 20, 1970. Ugo Pirro wrote the 1972-nominated screenplay and also is known for scripting *The Garden of the Finzi-Continis* (1972).

Anyone who has studied Luis Buñuel films will know they are much deeper than what's portrayed on the surface. His recurrent anti-clerical, anti–Catholic, sado-masochistic, iconoclastic and power-tripping themes are rife, often with a surrealistic bent. ***Tristana*** continues this practice but is deceptively pragmatic for the master of the fantastic and bizarre. The 1971-nominated Spanish motion picture features Fernando Rey, who collaborated with Buñuel on five films (four of them Oscar contenders), as an aging aristocrat down on his luck, charged with the guardianship of the young and beautiful Catherine Deneuve (star of three Buñuel films, including the unsubmitted

Heavyweights Catherine Deneuve and Fernando Rey act out an intimate scene from *Tristana* (1970), directed by legendary surrealist Luis Buñuel.

French product *Belle du Jour*). As she quickly matures from girl to woman, he seduces her, and for a time she becomes his paramour. But Tristana comes to loathe the old man, takes up with an artist her own age, and soon leaves the embittered Don Lope to start a new life. As Don Lope tells the lover: "You understand my grief. I look at her with the purest, disinterested love." At this juncture, the movie skips ahead and takes an unexpected series of turns that demonstrate how power can be illusory and control can sway from one person to another. This compelling color film earned a B+. It's an hour and thirty-five-minutes long and also stars Franco Nero who was in *The Battle of Neretva* (1970). Deneuve starred in *The Umbrellas of Cherbourg* (1965) and Rey in *The Discreet Charm of the Bourgeoisie* (1973) and *That Obscure Object of Desire* (1978). The cast included Antonio Ferrandis of *My Dearest Señorita* (1973) and *Volver a Empezar* (1983). The film opened in Spain March 29, 1970, and in New York City September 21, 1970.

The Swiss entry for the year, ***First Love*** (*Erste Liebe*), is an art film directed, acted and produced by Austrian *divo* Maximilian Schell. This is *The Graduate* meets *Elvira Madigan* but without the humor, unless one ponders how weird some characters are, especially the 16-year-old Alexander falling in love with 21-year-old Sinaida, daughter of a princess who has fallen on hard times. The kicker is that the adolescent's father, played by Schell, also falls in lust with the girl—played by lovely Dominique Sanda (also in *The Garden of the Finzi-Continis* in the next Oscar year)—to the boy's consternation. This film earned a C when viewed off a dubbed DVD borrowed from the Fitchburg (Wisconsin) Public Library. Since the dialogue was spare, the mediocre dubbing did not distract too much from the action. Indeed, one of the problems with the hour-and-thirty-minute movie was its plodding pace, especially when the two youngsters romp through the fields à la *Elvira Madigan*, touching and cooing and dreaming. The lack of popularity of the film in America can be assumed by the fact that only two critiques appeared on the International Movie Database (IMDb.com), although one of them was by prolific movie-watcher Roger Ebert. The film opened April 23, 1971, and in New York City October 7, 1970. Schell's résumé is well known, both as a director and thespian, including a Best Actor Award for the American film *Judgment in Nuremburg* (1961) and West German directorial nomination for *The Pedestrian* (1974).

When his father goes off to fight for the Viet Cong and his mother dies of cancer, an 11-year-old boy is left to survive with his baby sister on the dangerous streets of Saigon during the height of the Vietnam War. If young Hung is anything, he's cool and reticent. Filmed on location and based on a novel, ***Hoa-Binh*** (it means Democracy) is a French-nominated Oscar candidate by highly regarded cinematographer Raoul Coutard, who photographed most of the greatest films of French New Wave adherents François Truffaut, Jean-Luc Godard and Jacques Demy. He's a celebrated filmmaker but not particularly a seasoned director—indeed, this was his first (and only submitted) effort on his own, and it failed on many levels. According to Molly Haskell of the *Village Voice*, "In its most noteworthy accomplishment, the film achieves a rhythm and tempo— a controlled adagio—consistent with the calm, low-keyed response of the small boy, played by Phi Lan, to joy and bereavement alike." Another achievement may be in its understated political references, the most notable being occasional background sounds of war and a comment or two overheard to justify U.S. presence there. No, Hung is cool, calm and collected for a tyke under such stress. The big problem with *Hoa-Binh* today is its unavailability. It isn't found in libraries, and there's rarely anything listed on the usual online video sales sites. For this reason, this is one of the rare Oscar-nominated foreign films that have not been seen in the study, nor can it be rated or commented on directly. *Hoa-Binh* is an hour and thirty-three minutes long and opened in France March 11, 1970; the U.S. for a short run August 22, 1971; and only four other countries.

According to the online World Catalog, you'll have to go to the Bibliothèque Nationale de France in Paris if you want to see **Paix sur les Champs**, Belgium's 1971 Oscar entry. That's how rare it is. Surely it exists elsewhere, but that was the only sighting on WorldCat.org. We know the picture—also known as *The Fields Sleep in Peace, Peace in (or over) the Fields* and *Vrede over de velden*—is about a wealthy farmer in Flanders accused of murdering his fiancée twenty years before but acquitted. When his son falls in love with the victim's younger sister, the mother forbids the marriage. Riven with guilt and superstition, the father-suspect has a heart attack and admits to the homicide as he lies dying, but he also asks the mother for forgiveness. Based on a 1941 book by Marie Gevers and directed by Jacques Boigelot in his only Oscar submission, *Peace in the Fields* has touches reminiscent of *Crime and Punishment* and *Romeo and Juliet,* but is rooted in the beautiful Flemish rural landscape of the mid–1920s. Another of the handful of unavailable films did elicit a few translatable comments on European websites such as *Espacenord* and *Belfilm* from which to draw a smattering of information. The hour-and-thirty-four-minute feature opened briefly in France June 20, 1973, and was never released into distribution here or abroad. In the cast was Georges Poujouly, the young boy in *Forbidden Games* (1953).

1972

B+	*The Garden of the Finzi-Continis*	Italy
B	*Dodes'ka-den*	Japan
B	*The Emigrants*	Sweden
B–	*Tchaikovsky*	Soviet Union
C–	*The Policeman*	Israel

Italy's winning contribution to the 1972 Oscars, **The Garden of the Finzi-Continis** (*Il giardino dei Finzi-Contini*), takes place in 1938 as Benito Mussolini launches his persecution of Jews in much the same way Adolf Hitler had been doing in Germany for years. Only here, one aristocratic Jewish family believes itself above the fray, oblivious of the circumstances. The film is a snapshot of a period just before World War II in which time and space seem in repose just prior to the big bang. The garden represents the capsule in which this time-space continuum exists, and we're never allowed by director Vittorio De Sica to see all of it. The characters, too, are blind to their immediate future, even though one of them, who exists outside the bubble, knows of concentration camps and tries to alert the others of their existence. The Finzi-Contini family thinks itself safe from oppression behind the high walls of their kingdom-garden they never leave. Meanwhile, the central figure, the attractive, blonde, "unpredictable" daughter

Micòl, plays cat and mouse with her childhood sweetheart, Giorgio. She teases him sensually while at the same time holding the quiet calm of an innocent past to her breast and repressing his ardent advances to make love to her, saying "it would be too much like making love to a brother." Perhaps not the best of the Italian winners, *Garden* nevertheless is a well-made, entertaining but sad movie, which, as so many films of this era, draws starkly from the tyranny of World War II Europe. A B+ winner, the hour-and-thirty-four-minute film premiered first in Jerusalem December 2, 1970, and in Italy two days later. It opened in the United States December 16, 1971. In the cast were Dominique Sanda, who starred in *First Love* (1971), and Helmut Berger, who played in two American contenders, *The Damned* (1970) and *Godfather III* (1991). Five of De Sica's films were submitted including the first two from the category honored by the Academy, *Shoeshine* (1948) and *The Bicycle Thief* (1949); *Yesterday, Today and Tomorrow* (1965) was a winner and *Marriage Italian Style*, the next year, was the other nominee.

Cinematic genius Akira Kurosawa stepped completely out of his comfort zone when he made ***Dodes'ka-den***, Japan's nominee. The film stands out as a symbolic, spice-of-life, episodic motion picture that, given the unique quality of Japanese storytelling, might well have come from any qualified and talented director in the world. Kurosawa just knew how to adapt unusual tales to the screen. In this one he used color for the first time, filmed in standard 1:33 35mm instead of anamorphic widescreen, employed many little-known actors, and took his film company to an actual garbage dump—where all the action takes place—to shoot most scenes. It's about a collection of urban slum dwellers, each person or couple with a unique story of woe and suffering and, in some cases, unfettered violence. Critic-author Stephen Prince, writing for The Criterion Collection, said: "[Kurosawa's] characters aim to transcend their appalling circumstances not just with dreams and humor but also sometimes through simple, stubborn denial of what surrounds them." Indeed, the director was going through tough times and nearly took his own life a year after the film premiered. The theme (and title) is based around Roku-chan, a young simpleton who imagines himself one of the many trolleys he sees plying the streets outside of his dismal scrapheap world. As he continuously circles the junkyard on imaginary tracks, he makes the sound equivalent to "clickety-clack," which can be translated into Japanese onomatopoetically as *Dodes'ka-den*. It received a B, despite its poor showing at the box office (it didn't succeed topping the $300,000 it reputedly cost to make). The two-hour-and-twenty-minute film opened as a roadshow production in Japan October 31, 1970, and in the United States June 9, 1971.

Jan Troell's ***The Emigrants*** (*Utvandrarna*) tells a sincere, direct, often visceral tale of hardscrabble farmers in Sweden's remote Småland and their survivalist decision, naïve as it may have been, to uproot—lock, stock, barrel and brood—and travel to America in the pioneering mid–1800s. The 1972-nominated film was the director's first of three Oscar contenders, the second being a sequel, *The New Land* (1973), and third, *The Flight of the Eagle* (1983), and all in partnership with Max von Sydow. *Emigrants* is a raw, harrowing story of determination and suffering for the first half, laced with superstition and religious fervor. The second half is all adventure: leaving home; traveling over rutted roads to a port to board a ship, fetid and overcrowded as it was, for the weeks-long voyage to America; and then the long journey by train, steamboat and

Jan Troell's *The Emigrants* (1971) traces the migration of Swedish farmers by ship to the United States in the mid–1800s, and Max von Sydow (*foreground*) is their leader.

foot to new pastures in Minnesota. "One mile in Sweden is the same as six miles in America," says one character, dispelling a rumor that Minnesota was a mere 250 miles away from their port of call. Also in the cast is Liv Ullmann, the young wife Christine, whose babies come all too frequently, contributing to the couple's poverty in an already-impoverished world. She was nominated for Best Actress for her role, but that came a year later when Troell was a contender for Best Director and the script was nominated for Best Writing–Screenplay Based on Material from Another Medium. *The Emigrants* opened March 8, 1971, and in New York City September 24, 1972. The B–rated film appears often on a classic-film television channel, usually dubbed in English by some or all of the on-screen actors. Troell, incidentally, had a total of five films submitted to the Academy: Two didn't make the cut; this one and *The New Land* did; and a fifth, *Everlasting Moments* (2009), made the January shortlist.

Pyotr Il'yich Tchaikovsky was a troubled, depressed, likely homosexual 19th-century Russian composer, famous for his *Nutcracker Suite* and *Swan Lake*, among many other iconic compositions. Filmmaker Igor Talankin, in his only submitted BFF candidate, chose to tell his story in a fanciful biopic the Soviet Union submitted for a foreign film Oscar. Although the motion picture, shot in vignettes about the composer's life, gives a broad brush to actual events, Talankin's emphasis was on his music. *Tchaikovsky* touches on his youth, explores him as a student through the mentorship by Nikolai Rubinstein (the composer Anton Rubenstein's brother), cites his insufferable marriage to a former admirer and dwells on the long-lasting friendship with a patron, Natalia von Meck, whom oddly he never met. It does not mention his homosexuality or his controversial death, which while not fully understood is believed to have been suicide by drinking water laced with either cholera or arsenic. His death came shortly after the performance of his gloomy Sixth Symphony (*Pathétique*), seen by some as his own requiem. Not much is written about Talankin's two-hour-and-thirty-seven-minute epic, which was released in Moscow August 31, 1970—nearly two years before the Oscar ceremony—and in America during January 1972. One uncredited appraisal from *Digitally Obsessed!* points out many of the film's flaws. "Characters appear, are never properly introduced, so that we have no idea who they are or what relationship they have to anyone else, and then they vanish," the review site says. Despite the negative criticism, the author proffered a B– after watching the film. In the cast were Kirill Lavrov, a player in *Brothers Karamazov* (1970), and Antonina Shuranova, who was in *War and Peace* (winner 1969). One brief side note: the celebrated Russian-American composer Dimitri Tiomkin (*High and the Mighty, High Noon, The Unforgiven*) served as music arranger and executive producer on *Tchaikovsky*, for which he received a nomination for Best Music-Scoring Adaptation and Original Song Score.

The *Pink Panther* series starring Peter Sellers was a rage in the United States about the time **The Policeman** (*HaShoter Azulai*) from Israel hit the silver screen. The latter is now regarded as a classic of the Israeli cinema. Constable Sergeant Abraham Azulai is a patrolman in Jaffa. Like Sellers' Jacques Clouseau, he's honest and brave but exceptionally naïve. Unlike Clouseau's, his antics aren't slapstick, but there are parallels. His superior, Captain Lefkowitch (who coincidentally resembles Sellers), wants Azulai to retire after twenty years on the force but the veteran cop is reluctant to pack it in until he's been honored and promoted for leading, or thinking he has led, the arrest of a thief in what turns out to be a staged robbery. Directed by Ephraim Kishon whose *Sallah* (1965) was the first Israeli film submitted and nominated, *The Policeman* has been criticized for trying too hard to be funny when essentially it's a drama with comedic overtones. Indeed, it's fundamentally a character study of the patrolman: highlighting his foibles, ignorant associations with known criminals, connections to Arab politics, involvement with a prostitute, interaction with a jealous wife, and leader of troops who appear to genuinely like the guy. Called "too dated and silly" in the study, the hour-and-twenty-seven-minute film was only worthy of a C–. Even so, it won a slew of awards, including a Golden Globe, and is still revered in Israel. By the way, don't confuse the 2011 Israeli picture titled simply *Policeman* with this one; they are totally unrelated. The 1972 candidate opened in 1971 and in New York City April 6, 1972. It appeared only in four other countries. Among the cast were Zaharira Harifai, who was in *Sallah* (1965), and Avner Hizkiyaku, Joseph Shiloach and Shaike Ophir, characters in *The House on Chelouche Street* (1974). Shiloach also appeared in *I Love Your Rosa* (1973).

1973

A–	*The Discreet Charm of the Bourgeoisie*	France
B	*The New Land*	Sweden
C+	*The Dawns Here Are Quiet*	Soviet Union

| C | *I Love You Rosa* | Israel |
| C | *My Dearest Señorita* | Spain |

For Luis Buñuel, "there is no explanation" for his motion picture **The Discreet Charm of the Bourgeoisie** (*Le Charme discret de la bourgeoisie*), which won the foreign film Oscar in 1973. It reverses the theme of his 1962 satire *The Exterminating Angel*; in the latter, folks gather for a fancy dinner, eat and then cannot leave, for days and weeks. In the former, the egocentric and corrupt (both beside the point) middle-class but self-important characters, keep sitting down to eat but cannot or won't. Buñuel favorite Fernando Rey, playing a small, fictional country's ambassador to France, leads the group, taking them from place to place in his fancy Fleetwood Cadillac *avec* chauffeur, who at one point, being below middle class, becomes the butt of an experiment showing how *not* to drink a martini. In one segment, the peripatetic foursome arrives for luncheon at the home of a couple who are so enamored with each other they flee to the woods to make love instead of greeting their guests. Cynical, satirical, absurd, surreal: All of these describe Buñuel's film, his second nomination in three years. Give this one an A–. It runs an hour and forty-two minutes and opened in France September 15, 1972, and in the U.S. October 22, 1972. It reportedly cost around $800,000 to make. Buñuel received three nominations: also for *That Obscure Object of Desire* (1978) and *Tristana* (1971). The actor Fernando Rey appeared in all three. Delphine Seyrig had a part in this film and also was in *Stolen Kisses* (1969), the Truffaut vehicle. The cast also

(*Left to right*) **Delphine Seyrig, Jean-Pierre Cassel, Bulle Ogier, Milena Vukotic, Julien Guiomar, Stéphane Audran, and Fernando Rey enjoy a fine-dining experience, or another Luis Buñuel experiment in which the guests never get around to eating, in the *The Discreet Charm of the Bourgeoisie* (1972).**

included Michel Piccoli of *Dangerous Moves* (1985) and Stéphane Audran from *Coup de Torchon* (1983) and star of *Babette's Feast* (1988).

Rarely is an Oscar-nominated foreign film set wholly in America. ***The New Land*** (*Nybyggarna*), Sweden's submission, is an exception. It's the second part of Jan Troell's pair of sagas about Scandinavian settlers emigrating to the Minnesota frontier in the 1840s. The first film, cleverly titled *The Emigrants* and starring many of the same actors including Max von Sydow and Liv Ullmann, was a multi-award nominee in 1973, including Best Picture, but notably for Best Foreign Film the year before. Most of the first movie dealt with the subsistence-level lives of the farmers of the rural south of Sweden, their decision to pull up stakes to settle in America and their harrowing sea journey. *The New Land* picks up as they arrive at Lake Chisago where they find a new home in the Minnesota woodlands. It's just as difficult for them in America, however. Troell makes no bones about their struggle, particularly that of Ullmann's character, who suffers severely from homesickness and possibly numerous bouts of postpartum depression, and endures numerous challenges along the way. The central theme is marriage endurance and how, as film writer Terrence Rafferty concludes in a Criterion article, "Troell allows us to see that marriage itself is a kind of emigration: a matter of settling into another life, making the necessary accommodations, and gradually—over the years, over decades—finding that you think of this person who is not you, or this place that is not the land of your birth, as your home." The picture, at an hour and forty-two minutes, debuted February 26, 1972, and in New York City October 26, 1973. It has much the same cast as the other film: von Sydow, Ullmann, Eddie Axberg, among others. Troell had five films submitted and three nominated, the other one being *The Flight of the Eagle* (1983). While *The Emigrants* is relatively easy to find, even occasionally on television, it takes a little searching to find this successor. The Criterion Collection DVD from the local library received a B. Incidentally, the 1992 Swedish contender, Sven Nykvist's *The Ox*, which takes place in the 1860s and also stars von Sydow and Ullmann, is in many ways similar to Troell's duology.

Russian-style feminism during World War II serves as a theme of ***The Dawns Here Are Quiet*** (*A zori zdes tikhie*). Soviet gunnery soldiers at a small village outpost near Finland are distracted by the local "comforts," so they are replaced by an all-female unit. Senior Sgt. Vaskov remains behind to command the women, an order he's not so sure about, but he does warm to their charms. All is well until a couple of Nazis are discovered lurking in the woods. Vaskov takes a contingent of five co-eds to track them down, but they quickly find themselves the underdogs when the Germans suddenly expand to sixteen. This is a long film, three hours and eight minutes, and the first half is one lengthy exposition, letting us get to know the women, their backstories and former loves, one by one. The second half involves the battle in the forest, and most critics— of which there were few—believed this was the better part of the film. Director Stanislav Rostotsky, following the book by Boris Vasilyev, used close-ups, color and stylized imagery to convey intimacy and authenticity in the flashbacks, but employed conventional filming techniques and black and white the rest of the way. There's numerous "Die for the Mother Country" propaganda elements to the picture but it comes off well anyway; even so, it deserved merely a C+. It opened November 4, 1972; there is no indication it was distributed in the United States. Rostotsky in addition directed *White Bim Black Ear* (1979), which also included in its cast Andrey Martynov.

According to Deuteronomy 25:5, a deceased man's brother shall marry his widow if she has not had a son. That's the theme of *I Love You Rosa* (*Ani Ohev Otach Rosa*), this year's Israeli nomination. This slow, plodding film by Moshé Mizrahi explores the Old Testament passage using an 11-year-old boy as the protagonist expected to do his duty by marrying his 20-year-old sister-in-law. He adores her but is still too young to know what to do. The film—set in Jerusalem between 1887 and 1892, with opening and closing scenes in the modern age—was described as a "bittersweet romance." The obviously confused preteen, Nissem, tries to woo Rosa without success, but all is well that ends well as he grows into manhood. Mizrahi keeps the film on the up and up and refrains from anything that today would land a filmmaker or actor in jail on pedophilia charges. The hour-and-seventeen-minute picture is sentimental but not overtly so and has a satisfactory ending. This C film opened February 12, 1972, and in New York City February 16, 1973. It was the first of two consecutively nominated submissions by Mizrahi, the other being *The House on Chelouche Street* (1974), also starring Joseph Shiloach of *The Policeman* (1972).

The Spanish entry, **My Dearest Señorita** (*Mi querida señorita*), was controversial when it premiered in strongman Francisco Franco's Spain. It depicted a female who wanted to become a male at a time when transsexual operations were illegal in the ardently Catholic country. Even so, director Jaime de Armiñán and producer Luis Megino took on the taboo with the help of one of Spain's most prolific actors, José Luis López Vázquez, playing the part of Adela, a 43-year-old spinster who becomes Juan. Many scenes revolve around catalyst Isabelita, Adela's maid, played by another prolific actor, Julieta Serrano, who urges her boss to see a specialist. She gets fired for it, but Adela does follow her advice. Paradoxically, Serrano's character later emerges as Juan's love interest. The film, in color on a P.A.L. Spanish-language DVD from Colby College in Maine, appeared jerky and poorly edited (street observers pass by and stare into the camera); Chopin's "Third Étude" was chopped in here and there to set mood; and a lot of close-in facial shots don't appear to fit. The hour-and-twenty-minute picture, which garnered a C, opened February 17, 1972, in Chicago in November of that year, and subsequently only in three other countries. Armiñán was responsible for three submitted films, but the only other one nominated was *The Nest* (1981). Vázquez also starred in *Plácido* (1962), and Serrano was in *Women on the Verge of a Nervous Breakdown* (1989). Appearing in the cast was Antonio Fernandis, also in *Tristana* ((1971) and *Volver a Empezar* (1983).

In the Doldrums:
1974–1986

Not really. Not with such marvelous films as *Day for Night*, *The Tin Drum* and *Fanny and Alexander*, not to mention the István Szabó trilogy of "political parables" from Hungary or Akira Kurosawa's *Dersu Uzala* or *Kagemusha*. But of the sixty-five films nominated during this period, only a handful of them are well known, and some that are do not quite measure up. Indeed, a few of them are nearly impossible to locate.

This was a transitional time, when the film industries of many countries were in direct competition with television, a medium attracting a growing number of the best performers and, consequently, the majority of the film-going public. Japan is an excellent example of this. The Japanese cinema took a tumble after the popular period dramas of the '50s and '60s with a few exceptions. It wouldn't be until the turn of the century, with Hideo Tanaka's *Dark Water* and Yojiro Takita's *Departures*, before pictures other than *Yakuza* gangster potboilers and *anime* came back into prominence and the more prosperous, *true* cinephiles began to spend their money again.

Israel, which had created a number of decent international pictures earlier, reentered the scene with its *Operation Thunderbolt*, about the chest-pumping (and -thumping) raid on Entebbe, Uganda, in 1976, which, although nominated, was pretty much forgettable.

Another notable filmmaker during this period was Andrzej Wajda, who is credited for contributing to the birth of the Solidarity Movement in Poland with his 1982-nominated *Man of Iron*. It wasn't his only Oscar nomination. Another prominent Polish director was Agnieszka Holland. She recreated a World War II love affair between a Jewess and a Christian German farmer in *Angry Harvest*, a scenario regarded as controversial when the film hit the box offices.

And Yugoslavian moviemaker Emir Kusturica made a political feature, *When Father Was Away on Business*, which caused quite a stir.

It wasn't so much that laudable directors were struggling to find an engaged audience as it was turning out meaningful fare that would stand up today. There were some, of course, but for the most part, this period needed a serious lift out of the doldrums, and it took more than a decade for that to happen.

1974

A	*Day for Night*	**France**
A–	*The House on Chelouche Street*	Israel
B+	*L'invitation*	Switzerland
B	*Turkish Delight*	Netherlands
C	*The Pedestrian*	West Germany

Let's begin with the title: *La Nuit américaine,* which in French denotes the cinematic technique of filming night scenes during the day using filters and special film. This is a loose translation from the process's American name and title of the film: ***Day for Night,*** the 1974 Best Foreign Language Film winner. Call it a farce or film-within-a-film, but the fact is, this is director Francois Truffaut's homage to the movie industry. He takes an assortment of stereotypical characters in the industry and tells their various stories, showing along the way some of the more interesting techniques used in making motion pictures. The point here is that the French film-within-the-film he's making, *Meet Pamela,* will obviously be a stinker. It's not the movie we're watching, or for that matter the technical prowess that goes into shooting it, but the way people, in and out of the movie, react to each other and what they are supposed to be doing. This was a fun film and warranted a rare A. As happened now and then, *Day for Night* went on a year later to receive nominations in other Oscar categories: Truffaut for Director,

Séverine, played by Valentina Cortese in an Oscar-nominated role, needs cue cards during a scene in François Truffaut's film-within-a-film, *Day for Night* (1973). Jean-Pierre Aumont is pictured behind her.

Valentina Cortese for Supporting Actress, and Truffaut, Jean-Louis Richard and Suzanne Schiffman for Original Screenplay. It opened May 24, 1973, and in the U.S. September 7, 1973, and runs an hour and fifty-five minutes. Truffaut also was nominated for *Stolen Kisses* (1969) and *The Last Metro* (1981). Jean-Pierre Léaud, the lad, was also the male lead in *Stolen Kisses*.

It's a shame that such a fine film as **The House on Chelouche Street** (*Ha-Bayit Berechov Chelouche*), Israel's contribution in 1974, should receive so few reviews. Directed by Moshé Mizrahi, whose *I Love You Rosa* also made it through the nomination process the previous year, tells the tale of a family of working-class Sephardic Jews from Alexandria, Egypt—a widow named Clara, her older son Sami and her two daughters (as well as a younger boy who dies)—who struggle to survive in Tel Aviv in 1947 just before Israel became a state. Sami, 15, must work to help the family, and it's through his perspective that much of the story is told. His 33-year-old mother, played by Gila Almagor (*Sallah* 1965), is pressured by other family members to take a new husband—not easy since her primary suitor is a self-styled and nearly bald Don Juan whom she likes, but not that much. As the *Village Voice* noted at the time the picture came out: "'The House on Chelouche Street' is not a big film, but its heart and its camera are in the right place." Your author thought so, too, and gave it an A–. The picture opened in Israel in 1973 and came to New York City April 17, 1974, the only two distribution points. It also starred Joseph Shiloach and Shaike Ophir, both of whom appeared in *The Policeman* (1972).

How well do you know the private lives of your fellow office workers? That's the question posed in Claude Goretta's Swiss motion picture **L'Invitation**, which Switzerland proffered for the 1974 ceremony. Rémy Placet, a modest midlevel employee, invites his coworkers to enjoy a garden party at his home—but not just any home: Placet owns a luxurious country estate, purchased with an inheritance from his mother, and to serve at the party he has hired a fancy butler. His guests, particularly his bosses, are taken aback by this unexpected display of wealth and understandably show envy for the man's seeming affluence. Critic James Travers described *The Invitation* as "a modest comedy of manners, ... one of the cruelest and cleverest social satires of the 1970s." He continues: "...it is a film that is distinguished by its humanity, its perception and its thoughtful preoccupation with the related themes of class and identity." It was the first of two Goretta films submitted for consideration, the other one missing the cut. The movie, which opened first in Denmark November 16, 1973, and in New York City April 27, 1975, received a B+. Among the cast were Jean Champion—*The Umbrellas of Cherbourg* (1965), *Day for Night* (winner 1974) and *Coup de Torchon* (1983)—and Michel Robin, who appeared in the multiple award nominee *Amélie* (2002).

"You're a comedian," Olga tells Eric on their honeymoon. But Eric, always playful with his voluptuous bride, is anything but a comedian in **Turkish Delight** (*Turks Fruit*) from Holland. The hour-and-forty-eight-minute B-rated film alternates from Eric's prickliness and imagined violence to his quirky-but-edgy playfulness, and at times even feels more like a PG situation comedy. This is reflected in the segment when Queen Juliana comes to unveil his statue while his lover unveils her breasts to cool off, or the eschatological scene where the beet juice imitates cancer. But this film is not for the faint of heart. It's about a man no doubt in love with a lovely lady but also impulsive and troubled by a hungry need for sex and the young woman who is eager to give it to him. Eric, played masterfully by good-looking, blond Rutger Hauer, in short is unpredictable. Reflections play an important part in this film: images on sunglass lenses, a car's rearview mirror, the side of the queen's Rolls-Royce, a full-length mirror twice, a handheld mirror in a hospital, and even a voodoo statue. What you see is a reflection of what is perceived and perhaps not wholly real. This is realized by director Paul Verhoeven, who cast beautiful Monique van der Ven in this role. She later tried but never quite made it in Hollywood (see also *The Assault* 1987). She is sexy, but the acting is breathy and contrived. Hauer's is more spontaneous and natural. The DVD came from Pacific University Library in Forest Grove, Oregon, via the local library system and was of excellent quality. The movie as a whole could be considered sexploitation, since the Netherlands in the early '70s was fast becoming the mecca for free love and no-holds-barred, commercially produced or displayed sex products. And what of the title? One urban definition is that of performing an outrageous stunt or prank on your sexual partner before intercourse and then shouting, "Turkish Delight!" The first half of the film deserved a C, but as it progressed and what Verhoeven intended became more apparent, it was elevated to a B. After all, at one time the Dutch thought this the best movie ever made in their country! It opened February 22, 1973, and September 1974 in America. Verhoeven had seven films submitted for Oscar consideration, but this was the only one nominated (one other, *Black Book* in 2007, made the January shortlist). He also is responsible for the American blockbuster *Total Recall* (1991) and a film that perhaps should have been nominated, but wasn't: *Elle* (2017), which won the Golden Globe that year for Best Foreign Film.

   The Pedestrian (*Der Fußgänger*)—produced, directed and written by Maximilian Schell, also with a small part—might be considered the quintessential shame-induced anti–Nazi German-made product. Heinz Alfred Giese, played by Gustav Rudolf Sellner, a politically correct and essential engineer-industrialist twenty-nine years after the war, is suspected of being the local Nazi authority in a Greek village when two German soldiers are shot in the back by National Resistance fighters. Giese orders everyone in the village liquidated. Men are forced into the town square and executed. All women and children are herded into a church where Giese, it is alleged, and another Nazi, now a respected doctor, murder them and then torch the church. Now, years later, with authorities sitting on their hands, the German press hounds him. He runs a red light and causes a crash that also kills his beloved older son, Andreas—played by Schell—who it is believed wants to kill his father because of the atrocities he's committed—or it could be the other way around. Subsequently, authorities take away the industrialist's driver's license—hence the name *The Pedestrian*—and orders him to attend traffic school, where he is recognized by an older woman who survived the massacre. The newspapers believe the guy is guilty and publish the story. Giese denies it. The newsmen debate what is more important: convicting the aging man or leaving him to help the new Germany build on its economy. He is, after all, an important and talented industrialist. There are two other important matters: Giese has a mistress who is really his muse, and many of his feelings about the investigation run through her. She's unfaithful, however, and he eventually returns to his knowing wife. The other matter is Michael, his second son, a black sheep with long hair. It's through his appearance in the final minutes of the film that Germany's "shame" is particularly evident. "I don't want to be German anymore," he says. The film was viewed in English at the University of Utah library in Salt Lake City. It originally opened September 6, 1973, and in New York City February 28, 1974, and thereafter only in Denmark and Hungary. It rated a C. Two of Schell's films were submitted, but only this one was accepted; despite this, he appears in another nominated foreign film, *First Love* (1971), and was nominated three times for U.S. pictures, winning for his role in *Judgment in Nuremberg* (1962).

1975

B+	*Lacombe, Lucien*	France
B	***Amarcord***	**Italy**
B	*The Truce*	Argentina
C	*The Deluge*	Poland
C–	*Cat's Play*	Hungary

Not so much as a psychopath but as a naïve opportunist, Lucien Lacombe joins the Gestapo toward the close of World War II because the French Resistance won't take a reckless 17-year-old. He likes the new power, his automatic weapon, the fact he's no longer bored mopping floors in a medical ward. Louis Malle's morality play, ***Lacombe, Lucien*** (how the protagonist fills out forms in bureaucratic, Nazi-control Vichy France), shows how uninformed, provincial people acted and reacted to the politics around them in occupied France: blind, amoral and self-absorbed. Lucien is all of that, if power hungry, but as the war's inevitable end nears, he falls in love with a Jewish girl whom he protects, along with her family, from the cruel, desperate Nazis. Much has been said about this art film, not the least by cinema critic Pauline Kael of *The New Yorker*: "Malle's film is a long, close look at the banality of evil; it is—not incidentally—one of the least banal movies ever made…. There's no special magic involved in the moviemaking technique—it's simple, head-on, unforced." Malle, who enjoyed success with several American films, had three French films submitted for BFF consideration, of which this one and *Au Revoir les Enfant*s (1988) were nominated. *Lacombe, Lucien* was worthy of a B+, placing it above the winning film. It runs two hours and eighteen minutes, opened January 30, 1974, and came to the States September 29, 1974.

From Nino Rota's circuslike music to the flamboyant characters who populate all films of Federico Fellini, the great Italian director pulled out all the stops for his swan song. ***Amarcord*** sizzles with fun and delight and the reminiscences of a town thumbing its nose at austere fascism of 1930s Italy. Made in 1973, the motion picture won Best Foreign Film in 1975 and was nominated for two other Oscars: Best Director and Best Original Screenplay, both in 1976, which demonstrates how dispersed the Oscar awards could be. *Amarcord*, at just over two hours, recreates a time and place in Fellini's youth—specifically Rimini on Italy's Adriatic coast—but he refused to film there, to the consternation of his friends and family; instead, he built another Rimini at Rome's Cinecittà, saying it was necessary because filming in his own town would evoke sentimental memories that would distract from his script. Indeed, Fellini preferred that the town be fictional, recognized only for its universal or symbolic implications. *Amarcord* won acclaim for its political and social satire, stylistic playfulness, humor, humanity and the honest, if avant-garde, depiction of provincial Italy during a time of repression, delusion and false ideals. The movie is a celebration of the human spirit, seen from the points of view of various townspeople, not the least of whom would have been Fellini himself had he given himself a role. Admittedly, Fellini created autobiographical films, "feeding off his life, his fantasies, his earlier films," according to the late *Chicago Sun-Times* and television critic Roger Ebert. This was his last great picture, one that sums up in one way or another his other masterpieces: *La Strada, Nights of Cabiria, La Dolce Vita, 8½* and *Juliet of the Spirits,* arguably his most personal. Among the cast was Pupella Maggio, who appeared also in *Cinema Paradiso* (1990) and the Sophia Loren Best Actress award vehicle *Two Women* (1962). The film opened December 13, 1973, and in the United States September 19, 1974. It didn't stand out like the previous film but still merited a strong B.

It's a measure of a solid, character-driven plot when the story is so riveting you can't turn away, despite a dearth of cause-and-effect, onscreen action. **The Truce** *(La tregua)* is like that. Argentina's first entry, despite moments of melodrama, is moving from both perspectives of a man's highs and lows. The 50-year-old protagonist, Martin—with thirty boring years as a bean counter, twenty of them as a widower living

with his three children, now grown—falls in love with Laura, a coworker half his age. He dreams of retiring and living out the rest of his life as her lover, which she adoringly accepts. They keep this information from their colleagues, her parents and his children, in the latter case until his prescient daughter, who ironically is the same age as Laura, figures it out. Laura's allowed him to live again, and that's an important element of the film. A turn of events toward the end changes everything and Martin must be reminded, in the last line of the film, that it wasn't just his "girlfriend" who made him want to live again. The hour-and-forty-eight-minute motion picture received a B for the quality of acting. It was Sergio Renán's only submitted film and it opened August 1, 1974, but not in the United States; in fact, according to the International Movie Data-

French actress Magali Noël, as the hairdresser Gradisca, in Federico Fellini's often bizarre autobiographical last film, *Amarcord* (1973).

base (IMDb.com), the only other distribution was in Spain. Among the cast was Héctor Alterio—who appeared in *The Nest* (1981), *Camila* (1985) and *The Official Story* (winner 1986)—and Norma Aleandro of *Son of the Bride* (2002).

The Kingdom of Sweden invaded the Commonwealth of Poland and Lithuania in 1655. The war lasted three years and Poland, which won, still lost a third of its population because of fighting and war-related pestilence. When it was all over, the dualistic state's economy lay in ruins. This is the background for **The Deluge** (*Potop*), a patriotic feature few Westerners have seen. Directed by Jerzy Hoffman in his only submitted Oscar contender, the picture was based on the novel by Henryk Sienkiewicz and involved outstanding battle scenes and a torrid love story between hothead Andrzej Kmicic, played by Daniel Olbrychski—*The Promised Land* (1976) and *The Tin Drum* (winner 1980)—and Oleńka, played by Małgorzata Braunek. Another aspect of this national story is how some Polish-Lithuanian nobles turned against King Jan Kazimierz and traitorously sold out their Catholic country to King Charles X Gustav of Protestant Sweden. Oh, by the way, it is all of five hours and fifteen minutes long, maybe one reason it earned only a C when viewed over a streaming service in Polish. It originally opened September 2, 1974, and in the U.S. May 14, 1975; otherwise, further distribution was only conducted in Hungary and little Estonia.

Compelling performances by Margit Dajka as Erzsi and Elma Bulla as Giza make **Cat's Play** (*Macskajáték*) a little less dreary than would otherwise be the case in this strange, introspective Hungarian feature. There is little to draw on except the film itself: The only review by CD Universe simply borrowed the basic elements of the DVD's liner notes: "In the end, 'Cat's Play' opposes the bleakness of the outside world with themes of passion, love, and loyalty," they say. At the beginning of the film, when the camera is concentrating on septuagenarian Erzsi, she states, "But it's hard to bear old age when it masquerades as youth," and to that, one can decipher what this film is about. Replete with old-timey photos of the two women, both spinsters, and their entourages as they sauntered through their young years searching for love, the picture was described as a stylistic, "deeply involving drama," brimming with vivid imagery and character emotions. And, yes, there is a cat—one belonging to the "physicist"—who attaches itself to Erzsi. Directed by Károly Makk who had one other film submitted, *Cat's Play*—also listed as *Catsplay*—opened in Poland July 14, 1975, and was distributed only in Finland and Portugal, according to the IMDb—not in the United States, although it was available online. It received a C– in the study.

1976

B	*Dersu Uzala*	**Soviet Union**
B	*Sandakan No. 8*	Japan
B	*Scent of a Woman*	Italy
B–	*Letters from Marusia*	Mexico
C	*The Promised Land*	Poland

The former Soviet Union prided itself on large, expansive, slow-moving, heroic films emphasizing how the working class overcame strife for both mothers and the motherland. Japan's Akira Kurosawa produced a number of large, expansive, slow-moving, heroic films as well—notably *Ran* and *Kagemusha*—but that's where the comparison would appear to end. Not the case with the winning foreign motion picture for 1976, **Dersu Uzala**—a large, expansive, slow-moving ... you get the picture—filmed in the Siberian woods and Vladivostok region with a Russian cast and directed by the great Japanese filmmaker, who wrote the screenplay based on a memoir published in 1923 by explorer Vladimir Arseniev. The title is the name of the odd Asian hunter who is central to the fact-based tale of how two men, so profoundly different from each other in backgrounds, became fast friends and comrades over a series of exploratory adventures. Anyone familiar with Yoda in *Star Wars: The Empire Strikes Back* will recognize *Dersu Uzala*, a squat, 60-something Goldi tribesman from northern Manchuria, who for the most part travels the Ussuri basin of Siberia alone in search of sable. The captain of the various expeditions to map and survey the area befriends the scruffy little man and shares a number of exploits that most would find challenging, to say the least, in this hostile and forbidding land. It earned first place with a B in a year when two other films deserved the same grade. The picture, which runs two hours and twenty-four minutes long, cost an estimated $4 million to make. It opened in the Soviet Union January 5, 1976, in Japan August 2, 1975, and in the United States December 20, 1977. Other Academy-honored Kurosawa films included *Rashomon* (1952) and *Dodes'ka-den* (1972); two other films were submitted but not nominated.

The title of the Japanese entry for 1976 is simply an address, **Sandakan No. 8** (*Sandakan hachiban shokan*). Not just an address, it's a brothel, where young women are brought in to service locals from poor homes in Japan. There is a secondary title:

Yuri Solomin (*left*) and Maksim Munzuk are travel companions in *Dersu Uzala* (1975), a film from Russia by venerated Japanese movie-maker Akira Kurosawa.

Bokyo, possibly meaning "imaginary pot." This is a sad story, not only because of the trafficking of girls as young as 14, but also owing to the strange relationship that develops between Osaki, now an old woman with a past as a prostitute, and a female journalist, Keiko, who inveigles the story out of her. Nine years earlier, Osaki's son—embarrassed by his mother's avocation—rejected her to hide the stigma of who he was from his bride, who turns out to be the journalist. The story takes place in Malaysia, where Keiko seeks the so-called *Karayuki-san*—"Ms. Gone-Overseas"—the name given to those sold into prostitution by their families in other countries. Osaki tells her tale in bits and pieces over the several days the journalist lives with her in her squalid hovel, infested by insects and cats, which the woman collects as she once did men. In the end, Keiko breaks down (rather melodramatically) in admitting her ruse, but Osaki is just fine with it and asks her for a personal towel by which to remember her. Before the journalist leaves, she hacks her way through the jungle to locate the graves of the other *karayuki-san* she now has heard all about and is saddened to see the overgrown tombs. Upon clearing away the growth and debris, she also discovers a telling fact: all the gravestones are facing *away* from Japan. The B picture was the only nominee among three submissions of director Kei Kumai. The print arrived as a videotape from Lafayette College in Easton, Pennsylvania, via the local public library. The two-hour film opened November 2, 1974, and in New York City August 7, 1977; only Hungary received a distribution during this period.

Perhaps there's a statement in the fact that no traditional reviewers came forward with opinions on the fairly modern film, **Scent of a Woman** Italian style, directed by Dino Risi. Starring the "Lawrence Olivier of Italy," Vittorio Gassman, this earlier version of *Scent* (*Profumo di donna*) should not be confused with Al Pacino's 1993-award-winning version and differs from the later incarnation in that Gassman's character is anything but jolly or fun-loving; rather, he is irascible, misanthropic and misogynistic. Both, of course, are blind, with the self-proclaimed ability to sniff out a beautiful woman and seduce her. Each has a youthful, naïve sidekick to accompany him, in Italy's case from Turin to Naples to see his disabled comrade. But where Pacino's Fausto is reasonably lovable, overtly sentimental, and full of vim and vinegar, Gassman's is dark, bitter and an uncontrollable alcoholic. This film, hard to find but available, also was nominated for Best Writing from Another Medium. It runs an hour and forty-three minutes and opened December 20, 1974, with a first U.S. showing in New York City January 25, 1976. It received a generous B. Risi also directed five segments of the anthology film *Viva Italia!*, while Gassman appeared in *Big Deal on Madonna Street* (1959), *The Great War* (1960), *Viva Italia!* (1979) and *The Family* (1988).

Letters from Marusia (*Actas de Marusia*) by Chilean director Miguel Littín is a haunting look at how the rich and powerful exploited the masses of a small town in the foothills of the Andes to the point of rebellion, which was then crushed by ruthless military force. Based on events of 1925 in the Chilean saltpeter mines of Marusia, the hour-and-fifty-minute film demonstrates how the workers, laboring to break up rocks like prisoners on a chain gang, rose up on strike for better pay, work hours and conditions, only to be beaten down to almost the last man (who carries word of the massacre to the world through the "letters" of the title). About 500 workers and family members were killed out of a town of 2,400. This is a sweeping film, with broad cinematography that captures images not unlike *Ballad of a Soldier* and other "propagandizing" films from the Soviet Union. Reminiscent of Akira Kurosawa or even George Lucas, Littín also uses natural elements—particularly the wind that blows constantly and carries with it the grit of dirt and particles from the broken nitrate rock—to convey the bleakness of northern Chile's interior. After the overthrow of communist dictator Salvador Allende in 1973, Littín fled to Mexico and made *Marusia* using well-known Mexican actors. It was that country that entered this film into the 1976 Oscar race. It was viewed online in diffused color and garnered a B–. It first opened in Mexico April 8, 1976, and in the States July 11, 1985; Chile finally allowed it to be shown May 24, 2009. Also in the cast was Sergio Leone favorite Gian Maria Volonté, who appeared in *Investigation of a Citizen Above Suspicion* (1971). Littín was additionally responsible for Nicaragua's *Alsino and the Condor* (1983).

Poland in the late 19th century—a have-and-have-not age of rapid industrialization and hope among the poor working class—is the scene of the ironically titled **The Promised Land** (*Ziemia obiecana*). Three diverse friends partner to turn a rundown textile factory into a moneymaker in what the Strictly Film School website called "a wry, incisive, and elegantly realized Dickensian tale of greed, human cruelty, exploitation, and betrayal." Director Andrzej Wajda's second of nine submitted motion pictures (four received nominations), *The Promised Land* is based on an 1897 novel about the obsession of capitalism in the time of massive manual factories, rampant industrial growth and foul workhouses. The picture also served as a metaphor for what was happening in Poland at the time of its creation: the stirrings that would lead in 1980 to the Solidarity Movement, which political scientists regard as a beginning to the fall of Western Communism. A major thread of the storyline is the juxtaposition of the rough, often brutal lives of the factory workers and the ruthless pursuit of fortune by the uncaring and driven owners. The three-hour picture, worthy of a C, opened in Poland February 21, 1975, and at the Chicago Film Festival in November of that year, but it didn't generate an American distribution until it hit New York City twelve-and-a-half years later, starting February 5, 1988. Wajda's other nominees were *The Maids of Wilko* (1980), *Man of Iron* (1982) and *Katyń* (2008). Among the cast were Daniel Olbrychski and Wojciech Pszoniak, both appearing in West Germany's *The Tin Drum* (1980), and Andrzej Seweryn, whose credits include roles in *Man of Iron*, *Indochine* (1993) and the Best Picture of 1994, *Schindler's List*.

1977

B+	*Jacob the Liar*	East Germany
B	*Cousin Cousine*	France
B	*Seven Beauties*	Italy
B–	**Black and White in Color**	**Ivory Coast**
C–	*Nights and Days*	Poland

One night near the close of World War II, Jacob Heym, a sad-eyed Polish ghetto inmate, is caught after curfew and ordered to Nazi headquarters where he overhears a radio report about Russian troops advancing through Central Europe. He tells others, but because he knows no one will believe that he entered a Gestapo command center and came out alive, he makes up a tale saying he heard about the Soviet liberation force on his own clandestine wireless. His fellow Jews now want to hear more, and therein lies a dilemma: rather than admit he's lied, Jacob must now invent news, and by doing so, he becomes a hero among his trapped inmates. As he continues his ruse, he grows more guilt-ridden. The dramedy *Jacob the Liar* (*Jakob der Lügner*) was submitted by East Germany (GDR), and although it was made in an oppressive Communist dictatorship, it has surprisingly little, if any, straightforward propaganda. Directed by Frank Beyer who shepherded one other of the five submissions by the GDR, *Jacob the Liar* is, as Peter Stack of the *San Francisco Chronicle* noted, "a heartrending, brutally funny and ultimately devastating story." This is no *Life Is Beautiful*, Roberto Benigni's fanciful concentration-camp tragicomedy, although there are moments of awkward humor. It should be noted as well that it is superior to its American remake of the same title starring the late comic Robin Williams and merits a B+, despite not being the winner. The hour-and-forty-minute film, which opened in East Germany April 17, 1975, and in New York City April 24, 1977, stars Czech actor Vlastimil Brodský, who was also in *Closely watched Trains* (1968).

In *Cousin Cousine*, France's 1977 contender for best foreign film, two cousins by marriage fall in love, despite having spouses of their own who also just happen to be dallying with each other on the sly. It was, after all, the 1970s. The couple, played by

Vlastimil Brodský's Jacob Heym (*right*) appears bemused in *Jacob the Liar* (1974) after telling his fellow concentration camp Jews he owns a clandestine radio that has broadcast that the Russians are coming to liberate them.

Marie-Christine Barrault and Victor Lanoux, are engaging and their love story convincingly told, although what actually happens stretches the imagination. The two 30-somethings meet at a party and begin to dance knowing their significant others are off elsewhere. Eventually they move their affair into the open and others don't appear to mind at all. This is an exhilarating story, if not wholly credible. However, veteran and inveterate critic Pauline Kael of *The New Yorker* magazine called the picture "a rhythmless, mediocre piece of moviemaking." With delightful mixed metaphors, she continued: "With its wholesome carnality, '*Cousin Cousine*' is so pro-life that it treats sex like breakfast cereal." Barrault, who was also nominated for Best Actress, stars in *My Night at Maud's* (1970). Director Jean-Charles Tacchella's only submitted film was additionally nominated for Best Writing–Screenplay Written Directly for the Screen. It opened November 19, 1975, and in America July 25, 1976. The hour-and-thirty-five-minute picture stands as a B movie.

Pasqualino may not be the brightest bulb in the marquee, but he's an opportunist and, as one critic said, obsessed with notions of honor. He's the lead character in Lina Wertmüller's **Seven Beauties**, nominated in 1977 for four Academy Awards, including Best Foreign Film. The title refers to the Neapolitan thief's sisters, each uglier than the next, and despite his indiscretions, protecting their honor is utmost in his feeble brain. Through flashbacks we learn Pasqualino is more than a petty crook in prewar Italy, under whose aegis the motion picture was submitted. He kills and dismembers a man for trying to turn one sister into a prostitute, is sentenced to an asylum for his indiscretions, is released to serve in the Italian army during World War II, goes AWOL, is captured and deposited in a Nazi concentration camp where he services the sado-masochistic female commandant, becomes a *kapò* and is forced to murder his friend, and so on and on. This hour-and-fifty-five-minute picaresque film garnered a B. Wertmüller, responsible for two Academy submissions, was also nominated in the Best Director category for *Seven Beauties* and for its Writing-Original Screenplay, while her star, Giancarlo Giannini, was considered for Best Actor. Another film of hers was submitted but not accepted. The picture opened in Paris May 4, 1975, and in the States January 21, 1976. Also in the picture was Fernando Rey, a lead in three Luis Buñuel–nominated pictures: *Tristana* (1971), *The Discreet Charm of the Bourgeoisie* (1973) and *That Obscure Object of Desire* (1978), as well as 1972's overall Best Picture *The French Connection*.

As black retainers shoulder sedan chairs to transport Jesuit teachers along steamy trails of French West Africa in January 1915 they sing a song that translates, "My fat man is fat and lazy." Of course the arrogant Frenchmen don't understand this but ironically are quick to criticize their servants as indolent and stupid. They prove this by pointing out that whites can ride bicycles; never mind the fact a native is seen riding one in the next scene. This is **Black and White in Color** (*La Victoire en chantant*), a whimsical satire that surprised everyone by *winning* the 1977 Best Foreign Film over three arguably superior pictures. Another oddity was the fact the French-language film was submitted by the African country Côte d'Ivoire (Ivory Coast). The premise: The bored, lackadaisical and bigoted French colonialists learn World War I had started five months earlier and take it upon themselves to train and equip a band of natives to do battle with a nearby German contingent, a plan that does not go well. They march off with anticipation of great fun, singing and packing picnic baskets prepared by their wives, only to discover that war can be hell. (The first title given to this farce was *The Victory by Singing*.) The hour-and-a-half-long film was directed by Jean-Jacques Annaud in his only submission and opened in France September 22, 1976, and in the United States May 8, 1977. Although it has its moments, the film warranted only a B–, placing it fourth—not first—on the year's list.

At more than four hours long, **Nights and Days** (*Noce i dnie*) is truly epic, regarded by some as Poland's *The Forsyte Saga* or Proust's *À la recherche du temps perdu* in visual form—although, like *Remembrances of Things Past*, it did begin visually as a ten-and-a-half-hour TV miniseries. The twelve-part Polish nominee was directed by Jerzy Antczak, in his only submission, and was based on a renowned novel by Maria Dąbrowska in which the central character, Barbara Niechcic—a blithe, existential spirit with strong early feminist traits—goes through life from 1863 to the start of World War I, suffering many trials and tribulations along the way. These include the loss of a suitor, death of a young son, frequent stealing by another, a defiant daughter, a philandering husband who uses her money for his own gains, numerous deaths of those she loves, the forfeiture of her homes—all in agonizing detail and seen from only her perspective. This color film is not for everyone, unless a dedicated binge watcher or person with lots of time on his or her hands. The picture opened September 23, 1975, and in the United States at the Chicago Film Festival in November 1976. The distribution list only adds West Germany. It was a struggle to get through this C– film. One of the characters is played by Emir Buczacki, who was also in *Pharaoh* (1967).

1978

A–	*Madame Rosa*	France
A–	*That Obscure Object of Desire*	Spain
B+	*A Special Day*	Italy
C–	*Operation Thunderbolt*	Israel
C–	*Iphigenia*	Greece

Four months before **Madame Rosa** (*La vie devant soi*) was released in the United States, President Anwar Sadat of Egypt and Prime Minister Menachem Begin of Israel signed the Camp David Peace Accords. That was in 1977, and despite a solid truce between the two countries, never was there true peace in the Middle East for the rest of the century. *Madame Rosa*, the 1978 BFF winner, involves a frumpy, sick, sometimes fitful and dying character, played by Simone Signoret as an ex-hooker and Jewish Holocaust survivor who takes care of prostitutes' children in a sixth-floor walk-up so long and tedious of a climb that even the visiting doctor needs to be carried up the stairs. Momo is a North African Arab—Algerian—an adolescent who is just finding his way as a street criminal, trying to make things work and help his "adopted mother." One of the best scenes in the film comes when Mr. Kadir, after eleven years in an insane asylum, arrives to fetch Momo, his Moslem son. Madame Rosa recognizes the sham that he is and, in an Oscar Wilde sort of way, farcically tries to foist off on Kadir another, younger boy named Moishe, who was raised strictly as a Jew. Kadir won't have it, however, because of his own prejudices. All the while, Momo looks on, bemused, from the doorway. Another, more poignant scene involves Madame Rosa in her Jewish, basement hidey-hole, a place she goes to escape her fears of the concentration camp and by implication the hospital to which everyone except Momo is trying to get her to go. While Momo attends to her there, the last candle in her Menorah snuffs out. Symbolically, Rosa has left us, too. This hour-and-forty-five-minute film won the Academy Award among several good ones and deserved it. It earned an A–, the same as runner-up *That Obscure Object of Desire* from Spain. The director was Moshé Mizrahi—*I Love You Rosa* (1973) and *The House on Chelouche Street* (1974)—and besides Signoret, who won a Best Actress Award for *Room at the Top* (1960) and was nominated in the same category for *Ship of Fools* (1966), actor Michal Bat-Adam, who appeared in *The House on Chelouche Street*, has a part. It's not an easy film to find and was reviewed by only a handful of critics, none well known. It's available online if one is willing to hunt for it, as well as in some college campus libraries. It originally opened in France November 2, 1977, and in the States March 19, 1978. This is not a sequel to the '73 *Rosa*, by the way, but merely features a character with the same name.

Luis Buñuel and Fernando Rey collaborated a number of times on award-winning films, including nominees *Tristana* (1971), *The Discreet Charm of the Bourgeoisie* (1973) and ***That Obscure Object of Desire*** (*Cet obscur objet du désir*), this year's Spanish entry.

They also connected on two films from Mexico: *Nazarín*, submitted but not accepted, and the esoteric *Viridiana*. A master of surrealism (it was he, after all, who partnered with Salvador Dalí on the quintessentially surrealistic *An Andalusian Dog*), Buñuel relates the story of a post-middle-aged widower (Rey) besotted by a young virgin so elusive and schizophrenic that she is played by two actresses. He wants to bed her but won't marry her, fearing he'd lose presumed control over her, when in fact the reverse would be true. The relationship, which fluctuates as often as the two women change roles, is in chaos, just as the juxtaposed external views of the world—rampant terrorism, airplane hijackings, genocide, a pandemic—are exposed. After first

Ángela Molina, one of two actresses playing Conchita in Luis Buñuel's *That Obscure Object of Desire* (1977), enjoys a romantic moment with iconic actor and Buñuel favorite Fernando Rey.

viewing the feature, the author noted: "A very strange film, with an extremely off-putting ending that's not explained, either by me or any of a number of analysts online." But after viewing the hour-and-forty-two-minute movie a second time, it was evaluated to an A– picture. It opened in France August 17, 1977, the United States October 8, 1977, and Spain April 17, 1978, its delay owing to its controversial nature. Incidentally, Rey, whether a lead or costar, was a magnet for Oscar. He also won acclaim for the Academy's overall winner *The French Connection* in 1972, the 1977 BFF nominee *Seven Beauties* and the 1977 multiple Oscar contender *Voyage of the Damned*, among other award-winning films.

Sophia Loren and Marcello Mastroianni made seventeen pictures together and three of them, all from Italy—*Yesterday, Today and Tomorrow* (1965), *Marriage Italian Style* (1966) and this year's ***A Special Day*** (*Una giornata particolare*)—were nominated for Best Foreign Film. Antonietta, married to a macho fascist with six children, imposes on her neighbor, Gabriele, in an effort to rescue her escaped myna bird. It happens to be May 8, 1938, the "special day" when Adolf Hitler first visited Benito Mussolini in Rome, creating a lively background you hear and see throughout the movie. Everyone has turned out for the enormous parade and ceremony—everyone, that is, except Antonietta and Gabriele. She, doughty and haggard, pours out her soul to him and he admits being gay and afraid the government will arrest him and send him to a concentration camp in Sardinia. They get along fine—so fine, in fact, they wind up in bed, totally without guilt for reasons of their own. It was generally accepted that the motion picture turned out to be more a showcase for these fine actors than a true Oscar contender. The venerable critic Vincent Canby of the *New York Times* wrote that the picture "is pure theatrical contrivance, and this is part of the pleasure as we watch two extraordinary performers test themselves, take risks [and] find unexpected pockets of humor and pathos in characters that one doesn't easily associate with the public personality." The hour-and-forty-six-minute picture was credited with a B+. Italy submitted four of director Ettore Scola's films for consideration and three of them—this one, *Viva Italia!* (1979) and *The Family* (1988)—were chosen for nomination. Not a bad record. This film opened in France September 7, 1977, following nine days later in Italy and a further nine days in New York City. Mastroianni garnered a Best Actor nomination for the movie the same year.

Generally panned by most critics, ***Operation Thunderbolt*** (*Mivtsa Yonatan*), the Israeli entry, is one of a couple of films that purport to tell the true story of the Raid on Entebbe, Uganda, on July 4, 1976. Two Palestinian and two German hijackers commandeer an Air France plane from Tel Aviv to Paris after it lands in Athens, Greece, on June 27. They forced it to fly to Muammar Qaddafi's Libya, then on to Idi Amin's Uganda. There, the Jewish passengers and crew are separated from the rest and threatened with death if the Israeli government refuses to obtain release of fifty-three militant prisoners. After lengthy debate and pressure from the populace, an elite unit of 100 commandos is dispatched to the East African airport where it stages an implausible (but actual) rescue of 102 hostages. All of this was dramatized in the two-hour-and-four-minute film directed by Menahen Golan, which was characterized by the likes of Janet Maslin of the *New York Times* as "dull and propagandistic" and Andre Soares of the *Alt(ernative) Film Guide* as "cliché-ridden," devoid of "either psy-

Inspired Israeli actor-soldiers raid terrorists holding hostages at Uganda's Entebbe airfield in director Menahem Golan's *Operation Thunderbolt* (1977).

chological depth to any of the characters or nuances to the political underpinnings of the crisis." It is no wonder there were relatively few critical analyses available for this C– movie. Despite the negative publicity and an estimated $2.5 million budget, it's interesting that Golan—gregarious and eccentric—also directed a slew of comic-book science-fiction flicks in Hollywood, a good body of work for whom *Film Comment* referred to as a "lowly assistant to Roger Corman" and grind-market hack. So it goes. Appearing in the film was Gila Almagor, noted for her roles in *Sallah* (1965) and *The House on Chelouche Street* (1974). It opened January 27, 1977, and came to America January 27, 1978.

A bleak, stylistic period piece, ***Iphigenia*** required two viewings several months apart to get a true feeling for director Michael Cacoyannis' pre–CGI (computer-generated imaging) staging of this quasi-Homeric tragedy about child sacrifice to appease the gods. Most viewers will be somewhat familiar with the story of Helen of Sparta ("the face that launch'd a thousand ships," according to Christopher Marlowe) and how she left her husband, Menelaus, to elope with Paris to Troy, how her brother-in-law Agamemnon marshaled the great Greek expeditionary force to pursue her, and how this resulted in the fabled Trojan War. Lesser known, perhaps, is the mythological aspects of the story, presented in one version by Euripides, alongside Sophocles and Aeschylus one of the three great Athenian tragedians. The film is set on the beach at Aulis before the launch. High winds prevent the vessels from sailing and the army is getting restless. They are permitted to hunt domestic and wild animals near a temple and a rare stag is inadvertently killed, enraging the goddess Artemis who demands payment in kind by having Menelaus' daughter, *Iphigenia*, sacrificed before the deity will allow the ships to sail. From this early stage of the film, a great deal of maneuvering takes place with Iphigenia escaping, being recaptured and eventually submitting to her fate. Cacoyannis, who also made *Electra* (1963), ends this two-hour-and-seven-minute tragedy on a nebulous note, with the girl disappearing over the rise of a hill but never shown being sacrificed, dead or dying. Most prominent in the film is the actress Irene Papas playing Iphigenia's protective aunt, Clytemnestra; she also played Electra and was joined in both films by Kostas Kazakos. The number of extras employed on the beach set is prodigious. The color film opened September 10, 1977, and in the States November 20, 1977. This stagey movie was not deserving of more than a C–.

1979

B+	*Get Out Your Handkerchiefs*	France
B	*Viva Italia!*	Italy
C	*The Glass Cell*	West Germany
C	*White Bim Black Ear*	Soviet Union
C–	*Hungarian Rhapsody*	Hungary

It's difficult to make out the true purpose of **Get Out Your Handkerchiefs** (*Préparez vos mouchoirs*), the 1979 winning Best Foreign Language Film from France. It's a comedy it's a satire; it's a sexual fantasy with more than a touch of pedophilia thrown in for good measure. Gérard Depardieu stars as the disgruntled but caring husband so concerned about his depressive wife that he pimps her out to another man in an effort to make her happy. When that doesn't work, the two "man-children" come up with the brilliant idea to solicit help from a 13-year-old, and the true child succeeds where the others have failed. Everyone lives happily ever after—more or less. The movie, considered a "romantic comedy," ran into mixed reaction before and after the awards ceremony. The nicest thing said about the hour-and-forty-eight-minute feature and its director Bertrand Blier was that it's "an exuberant and highly inventive comedy." The *New Yorker*'s Pauline Kael opined "seeing 'Handkerchiefs' is like a vacation in a country you've always wanted to visit." But the writer Janet Maslin on the *New York Times* also noted it was hard to care about these people. "Mr. Blier's penchant for depicting behavior like this is certainly daring, but whether it amounts to anything truly provocative is another matter. Genuinely challenging an audience is one thing, and simply upsetting it is something else." Incidentally, it was Blier's only submitted film. It's a likable picture and worthy of a B+, keeping it at the top of the year's list. It opened January 11, 1978, and December 17, 1978, in the United States. Depardieu, who despite a late start in his career had more than 220 acting credits at the time of this writing, also starred in BFF nominees *The Last Metro* (1981), *Camille Claudil* (1990) and *Cyrano de Bergerac* (1991).

Viva Italia! (*I nuovi mostri* or *The New Monsters*) is a portmanteau film of fourteen different anecdotal tales reminiscent of Italy's 1964 winner for Best Foreign Film winner *Yesterday, Today and Tomorrow*, but also *The Yellow Rolls-Royce* and *The Red Violin*, where objects (car and a musical instrument) pull separate stories together. The idea, of course, is to illustrate, comically if possible, Italian quirkiness: a scenario that aptly fits any national group. Prominent among the actors are Alberto Sordi in three segments and Vittorio Gassman in five. The directors used included Ettore Scola for seven segments, Dino Risi for five and Mario Monicelli for two. All three have a combined total of eight submissions of which a remarkable seven were nominated. One is more amused by the action than the dialogue, but it isn't too difficult to get the point. A few of the "episodes" are laugh-out-loud funny; some are confounding; it's generally about how mean spirited the middle class of Italy is. The picture falls into the B category as a whole, but seen individually, the sketches operate between an A– and C–. The film, viewed online at an hour and a half but without subtitles, debuted December 22, 1977, and in New York City July 9, 1978.

The late novelist Patricia Highsmith—whose name is no stranger to Hollywood owing to *Carol*, based on *The Price of Salt*, and the Ripley series which must always include the French-made *Purple Noon*—wrote *The Glass Cell*, a psychological thriller published in America as a Crime Club selection in 1964. West German director Hans W. Geißendörfer in his only nomination (he had two films submitted) adapted it to the silver screen under the German title *Die gläserne Zelle*. It's about a Frankfurt architect named Phillip who is released from jail after being wrongfully imprisoned for five years. He discovers that his wife has not been faithful, that she had a brief fling with his defense attorney during the incarceration, but even though she says it's over, she continues to see him. Phillip's growing jealousy gets the best of him, however, to the point he murders the scoundrel. There's a scene in *The Talented Mr. Ripley* (a Highsmith invention) in which Tom beats the suspicious Freddie Miles to death with a statue, much in the same way Phillip kills the lawyer. The only complaint about the movie involved the almost nonexistent character development, except perhaps Phillip's; the ditzy, vacuous wife's portrayal; the poor color saturation and at-times a strangely literal translation of English subtitles (one line: "Your lawyer overuses my nerves"); and why make young Timmie a virtuoso flautist at the beginning without showing his talents again? That's why this nominee warranted only a C in the study. It first opened in West Germany April 6, 1978, and in America in May 1981, with only Australia and Denmark listed for distribution. It runs an hour and thirty-three minutes, is exceedingly hard to find and consequently is virtually unknown to filmgoers. In spite of its poor showing, the film included two notable actors: Brigitte Fossey, the little girl in *Forbidden Games* (1953) and adult Elena in *Cinema Paradiso* (1989), and Helmut Griem, who took part in multiple Oscar winner *Cabaret* (1973). Region 2 P.A.L. copies of *The Glass Cell* exist in several U.S. Midwest and East Coast college libraries, according to WorldCat.org, but Amazon and eBay list none.

Animal adventure films abound on Netflix, Amazon Prime, YouTube, but none is quite like **White Bim Black Ear** (*Belyy Bim Chernoe ukho*) from the former Soviet Union. This is no kids' film—no *Benji*, *Bolt* or *Homeward Bound*—and even adults should be warned. Bim is a runt, a mottled white Scottish setter with a black ear, making it impure among breeders. Its owner develops a serious heart condition, and when the dog is given away, it becomes anxious and sets off across Moscow to find its master, only to discover a world full of people, both kind and cruel. Bim gets into trouble, is injured by a train-track switch and runs into inhumane situations. It's amazing how few reviews were available (one Finnish critic listed on IMDb and four minor user comments). The three-hour-long film, by Stanislav Rostotsky (whose *The Dawns Here Are*

Quiet was nominated in 1972) is remarkable in the way the dog(s) performed for the camera (two English setters, Stepan and Dandy, were used in the shooting, coached by Viktor Somov, according to a Russian interview). A concern for some viewers might be how some of the scenes may have been shot in 1970s Soviet Union using animals that were not likely mechanical or anatomical. But there is no evidence any pain was inflicted. Also starring was Vyacheslav Tikhonov, who performed in *War and Peace* (winner 1969) and *Burnt by the Sun* (winner 1995). This is a C film.

Trying to make sense of **Hungarian Rhapsody** (*Magyarok* or *Hungarians*) is like building sandcastles in a hurricane, and the film, indeed, has plenty of dusty breezes to contend with. The feature, from Hungary of course, is basically a dream sequence, with marching *and* dancing soldiers, candles blowing in the noisy wind, a noble woman's fiery floating funeral, a girl who's treated like dirt as she's flung to the dusty ground, lots of military music, and numerous deaths by Russian roulette. The final shots are reminiscent of the Last Supper, with twelve leads lined up on a long table as the rest of the large cast marches into the scene in serried ranks. There's inexplicable nudity, mostly young ladies, and several scenes in which drunken soldiers are challenged to shoot themselves in the head, and usually do despite the one-to-six odds. Even a horse, off camera, is shot because a soldier is told to do it and he does so, poorly one might add, without question. That was one of the themes: that we do what is asked of us and obey our superiors. In that case, it goes for women, too. There's not much in this film that one could see as redeeming. Garnering only a C−, the picture was directed by Zóltan Fábri, who also did *Boys of Paul Street* (1969), the only other nominated film of four submitted, and it runs an hour and forty-seven minutes. It was released February 8, 1978, and in New York City November 20, 1981; apparently additional distribution only included East Germany and Spain. The VHS tape viewed came from California University of Pennsylvania via the local library, and while watchable, it showed a lot of wear and tear. In fact, much of the film was shown as though on a large stage with featureless principals going through their odd ballet, the camera slowly swaying back and forth. Also uncredited in the cast was György Cserhalmi, *Mephisto* (winner 1982), *Hanussen* (1989) and *Želary* (2004).

1980

A	*The Tin Drum*	**West Germany**
B+	*Mama Turns 100*	Spain
C+	*A Simple Story*	France
C	*The Young Girls of Wilko*	Poland
C−	*To Forget Venice*	Italy

Described by many as a "surrealistic black comedy," **The Tin Drum** (*Die Blechtrommel*) won the Academy Award for Best Foreign Film in 1980. The two-hour and twenty-two-minute film, directed by Volker Schlöndorff, is about a little boy named Oskar who adores tiny bandbox drums and beats them incessantly. His drumming is a protest against what he, a 3-year-old, is witnessing in his tiny world. It's tumultuous, brutal, highlighted by the rise of Nazism. Though he doesn't fully understand it, the inhumane

Little David Bennent, as Oskar Matzerath, pounds his toy instrument in protest during a scene from *The Tin Drum* (1979), the Academy Award-winning film version of the Günter Grass novel.

forces are driving him to seek escape from it all by causing him to stop growing. It's allegoric, following the plan of author and fill-in screenwriter Günter Grass, whose 1959 book by the same title was a worldwide bestseller. The A movie was Schlöndorff's only nomination out of two submitted and opened May 3, 1979, and then in the United States April 11, 1980. Among the cast were Mario Adorf, a prolific thespian with 216 acting credits, who played in *The Devil Strikes at Night* (1958)—also Tina Engel from *The Boat Is Full* (1982) and Ernst Jacobi of *The White Ribbon* (2010).

Mama Turns 100 (*Mamá cumple cien años*) by Carlos Saura, who also directed *Carmen* (1984) and *Tango* (1999), was an unexpected delight. It's rarely seen and hard to find, and indeed had only two brief critiques listed on the International Movie Database (IMDb.com). Geraldine Chaplin (Best Picture candidates *Doctor Zhivago* in 1966 and *Nashville* in 1976)—Charlie's daughter and Saura's lover for twelve years, who speaks fluent Spanish and French—is a token star of the Spanish film, playing a nanny who returns home with her horny husband to celebrate a birthday. But the real star is Rafaela Aparicio, "Mama," who is turning 100. She lives in the family home in rural Spain, and her dysfunctional offspring have gathered to celebrate her birthday and wish her dead so they can save the home for themselves. There are some very funny moments—not the least of which is when Mama enters her birthday party on a slowly descending makeshift platform whose wires are decorated with leaves. Other moments include her several "fits" that require a drop of medicine to remedy, a telling point of what happens at the end. The only grumble—and it's silly—was knowing Aparicio's age, 73, when she's supposed to be on the brink of 100, and the fact she had a number of daughters and sons who barely fit middle age. Chaplin, who should be older than the kids she took care of, was only 35 when she made the film. Nevertheless, it was a fun romp. The 100 minute film—which opened in Spain September 17, 1979, and as late as September 1988 in America after appearing at two earlier film fests—received a B+. Another actor appearing was Fernando Fernán-Gómez—*Belle Époque* (winner 1994), *The Grandfather* (1999) and *All About My Mother* (winner 2000)—who had a remarkable 213 acting credits.

The French entry for 1980, *A Simple Story* (*Une histoire simple*), is about Marie, a 39-year-old divorcee, who decides to have an abortion and at the same time kicks

Serge, the father, out of her life without telling him about the baby. She hooks up again with her former husband, Georges, a businessman in the fashion world, with whom Marie had Martin, now 16. They have an affair and she gets pregnant again. Meanwhile, Georges decides there's nothing left for him in his job and decides to go to Marseilles as a mentor to young boys. Marie is happy. She's greeted by her friends in a café to announce her pregnancy. "Will you tell him?" she is asked. "No," she admits, still smiling. Life is good. Sounds "simple" enough, and more like a Lifetime Network feature—right? It would fit well, except that it's in French and, like so many good French flicks of that period, it's an ensemble film revolving around one central cast member. There are other characters: loser Jerome who can't get his act together—indeed, who struggles in a later successful effort to commit suicide—and Gabrielle, who had lovingly put up with Jerome, but after his tragic death takes up with Marie's ex-boyfriend Serge and attempts to make a good man out of him. (Are you following this?) Romy Schneider stars; Claude Sautet directed in his only submitted film. The VHS print, an hour and fifty minutes long, came from the Wellesley (Massachusetts) Free Library and was better quality than most tapes of this age. It's an odd story with a hackneyed, soap-operatic storyline. It opened November 22, 1978, and came to the States one year later. It garnered a C+. Also in a small role was Madeleine Robinson, *Camille Claudel* (1990).

After fifteen years as a soldier and handyman at a monastery, 40-year-old Wiktor Ruben returns to visit his aunt and uncle in rural Poland. His first stop is Wilko, the home of an old woman and her five daughters, all but one of them married or separated, some rearing preteen children. At one time they all adored Wiktor, and in his insouciant way he liked them back. Another daughter, Fela, he loved the most, but at this surprise reunion with the others he learns she has passed away. This is the premise for **The Young Ladies of Wilko** (*Panny z Wilka*, also titled *The Maids of Wilko*), directed by Andrzej Wajda. Wiktor takes up where he left off but settles on the youngest girl to woo because Tunia most resembles Fela. We learn that Fela died mysteriously, presumably of a broken heart after the protagonist abruptly disappeared. Wiktor doesn't seem to know what he wants, nor do we, and only recently had he begun to question his own place in life. As Vincent Canby wrote in his *New York Times* review shortly after the movie's release: "...Wiktor has always been slippery in his relations with those he loves." One of the sisters notes that, unlike the handsome 20-something guy who strode off to college and then war, Wiktor had begun to wilt at around 40. Considered a dark comedy, *Wilko* can be incredibly boring at times and deserved no better than a C. Wajda was always prolific when it came to Academy submissions: Of his eight films sent in by Poland, four of them—including *The Promised Land* (1976), The *Man of Iron* (1982) and *Katyń* (2008), as well as this film—received nominations. This movie opened in March 1979 and only appeared in regular release in America, as far as we know, at the New York Film Festival October 11, 1979. It is two minutes shy of two hours long.

The Italian entry, **To Forget Venice** (*Dimenticare Venezia*), is not a travelogue, nor a drama filmed in a stunning environment. In fact, the entire setting is in a manor or on its wooded grounds. Chockablock with full-frontal nudity, the picture revolves around a retired, aging opera diva, whose brother and his male lover has returned to visit her and her adopted niece and *her* female lover. To the couples, much of this world is fantasy based on memories of wonderful days cavorting as youngsters. But the sudden death of the "aunt" changes everything, even sexual preferences. This hour-and-fifty-minute color film, directed by Franco Brusati in his only submission, was viewed on tape from William Paterson University of New Jersey, via the local library, and was dubbed and rather horrible, no better than a C– film. It's easy to forget *To Forget Venice*. For the record, *La Cage aux Folles*, also from Italy, which garnered three Oscar nominations including Best Director (Édouard Molinaro), Best Writing from another medium, and Best Costume Design, would have been a much better submission for this year's contest.

1981

A–	*The Last Metro*	France
B+	***Moscow Does Not Believe in Tears***	**Soviet Union**
B+	*Confidence*	Hungary
B	*Kagemusha*	Japan
B–	*The Nest*	Spain

During the Nazi occupation of Paris, a forced nighttime curfew required all entertainments to end early enough for the patrons to take the last subway home. So it's true in François Truffaut **The Last Metro** (*Le Dernier Métro*), France's 1981-nominated Best

Gestapo soldiers were among the many regular attendees at Théâtre Montmartre, where Catherine Deneuve, as actress-manager Marion Steiner, holds court in *The Last Metro* **(1980).**

Foreign Film. Starring two of the top box-office stars of the period, Gérard Depardieu and Catherine Deneuve, as well as a solid cast of characters that people the fictitious Théâtre Montmartre where most of the play resides, the story is about how the small acting troupe deals with events surrounding them. Deneuve, as Marion, is married to a German Jew who flees to Paris to escape oppression only to be followed there by the Wehrmacht. The fugitive confines himself to the cellar beneath the stage where he writes production notes to the actors performing above. The lead actor is the upstart Depardieu, as Bernard, who moonlights as a Resistance fighter and attempts to seduce Deneuve, both elements adding tension to the storyline. According to critic Armond White, writing for The Criterion Collection: "The film's tone originates in Depardieu's Bernard, with his brash, spirited commitment to both theater and liberation." Of course, throughout this feature, there are plenty of Nazis to contend with. This was the third Truffaut film proffered for an Oscar and the third nomination; *Stolen Kisses* garnered attention in 1969 and his second, *Day for Night*, won in 1974. For this survey, *The Last Metro* deserved to be ranked higher than the winning film and warranted an A–. It's two hours and eleven minutes long. Deneuve, of course, starred in Oscar-contender *The Umbrellas of Cherbourg* (1965); Depardieu was lead in nominees *Get Out Your Handkerchiefs* (1979), *Camille Claudel* (1990) and *Cyrano de Bergerac* (1991). (Incidentally, there actually was a Théâtre Montmartre, located at 1 place Charles Dullin, from 1822 to 1914. It's still there as the Théâtre de l'Atelier.)

The 1981 winning foreign-language film, **Moscow Does Not Believe in Tears** (*Moskva slezam ne verit*), is the Soviet version of "Where are they now?" It's a two-and-half-hour-long romantic comedy whose first half is about three young country girls who move to the city to live and work together in 1958. During their stay, they develop distinct personalities and discover love in all the right or wrong places. Jump ahead twenty years and we find the same women in positions that fate has dealt them, for better or worse. The picture depicts what women of the proletariat might have endured during those difficult, hardscrabble years under communism (see title), but being a Kremlin-approved submission, it tries to instill a tongue-in-cheek innocence into what is essentially a melodrama. Despite its winning ways, the motion picture did not fare well with critics, receiving such comments as "almost unbearable," "overly long" and "unconvincing" in their descriptions. One critic, a blogger named Richard Winters, wrote that "this film lacks anything profound and comes off as a typical drama that is passable and entertaining, but not great." He nonetheless did mention that the main "characters are well rounded and believable." With an estimated $900,000 budget, Vladimir Menshov directed the picture, his only submission, which debuted February 11, 1980, and in New York City May 8, 1981. Surprisingly, even though it was considered the Best Foreign Film, there's a dearth of reviews for this movie, and none from the heavies. It's an entertaining motion picture and merited a B+.

There's a certain air of desperation at the beginning of **Confidence** (*Bizalom*), Hungary's contender. Kata is stopped on an empty, rain-slickened street in Budapest by a man who informs her the occupying Germans are ransacking her house and detaining her husband. At first we don't know why, but we soon learn she's the unknowing wife of a Resistance officer, an anti–Nazi organizer who's been exposed. She's given a new name and a room in a boardinghouse where she's surrounded by a collection of old people and borderline Nazis. Her sponsor, who takes on the role of her fake husband, continuously reminds her to stay the course, not to mention any details of her life, not to worry about her husband, not to leave the safe house without permission, and not to keep but burn all photos of her spouse and child. "Look, we're both in a dark forest," says her underground savior. The motion picture is full of suspenseful moments, utter anxiety, hopelessness, fear and a dire need to trust each other, if that's possible in this world of paranoia. It's claustrophobic, with muted color tones and murky dimness, and the drabness of war-weary Eastern Europe is everywhere, in the rattling trolleys, the desolate streets, even Kata's dirty toilet bowl. As the picture progresses, she falls madly in love with her rescuer—a self-professed coward, despite his humanity and good looks, bearing the assumed name of János Biro—and even a night with her reclusive husband doesn't change her mind. Caught up in their cramped rented room, she and János act much like husband and wife, caressing one minute and fighting the next, but as the conclusion approaches, things change. We shall leave it there. *Bizalom*—it actually translates as "trust"—is a B+ movie enjoyed to the very end. The director, István Szabó, was among Hungary's most prolific filmmakers with seven features submitted to the Academy of which four were nominated, and one, *Mephisto*, took home the Oscar in 1982. Szabó's other two nominated pictures were *Colonel Redl* (1986) and *Hanussen* (1989). Among the players are Ildikó Bánsági and Péter Andorai, who appear in *Mephisto* and *Hanussen*, and Oszkárné Gombik, also in *Mephisto*. *Bizalom* is not an easy picture to find, but one day it turned up in full on YouTube.com, and with decent English subtitles. It should be noted that some hard-to-find films can suddenly appear on YouTube one day and abruptly be removed the next, citing copyright infringement.

From swashbuckling samurai films to the fairly recent black comedy *Departures* (2009), the Japanese know how to make a movie. Arguably the country's greatest filmmaker was Akira Kurosawa, who directed only thirty films in his fifty-seven-year career, among them *Seven Samurai, Yojimbo, Sanjiro, Rashomon, Dersu Uzala, Ran* and *Ikiru*, and is credited for putting postwar Japan on the world's cinematic map. The film **Kagemusha**, a historical *jidaigeki* samurai drama, is said to be responsible also for reinforcing the Japanese film industry when it was most needed; after a robust list of nominations since the first hon-

Tatsuya Nakadai commands the battle throne, serving as a dead warlord's double in Akira Kurosawa's *Kagemusha* (1980).

ored foreign film in 1950, it had produced only a couple of mediocre nominations and then suffered a dry spell before *Woman in the Dunes* in 1965 and *Kwaidan* the next year. *Kagemusha*, like unsubmitted *Ran* five years later, was produced on a grand scale and required financial backing from two giants of the silver screen, George Lucas and Francis Ford Coppola, both of whom were great admirers of Kurosawa. The budget was reported to be an estimated $6 million. The story takes place in the pre–Tokugawa period when warlords were vying for control of the country, manifested in the *Shogun*, or Generalissimo, who was venerated above all but the Emperor. One of the lords dies of a battle wound, but his attendants employ a low-life lookalike to impersonate him as a ploy to keep the other warlords at bay. The title translates to "Shadow Warrior," meaning a political decoy. Much happens in the three-hour film (later cut by twenty-nine minutes), including an impressive battle scene using real extras to rival a Peter Jackson encounter of thousands of computer-generated warriors. Kurosawa first laid out his epic in elaborate, multimedia storyboards that today are revered as a separate art portfolio. He tried to peddle the film using these drawings rather than the rough screenplay, as was tradition, and for the most part it worked. The feature also received a Best Art Direction-Set Decoration nomination. It opened in Japan April 26, 1980, and in the States October 10, 1980. Players included Tatsuya Nakadai, who was in *Immortal Love* (1962), *Kwaidan* (1966) and *Ran* (unsubmitted 1985), and Tsutomu Yamazaki, who starred in *Departures*. *Kagemusha*, a B movie, was viewed on a double DVD that included film essays on Kurosawa, his partnership with Lucas and Coppola, and how he produced his storyboards, considered artworks in themselves.

Despite its theme of perceptible pedophilia, **The Nest** (*El Nido*) is quite engaging. Seen on VHS tape at the University of Washington in Seattle, the full-screen color film from Spain partnered a 60-year-old widower with a 13-year-old girl in an offbeat drama of pseudo-romance and control. Was it pedophilia? Would the townsfolk, including a police-sergeant neighbor and the girl's father, eventually chase down the older man and string him up for messing with the girl? Actually, we would learn, it's the girl messing with *him*. Although he's an accomplished man living in a rambling rambler, who loves chess and gadgets and classical and operatic music that he likes to conduct, he's completely at the girl's mercy toward the end—remarkably to the point of being asked to commit and attempt murder. The child—pretty, a little sexy, her hair atumble but well groomed—has quite a lip on her and mirrors the nastiness of her harridan mother, who manipulates her father; indeed, in one scene, the mother demands her husband give the girl a good thrashing, and the father and daughter retire to the bedroom where he belts the hell out of, not her, but the bedding, bringing a smile to the unseeing, unknowing wife, who remarks: "And she doesn't even cry out." Directed by Jaime de Armiñán, who authored three submitted films and two nominations including *My Dearest Señorita* (1973), the film is an hour and thirty-seven minutes long and opened January 30, 1981, and August 9, 1982, in New York City. It stars Héctor Alterio from *The Truce* (1975), *Camila* (1985) and *The Official Story* (1986). Unfortunately, the dialogue was dubbed in English. At times a scene is dreamlike, with the girl and older man cavorting on a knoll next to a tree where they often met. At the end, the girl goes to the hill to console her loss and sees a white stallion the old man used to ride, running free and symbolically. The rating? An overly liberal B–.

1982

B+	*The Boat Is Full*	Switzerland
B	***Mephisto***	**Hungary**
B–	*Muddy River*	Japan
C+	*Three Brothers*	Italy
C	*Man of Iron*	Poland

The recent migration of war refugees from the Middle East to Europe has dominated international news since the spring of 2014. More than a million men, women and children—most from Syria, Afghanistan and Iraq—fled in 2015 alone. The Swiss film ***The Boat Is Full*** (*Das Boot ist voll*) nominated in 1982, tackles the question of what one country can, should or fails to do in welcoming asylum-seekers, only in this case it centers on Switzerland's actions during the Holocaust. Six individuals—four Austrian Jews, a French youth and a deserting Nazi—seek shelter across the border in neutral Switzerland after a harrowing flight from the Third Reich. They become embroiled in local politics around the issue of how many refugees would be allowed into the country by the Swiss. Sound familiar? Indeed, during World War II, the Swiss set severe rules and restrictions and accepted only 7,000 asylum-seekers, mostly women and children, to resettle there and sent as many as 30,000 packing back to Germany where their fate was, more than likely, a free train ride to the extermination camp. The escaping band, the focus of director Markus Imhoof's German-language motion picture whose title infers that "Switzerland Is Full," receives shelter from a kindly couple but is inspected by a village constable and found not to fit the strict Swiss guidelines for immigration. There is much anxiety and tension throughout the movie, but at times events seem too implausible or superficial, and even the main characters fail to attract much sympathy. Nevertheless, it's a B+ film and considered one of the better of scores of Oscar-nominated Holocaust films, and a superior pick for this year's Oscar. It was also available on Amazon Prime. Imhoof films were submitted for a Best Foreign Film nomination three times, this being the only one selected. It runs an hour and forty-one minutes and opened first in the United States October 21, 1981, and in West Germany December 18, 1981. It also stars Tina Engel, who appeared in *The Tin Drum* (1980).

Powerful and passionate, ***Mephisto*** from Hungary was the winning foreign film in 1982, and most of it had to do with the tour de force performance of Austrian thespian Klaus Maria Brandauer as Hendrik Hoefgen, the actor who rises as a star in parallel to the Nazi Party, and Hungarian director István Szabó, whose craftsmanship, style and intelligent script captivate the senses on almost every level. The title is short for Mephistopheles, the devil, whom Hoefgen plays on stage, a complement to the Nazis who make it all possible for him. He's ambitious, willing to cast aside lovers who unintentionally block his upward mobility, with the one exception of a black woman, Juliette, who knows how to dominate him. But for the most part, the actor's climb is really a descent into the hell that is Germany. The movie was based on a book by the son of 19th-century novelist Thomas Mann, Klaus Mann, who used as his model his brother-in-law, the actor Gustaf Gründgens. The motion picture is the first of three films involving the partnership of Brandauer and Szabó, all of them Oscar candidates; the others were *Colonel Redl* (1986) and *Hanussen* (1989). He also did *Confidence* (*Bizalom*), a contender in 1981. (Three other films were submitted but not nominated.) Besides Brandauer—selected in 1986 for Best Actor in a Supporting Role for multiple Oscar winner *Out of Africa*—*Mephisto* stars Krystyna Janda, who appeared this same year in the Polish film *Man of Iron*, and included György Cserhalmi, who also appeared in *Hungarian Rhapsody* (1979), *Hanussen* (1989) and *Želary* (2004). As much as *Mephisto* excels, it still falls into the B category, which lowered it to second place. It runs two hours and twenty-four minutes and premiered in Hungary February 11, 1981, coming to America March 22, 1982.

Klaus Maria Brandauer brilliantly portrays the actor Hendrik Hoefgen, depicted here as Mephistopheles, in István Szabó's winning drama, *Mephisto* (1981), which parallels Hoefgen's nefarious rise with that of the Third Reich.

Another Japanese film viewed without subtitles on DVD and in P.A.L. mode at the University of Washington in Seattle was ***Doro no Kawa*** (*Muddy River*). A child-driven film, it's about a young boy in modern postwar Japan living with parents in a ramshackle house on a riverbank and his fascination with a dumpy little trawler parked opposite their home. Nothing escapes him along the river, or for that matter outside the teashop his family runs. In an early scene, a kind blowhard vendor, in an effort to get his horse-drawn cart out of the mud, is thrown to the ground when the nag is spooked by a passing car. The cart runs over him and he dies. The boy sees it all, and it's most affecting. The black-and-white, B– film, directed by Kohei Oguri, has outstanding sound and cinematography (check out the excellent camera angles). The hour-and-forty-five-minute film debuted January 30, 1981, and in New York City January 21, 1983. Oguri had one other submission for BFF, but it was not selected as a nominee.

Director Francesco Rosi was a leader in the post–New Wave period of Italian cinema in which films with political themes prevailed. ***Three Brothers*** (*Tre fratelli*), his only submitted candidate, is one of those films, but less a statement about Italy's politics than a reminder of filial duty and social necessities arising from the former fascist country's earlier neorealistic concepts of postwar poverty and corruption. The picture was in color, but not clearly so, and at times appeared more of a black-and-white creation. Three diverse brothers—a prominent judge, a social worker and an industrial laborer—are brought back together by their distraught father upon their mother's death. Each man is troubled by work entanglements (the judge fears assassination, for instance) or domestic problems. They have been estranged in their urban empires, having forgotten much of their halcyon early lives in the rural world of their parents. There are moments of poignancy, such as when the father visualizes his wife waving good-bye to him along a bucolic country road moments before he urges his sons by telegram to return home for the funeral. Critics mention the movie's parallels to the Stalinist years of the Soviet Union, since the short story upon which the film was loosely based was written by Russian novelist Andrei Platonov, also citing social and political commentary. The film, which garnered a C+, opened March 19, 1981, and in New York City February 19, 1982, and runs an hour and fifty-three minutes. It should be noted that one of the brothers was played by celebrated French actor Philippe Noiret who starred in Best Foreign Film (BFF) nominees *Coup de Torchon* (1983), *The Family* (1988) and *Cinema Paradiso* (winner 1990). He was also in Best Picture *Gigi* (1959) and *Il Postino: The Postman* (1994), which, while it didn't receive a BFF nod, was nominated for Best Picture, Best Actor (not Noiret), Best Director, Best Writing (from previous material) and, as a winner, Best Dramatic Score.

Seen as a semifictional account of the beginnings of the Solidarity Movement that eventually brought the Polish Communist government to its knees, Andrzej Wajda's **Man of Iron** (*Człowiek z żelaza*) was developed during a brief thaw in that country's censorship laws (1980–81). The main character, Maciej Tomczyk, is said to represent Nobel laureate Lech Wałęsa, leader of the anti–Communist labor movement at the Gdańsk Shipyard, who actually had a small part in the film. According to Kevin Wilson of Thirtyframesasecond.com, "'Man of Iron' remains an important film, a document of a declining regime and the collective action that accelerated it, but also an example of the clever interweaving of documentary footage and fiction to represent a historical significant set of events." There is a story here; Wajda is an excellent storyteller, as evidenced by his '50s war trilogy including could-have-been-nominated *A Generation*, *Kanal* and *Ashes and Diamonds* (Poland's first submission and nominee was Roman Polanski's *Knife in the Water* in 1964). But the story was almost secondary to the overall historical perspective the film delivers. Over time, eight of Wajda's films were submitted to AMPAS and half of them received nominations; along the way, he also garnered an honorary Oscar for his work in 2000. The film, which opened July 27, 1981, and in New York City October 11, 1981, is two hours and thirty-six minutes long and merited a C. Also starring was Krystyna Janda, who appears in another nominee from this year, *Mephisto*.

1983

A–	*Coup de Torchon*	France
B+	*Private Life*	Soviet Union
B	*Alsino and the Condor*	Nicaragua
B–	***Volver a Empezar***	**Spain**
B–	*The Flight of the Eagle*	Sweden

Bertrand Tavernier's **Coup de Torchon**, which translates to "Clean Slate," was an enigma. First, actor Philippe Noiret was in practically every scene; everything in the motion picture, for better or worse, appeared to revolve around him. The French film

Lucien Cordier (Philippe Noiret) looks on as his lover Rose (Isabelle Huppert) shoots to kill in *Coup de Torchon* (1981).

takes place in the fictional backwater town of *Bourkassa* in ... well, the film is shot in Senegal ... where the main character, Lucien Cordier, is the do-nothing sheriff. He's so passive that his wife who has some incestuous relationship going on with her imbecilic brother, two well-dressed and sadistic pimps, Lucien's boss in the big city from whom he seeks advice, and a nondescript company bigwig who won't move his latrines from in front of his ramshackle abode—all of them ridicule and take advantage of him. Most of these people are despicable and, contrary to Cordier, treat the black natives like chattel. When he refers to 1,275 "souls" in the village, he's questioned as to what he means by "souls" since he's obviously referring to the natives. He meets the new schoolmarm, Anne, who's charming and innocent; he befriends and has sex with the nymphomaniac wife of a violent husband. These two women make his life a little, er, nicer. But around the thirty-minute mark, the comedy takes a bloody turn and it builds melodramatically from there. At the close, one isn't sure if this fellow is a good guy or a bad guy, hence a Tavernier trait of employing ambiguity to make you think, according to some critics. It deserved an A−, the highest among the five films nominated for the 1983 prize, the winner falling to fourth in this survey. The two-hour-eight-minute film—Tavernier's only submission, although his filmography is long and impressive—opened November 4, 1981, and came to New York City December 20, 1982. It also starred Best Foreign Film nominee veterans Isabelle Huppert—*Entre Nous* (1984) and Eva in *Amour* (winner 2013)—and Stéphane Audran—*The Discreet Charm of the Bourgeoisie* (winner 1973) and the wonderful chef in *Babette's Feast* (winner 1988). Noiret's list is prodigious, starting with an uncredited appearance in Best Picture *Gigi* (1959) and including the lead role in *Cinema Paradiso* (winner 1990).

Private Life (*Chastnaya zhizn*) opens with a bureaucrat tearing up documents while Lenin peers down from a portrait on the office wall. In this Soviet Union nomination, we learn that two companies have merged and our hero has just been fired, replaced by his lackluster protégé. At first, he's at a loss what to do, but as the film progresses he figures out how to be normal again, take interest in his family, and learn how to get around on public transportation. It's an introspective piece that takes him through the process of making choices and change. There's an interesting exchange between him and his wife toward the end of the film that says it all:

> SERGE: "Where'd it all go?"
> NATASHA: "It all drifted away.... I am what you made me.... I felt as long as you were with me, nothing else mattered."
> S: "You really think so?"
> N: "It has nothing to do with us."
> S: "Natasha, I love you very much."
> N: "And I love you."
> S: "You do?"
> N: "Yes."
> S: "Then why is everything so difficult?"
> N: "You were gone for so long."

The hour-and-forty-two-minute drama, created by Yuli Raizman as his only submitted title, received a B+. At the time of this writing, there was virtually no critical reviews or user comments listed on the International Movie Database (IMDb) or other popular websites, indicating a dearth of interest in this picture outside of Russia. Two of the actors appeared in two other foreign film nominees: Mikhail Ulyanov in *Brothers Karamazov* (1970) and Irina Gubanova in *War and Peace* (winner 1969). It first opened August 23, 1982, in the Soviet Union and February 27, 1983, in New York City.

Alsino and the Condor was a child-driven film that takes place in rural Nicaragua. It's in a way a coming-of-age film about a 12-year-old boy named Alsino who learns to survive while soldiers wage war against the peasantry. Alsino encounters a peasant girl for his first kiss, loves to climb trees, and can jump from the upper branches to "fly" like the condor, hence the title. Being in the tree, where snipers usually abound, gets him into trouble, but that turns out to be okay because the American adviser, played exceptionally poorly by Dean Stockwell, takes a shine to the kid. He gives him a helicopter ride, ostensibly to be interrogated, then takes a selfie with the boy next to the aircraft before setting him free. The film was of medium quality on VHS tape, its color beginning to fade; the subtitles had typos; and the music was sappy. But some of the dreamlike aspects of the story, especially after the boy falls from a tree and is injured, are well done. To date, the hour-and-twenty-nine-minute, B film is the only one of three submissions from Nicaragua to be nominated and was directed by Miguel Littín, responsible also for *Letters from Marusia* (1976). *Alsino ...* opened in 1982 and came to New York City May 1, 1983. Stockwell, prolific with 203 film credits, was nominated for Best Supporting Actor for *Married to the Mob* (1988) and had a part in *Blue Velvet* (1987).

The English titles of *Volver a Empezar*, the first feature from Spain to win the Academy Award for Best Foreign Film in 1983, are *Starting Over* and *Begin the Beguine*. The latter is appropriate, since the protagonist, Antonio Albajara, a world-renowned author and Nobel laureate, has returned to his homeland after a fifty-year exile caused by the Franco civil war, to be reacquainted with Elena, his long-lost love. The second title, the Cole Porter song made famous by Fred Astaire (who is mentioned), plays throughout the movie, interspersed with the sadder Classical piece "Pachelbel Canon," which only comes up when the film focuses on Albajara's illness. See, he's dying from cancer, a major reason he must return to his hometown of Gijón one last time to see his old flame. It's a requited love story, and it involves two 70-somethings over the course of just a few days during which the protagonist, also a professor of Medieval Literature at the University of California, Berkeley, receives honors from his Spanish colleagues. At the end, he must leave Elena to teach again in his adopted home until the time his affliction takes him. This hour-and-twenty-seven-minute feature opened March 1, 1982, and in New York City April 22, 1983. The author viewed *Volver* in Spanish at the Knight Library on the campus of the University of Oregon in Eugene and gave it a B–, quite low for a winning picture. While it has its place, the screenplay by director José Luis Garci (*Double Feature* in 1985, *Course Completed* in 1988 and *The Grandfather* in 1999) is not particular unusual. The plot is actor-driven and some of the cinematography is exceptional, filmed on location in Asturias, Spain, for the most part. It also stars Antonio Ferrandis (*Tristana* 1971 and *My Dearest Señorita* 1973). One last thing: This film is not easy to find; WorldCat.org lists it in very few locations around the United States, and perhaps having won an Oscar, one would think it should be more available. Why is never explained, except that after the award was given, it had a meager run in art houses. Someone would do well to find originals of as many of the Oscar winners as possible and put them all, as a collection, on durable DVDs.

Jan Troell's ambitious exploration film ***The Flight of the Eagle*** (*Ingenjör Andrées luftfärd*), Sweden's entry, includes international star Max von Sydow as scientist and adventurer Salomon August Andrée, who with Nils Strindberg and Kurt Frænkel attempted to "conquer" the North Pole for Sweden by flying there in a hydrogen balloon in 1897. Like British explorer Robert Scott, who perished trying to become the first person to the South Pole (Norwegian Roald Amundsen beat him there and survived), Andrée and his team also didn't make it. The story stems from a book based on the diary and photographs found at the team's last camp, as well as pure speculation. It was Troell's third nominated film in the category, following *The Emigrants* (1972) and its sequel *The New Land* (1973), and both also staring von Sydow. In *Flight*, Troell's photography of the Arctic's wild, icy expanses, polar bears and other creatures, and the giant balloon in flight are spectacular. The acting is credible, as are the attention to production details and 19th-century props, and especially the makeup of the deteriorating men in the harsh elements. Interspersed throughout are flashbacks to romantic interludes enjoyed mainly by Strindberg and Frænkel and Andrées' odd relationship with his mother. One of the hard-to-find films, a copy was available at Simon Fraser University in Burnaby, British Columbia, Canada. A decent assessment would be a B–, mainly because of the long, drawn-out and repetitive process of showing the three men trying to survive against the odds over what was thought to be just two weeks. The two-hour-and-twenty-five-minute film opened August 26, 1982, and in New York City April 8, 1983.

1984

A–	*Fanny and Alexander*	**Sweden**
B+	*Carmen*	Spain
B	*Entre Nous*	France
B	*Le Bal*	Algeria
B–	*The Revolt of Job*	Hungary

Fanny and Alexander is an exhausting film of multiple textures, bright and dull colors, luxuriant and boring settings, and a collection of real and unreal characters. Considered in some circles among the best films ever made, the three-hour-and-eight-minute masterpiece of Swedish director Ingmar Bergman—his "last" film nineteen years before he really stopped, and that due to his own demise—is seen from the perspective of two children. In particular, it's Alexander's point of view, as he sees a well-to-do family suddenly transported to a drab, relatively poor living situation upon their father's death and mother's remarriage to a cruel, mean and overtly rigid member of the clergy. Bergman, who said the film was mostly autobiographical, uses mysticism and supernatural characters as envisioned by Alexander to move dreamlike scenes along, and many of these vignettes are hypnotic and believable. Singled out among many positive points of the film is the outstanding cinematography by longtime Bergman collaborator Sven Nykvist, who contrasts scenes of sumptuously rich life in the first third of the film

Fanny and Alexander (1982), performed by tweenagers Pernilla Allwin and Bertil Guve, are caught up in a desperate struggle for acceptance by their austere stepfather in Ingmar Bergman's Oscar–winning film.

with those of a dangerously austere and fecund existence later under the stepfather's guidance. There is a made-for-television adaptation, also offered by Criterion, which runs a mere 312 minutes, but the theatrical version—the 1984 winning foreign film— is the one to watch. It also scored Best Cinematography (Nykvist), Art Direction-Set Decoration and Costume Design, as well as a nomination for Best Director and Best Writing-Directly to the Screen. It garnered an A–. Eight of Bergman's films were submitted to the Academy of which three were not only nominated but won the coveted prize. The other two were *The Virgin Spring* (1961) and *Through a Glass Darkly* (1962). Nykvist eventually tried his hand at directing with *The Ox* (1992). The cast included Jarl Kulle—*Babette's Feast* (1988) and *Käre John* (1966)—Christina Schollin—also *Käre John*—and Kerstin Tidelius—*Adalen 31* (1970).

Life imitates art in Carlos Saura's **Carmen**, Spain's entry. He marries Georges Bizet's opera *Carmen* with the art of flamenco in this second film of a trilogy about the Andalusian dance form. Antonio Gades, the flamenco impresario and choreographer, starred in the 1968 contender from Spain, *Bewitched Love* (*El Amor Brujo*), in playing Bizet's Don José. In the musical, he searches for the right woman to dance his interpretation of the fiery Gypsy seductress of the French opera and finds her in the attractive, enigmatic Laura del Sol, whose name in the film just happens to be Carmen. Using guitars, castanets, handclapping and plenty of foot stomping, Saura creates a real world of dance-infused allegory that takes us from Gades' and del Sol's falling in love, through his jealousy and her infidelity, to the final fatal operatic climax, as stated, with life imitating art. This is a classy story that would appeal to more than just opera buffs and terpsichoreans. The color is muted and the staging minimalist, and it is chockablock with dancing—and not particularly à la Fred Astaire. It warranted a B+. *Carmen* opened May 6, 1983, and came to New York City October 20, 1983. It runs an hour and forty-two minutes. Saura also directed *Mama Turns 100* (1980) and *Tango* (1999).

Lena's marriage is conventional—too conventional—even though it starts out as a marriage of convenience. Played by Isabelle Huppert as Lena, a Jew, the central figure of the French entry **Entre Nous** (*Coup de foudre*) chooses marriage over deportation to a Nazi concentration camp. Her husband, a Foreign Legion guard, marries her and following the war takes her away to Lyon where he opens an auto-repair shop. The two have a pair of little girls and life becomes harmonious—or is it? Lena's motherly-wifely instincts are as expected—at least from a postwar male's point of view—but she grows uptight about her union, finding little in common with her husband, and she begins to search elsewhere. Then by chance, in 1952, she encounters an artistic free spirit named Madeleine, played by Miou-Miou, and the mood changes. The two women discover they are sympatico and actually go farther than a casual friendship. The two leave their husbands and together open a women's clothing boutique. Toward the end, Lena's poor cuckolded husband has a violent fit and tears the dress store apart. Such is this exceptional film by Diane Kurys, upon whose mother Lena's character was loosely based. She also co-wrote the movie. The title means "between us" and reflects the restrained relationship the two women maintain. *Entre Nous* deserved a B. It first opened April 6, 1983, and in the States January 25, 1984. It was Kurys' only submitted film and runs an hour and fifty minutes. Huppert also appeared in such nominated films as *Coup de Torchon* (1983), *Amour* (2013) and *Elle* (2017), which failed to achieve a BFF nomination but perhaps should have. Even so, Huppert as Elle was nominated for Best Actress. Another cast member, Guy Marchand, is known for his parts in *Cousin Cousine* (1977) and *Coup de Torchon*.

Although Algeria's entry **Le Bal** takes place in Paris over a period of fifty years going back to the 1930s, it is directed by an Italian, Ettore Scola. It's remarkably different—strange even—as though Federico Fellini directed *Ballroom Dancing*, only with an ensemble of Marcel Marceaus—no dialogue at all, only music. (No Academy rule disqualified a film without dialogue, just one predominately in English.) Set in a ballroom made for taxi dancing shortly after World War I, the picture takes its series of memorable characters through different eras using the music, costumes and mannerisms of the various times. Most interesting was the tall, big-chinned fellow—not unlike "La Goulue," the caricature in Toulouse-Lautrec's painting—who eventually becomes the officious Nazi SS officer in the World War II sequence, remarkable because in all the other scenes he's either clinically shy or a two-fisted drinker. Actually, however, he isn't; he has an alter ego, one thwarted by two women who are the only dancers on the floor during the particular scene. At first the lack of dialogue is disconcerting, but one becomes more intrigued as the film goes along and, in the end, it warranted a solid B. The DVD, if one can find it, runs an hour and forty-nine minutes. Scola was responsible also for *A Special Day* (1978—writer, too), a portion of *Viva Italia!* (1979), *The Family*

Filmed without dialogue, the humorous *Le Bal* (1983), directed by Ettore Scola, explores 50 years of ballroom dancing. Here, Monica Scattini shows interest in one of her suitors, played by Michel van Speybroeck.

(1988) and two other films submitted but not nominated, and all of them from Italy. *Le Bal* opened in Paris December 21, 1983, and in New York City March 23, 1984.

Another Holocaust film set in 1943–44 Hungary, ***The Revolt of Job*** (*Jób lázadása*), tells the story of a Jewish farmer, Job, and his wife, Roza, who adopt an uncircumcised Christian boy, Lacko, to carry on their legacy once the couple is captured and sent to Auschwitz, as anticipated. It's a sweet story, for the most part, with Job teaching the 7-year-old about life, farming and religion and how, when the time comes, he must go out and seek the Messiah. Principal writer-director Imre Gyöngyössy took a passage from the Bible, "You shall teach it to your children," as the theme. Nazi occupation of Hungary came late in the war and Jews escaped the Holocaust until May 1944 when tens of thousands were rounded up and sent to the Polish death camp. Many of the extras used were acquainted with the real Job, Roza and Lacko and felt it their duty to participate in the color film, which runs an hour and thirty-eight minutes. It was first released in Hungary December 1, 1983; in New York City March 28, 1984; and nowhere else but East Germany. The main characters in this B– film were easy to embrace whole-heartedly and the obvious ending made one quite sad. It was the second-consecutive Gyöngyössy product submitted, the other being passed over. It should be noted he also shared the directing duties with Barna Kabay. Among the cast was Hédi Temessy, who appeared also in *Mephisto* (1982).

1985

B+	*Dangerous Moves*	**Switzerland**
B	*Camila*	Argentina
B	*Beyond the Walls*	Israel
B	*Wartime Romance*	Soviet Union
—	*Double Feature*	Spain

Dangerous Moves (*La Diagonale du fou*) from Switzerland won the Best Foreign Language Film award in 1985, surprising just about everyone—not that this year's competition was particularly spectacular. It's about a fictional world chess championship match not unlike the 1972 Bobby Fischer-Boris Spassky match in Iceland that put the strategic game on the map, also recently dramatized in the American film *Pawn Sacrifice*. The Swiss entry thirty years earlier is said to be loosely based on the 1978 World Chess Federation match between Russians Anatoly Karpov and Viktor Korchnoi (who had defected to the West). That competition was almost as strange as the one in Reykjavik six years earlier. Directed and written by Richard Dembo in his only submitted effort, the color film is set in Geneva, Switzerland, in 1983 and dwells on the psychology of the match. One player makes the other wait; the opponent hires a psychic to weird out the other; the tardy player wants the lighting changed and complains about the weight of the pieces. In short, there's a lot of emotional tension—and politics—at play. One positive point involves the competitors' wives, played by veteran actresses Leslie Caron and Liv Ullmann, but neither has much of a part. This hour-and-forty-minute film was judged a B+ film, despite its shortcomings. The picture had a rather limited run, first in West Germany starting April 15, 1984, and in America May 24 the next

Would-be chess champion Pavius Fromm (Alexandre Arbatt) consults with his wife (Liv Ullmann) in Richard Dembo's Oscar-winning *Dangerous Moves* (1984).

year, but also France, Argentina and Portugal. Also in the cast was Michel Piccoli, one of the most prolific actors with 234 acting credits, who appeared also in *The Discreet Charm of the Bourgeoisie* (1973) and Louis Malle's multiple-Oscar nominee, including Best Picture, *Atlantic City* (1980).

Forbidden love and repressive politics feed ***Camila***, the Argentine nominee for the year. Based on a true story, the film is about a free-spirited, upper-class 19-year-old in mid–19th-century Argentina. She rails against the dictatorship of Juan Manuel de Rosas, but even more blasphemous, she falls in love with a Jesuit priest, despite the Catholic authority condemning such sacrilege. The couple escape to the hinterlands where they teach school and enjoy an idyllic life until a visiting cleric recognizes them. On orders from the warlord, the two lovers—Camila O'Gorman, performed by Susú Pecoraro, and Ladislao Gutiérrez, played by Imanol Arias—were condemned to death without trial. The director, María Luisa Bemberg, took liberties with actual events, perhaps under some pressure from the church; for example, the fact Camila was eight-months pregnant when she was killed was left out of the story. The few western critics who reviewed this film thought it overly dramatic and soap-operatic, but it merited a B rating. *Camila*, with a runtime of an hour and forty-five minutes, was Argentina's second nomination for Oscar, *The Truce* being the first a decade earlier. *Camila* was released simultaneously in the United States and Argentina March 15, 1985, and was the only nominee of two submitted films by Bemberg. Veteran actor Héctor Alterio, with 173 acting credits, had a part, as he did in *The Official Story* a year later, as well as *The Truce* (1975) and *The Nest* (1981).

Brutal, inhumane, at times difficult to watch, the nominee **Beyond the Walls** (*Me'A-horei Ha-Soragim*)—described by one critic as "a political allegory of Arab-Israeli relations"—tells the tale of life in a crowded Israeli prison full of Jews and Arabs. It takes place at the time of the Lebanon civil war during the turbulent 1970s and '80s when a radio news flash about the deaths of Israeli civilians, including children, could easily trigger a riot. *A Prophet* (2010) seems almost tame by comparison. Excellent acting in a near-documentary style makes the film worth watching. There are moments in the movie when things appear calm and pleasant: when the "Nightingale," an inmate with musical talent, sings and plays his guitar on national television from a makeshift prison stage of a festival-contest; or moments when a father and daughter are trying to connect within visiting hours. But drug-infused, anti–Jew, anti–Arab, anti-guard moments are far more common in this picture, directed by Uri Barbash—his only nominee of two submissions. Considered a B movie in a year full of B films, this hour-and-forty-three-minute VCR tape arrived from Holy Cross Libraries in Worcester, Massachusetts. It was originally released September 27, 1984, and started a run in the United States February 25, 1985.

Jules et Jim it is not—the Soviet entry for 1985, **Wartime Romance** (*Voenno-polevoy roman*). But it does have a "love triangle" of sorts. During the war, Sasha falls for his commander's blonde girlfriend, Lyuba. Spin forward a few years. Sasha, the war over, marries Vera, a teacher, and while walking one day in a Moscow square discovers his former lover, Lyuba—bundled in old clothes against the cold, obviously indigent and now with a daughter—selling pies to passersby. He tries to take up where he left off, but his wife finds out and rather than raise Cain, she invites the former nurse to live with them. Strange bedfellows? (One is reminded of *Gervaise* from 1957.) Well, it doesn't take Sasha long to learn one rule of love: what appears everlasting can be a fleeting notion. He abandons his former paramour and his wife welcomes him back. The picture, directed by Pyotr Todorovsky in his only submission, was available on DVD from an East Coast library. The International Movie Database (IMDb.com) listed no critical commentary, except from "users," who for the most part found the hour-and-thirty-two-minute film "weird." A B film, *Wartime Romance* opened November 7, 1983, and for a brief time in America in February 1985. Hungary, West Germany, Finland and the Czechoslovakia also had short distributions.

Renowned Spanish director José Luis Garci, one of the more prolific of the post–Francisco Franco filmmakers, was gracious in thanking all the right people during his acceptance of the Academy Award for Best Foreign Film in 1983 when *Volver a Empezar* (*Begin the Beguine*) took first place. But he admitted in interviews afterward that he did not make films to win trophies. Indeed, some of his motion pictures are virtually unheard of, even those nominated, and it takes a great deal of research to learn even what they are about. One of those is **Double Feature** (*Sesión continua*). A clip or two can be found online, but nothing substantial enough to get the gist of what it's all about. IMDb described the plot this way: "The film tells the story of the relationship and friendship of two men who are both very much affected by the cinema: Both of them are writers, one of books [and] the other of screenplays." *Eso es todo!* No critical or "user" reviews exist as of this writing. This emptiness continues for another Garci film, *Course Completed*, which was nominated for the 1988 ceremony. This film has not been ranked because it has not been seen. For the record, however, Garci, with six submissions, is also responsible for *Begin the Beguine* and *The Grandfather* (1999), both of which are well documented. Actor Jesús Puente was in this and *Course Completed*. *Double Feature*, at an hour and fifty-five minutes, opened in Madrid, Spain, September 10, 1984, and in Argentina April 11, 1985, but that was it as far as known distribution is concerned.

1986

B	*The Official Story*	**Argentina**
B	*When Father Was Away on Business*	Yugoslavia
B	*Colonel Redl*	Hungary
B–	*Angry Harvest*	West Germany
D	*Three Men & a Cradle*	France

During Argentina's "Dirty War" from circa 1974 to 1983, in which authorities kidnapped, killed and/or tortured literally thousands of so-called "Socialists," an estimated 500 children disappeared as well. Over the years since, more than 100 have been found in the hands of other families, the result of secret adoptions of kids largely forced from imprisoned mothers. The 1986 Argentine winning Best Foreign Language Film, **The Official Story** (*La historia oficial*), tackles this highly charged political theme. It's a heartbreaking, painful drama. Alecia, the main character, begins to suspect that her adopted child, Gaby, may be one of the missing; her husband had brought her home as a babe. She befriends an older woman named Sara whose grandchild was stolen from her incarcerated mother, and indeed she just might be Gaby. Despite being on opposite sides of the issue, Alecia and Sara develop an endearing relationship, considered by critics as one of the more powerful points in the film. The Official Story comes out, the adoptive father is blamed as a participant in the nasty business, and all is not well. The picture was directed by Luis Puenzo and was his only nomination and win among the three submitted to the Academy. It opened April 3, 1985, and in the U.S. November 8, 1985, and also starred venerable actor Héctor Alterio, who was in *The Truce* (1975), *The Nest* (1981) and *Camila* (1985). This hour-and-fifty-two-minute winning drama warranted a B, virtually tying it with the next two films. A side note: According to *A Short History of Film* by Dixon and Foster, *The Official Story*, with its cover-up, is an example of what they labeled Latin America Realism. The other films they cite and the realism they display include Brazil's *Central Station* (1999), humanism; Argentina's *Son of the Bride* (2001), midlife crisis; and Brazil's *City of God* (2002), brutal slum life, and lest we forget the desperation of Mexico's *Biutiful* (2011), which came out after Dixon and Foster's volume. Also in the cast of *The Official Story* was Pablo Rago, seen in *The Secret in Their Eyes* (2010).

Not a Willy Loman story despite its name, the Yugoslav dramedy **When Father Was Away on Business** (*Otac na službenom putu*) takes place in Sarajevo in 1950 at the time of the break between Tito and Stalin. This contender is additionally about a family divided because of politics, which director Emir Kusturica is careful to mask with humor and ambiguity. The story is related by 6-year-old Malik who, age notwith-

In *When Father Was Away on Business* (1985), life goes on for the family of Mesha, who's in prison for opposing communist dictator Marshal Tito and believed to be "away on business" by young son Malik (Moreno D'E Bartolli), playing the accordion. The other actors, from right, are Mira Furlan, Emir Hadžihafizbegović, Predrag "Miki" Manojlović and an unidentified guitarist.

standing, is sensitively aware of what is going on regarding his womanizing father, his long-suffering mother, his nerdy brother and others. Even so, he takes up sleepwalking, which *CineScene*'s Howard Schumann opines "perhaps (is) a wry metaphor for the status of the people under Marshal Tito." When the father innocently utters a wisecrack about a political cartoon he's seen concerning the Stalin-Tito break, his mistress snitches on him and he's arrested by his bureaucrat brother-in-law and sent away to work in a mine—hence the title, the excuse the mom gives Malik to explain his absence. There are a number of lighter moments, even poignant ones, especially when the family is reunited. Although another Communist-era film, this one had a good cast, fine direction and riveting screenplay, and deserved a B. It opened in West Germany September 12, 1985, and in the States twenty years later on October 11, 2005, seven months after it first appeared in Belgrade at its annual film festival. It did finally open in distribution in Serbia June 23, 2014, nearly thirty years after its premiere. For what it's worth, Josip Broz Tito died in 1980. Kusturica, by the way, had three films submitted for consideration but only this one nomination.

Alfred Redl served as one of history's most infamous traitors, "more sly and false than intelligent and talented," according to a 1907 Russian document. He headed the spy unit of the Austro-Hungarian Empire but sold out to Czarist Russia. It is said his counterespionage between 1903 and 1913, just before the outbreak of the Great War, resulted in the death of tens of thousands of his countrymen. *Colonel Redl*, Hungary's nominee for 1986 and a B film, is the second historical movie in director István Szabó's trilogy, led by the 1982 winning film *Mephisto*. Both films starred Klaus Maria Brandauer, "one of the most underrated actors of his generation," according to *Bonjour Tristesse*, a blog about foreign indie and cult cinema. Critics pointed to Brandauer's body language and facial expressions, captured expertly by the most honored Hungarian filmmaker, as the essence of the film. The two-hour-and-twenty-four-minute feature opened February 20, 1985, and in the United States October 4, 1985. Szabó also made *Hanussen* (1989)—also starring Brandauer—which did not win. He had a total of seven films submitted for consideration and four nominations, *Confidence* (1981) being the other. Brandauer also received a Best Supporting Actor nomination for the multiple-award-winning English-language film and Best Picture *Out of Africa* (1986). The cast of *Colonel Redl* included Armin Mueller-Stahl, who appeared in *Jacob the Liar* (1975) and *Angry Harvest*, up next.

Angry Harvest (*Bittere Ernte*) is a film by West German director Agnieszka Holland (*In Darkness* 2012), which controversially made the cut for the 1986 contest. Better titled in literal translation *Bitter Harvest*, the hour-and-forty-one-minute feature—a B– film—is about a sophisticated Jewish woman who is separated from her husband and children when they escape from a death train in the winter of 1942. She finds herself a captive of an unmarried, sexually repressed farmer named Leon in the German-speaking Silesia area of Poland. Over time, and despite the brutish nature of the bumpkin, the two become lovers. Critics smacked the film for being too melodramatic with incredulous scenarios, whereas Armin Mueller-Stahl, playing Leon Wolny, was roundly praised for his acting. He starred as well in the nominated foreign films *Colonel Redl* (1985), honored this same year (see above), and *Jacob the Liar* (1975); he even had a part in the later, American version of *Jakob the Liar* with Robin Williams. His best role might have been as Peter in *Shine* (1997), a seven-nomination (including Best Picture) English-language motion picture in which Mueller-Stahl received a bid for his supporting role. A side note on the director: Holland's better film, *Europa Europa*, about a young Jewish boy who masquerades as an Aryan during the Holocaust, was passed over by the Academy as "junk" when, in fact, crowds flocked to art houses worldwide to see it. The committee also refused its submission because it was filmed for the most part in Poland, not West Germany, and therefore was not in compliance with Academy rules. *Angry Harvest* opened January 9, 1986, and in the U.S. two months later. Also in the cast was Wojciech Pszoniak, known for *The Promised Land* (1976), *The Tin Drum* (winner 1980) and *Dangerous Moves* (winner 1985).

There must be something about **Three Men and a Cradle** (*3 hommes et un couffin*) that made the French nominee worthy of consideration. We know it borrowed heavily from the 1948 *Three Godfathers* with John Wayne, it was remade in America as *Three Men and a Baby*, and it yielded three Indian spinoffs. But to read critical commentary, you would think this the worst movie *ever*—worse even than *Ishtar* or *Gigli*. Simply stated, it's about three swinging bachelors in Paris who receive an expected "package" at their apartment, but it turns out to be a baby, not the drugs they'd ordered. The infant apparently is the progeny of one of the bachelors, a flight attendant who's working out of town. Drug pushers are on the chase. Narcs get into the act. It's sheer chaos—the plot as much as the action. Charles Tatum, eFilmCritic.com, said the picture "gives many foreign films a bad name." Venerable reviewer Roger Ebert, not known for holding back, had this to say: "I hated every second of this movie because it was so blind to psychology and reality and so willing to settle for every relentless cliché and dim-witted, knee-jerk emotional response in the book." The only good thing about it, he continued, was the acting of the two infants who played the baby. This hour-and-forty-six-minute slapstick comedy was evaluated with a D and definitely not worth seeing again, as many of the features in this study were. It was directed by Coline Serreau in her only submission and opened September 18, 1985. Despite its absurdity, it made $2,052,466 when it came to the States. In the cast was André Dussollier, who played in *Amélie* (2002), which had five Oscar nominations including Best Foreign Film. Quite a contrast.

Fabulous Flicks:
1987–2000

From the mid-'80s through the '90s, some sixty-nine films received nominations and of them no more than 20 percent are very memorable. Several are outstanding—*Babette's Feast, Cinema Paradiso, Mediterraneo, Antonia's Line, Kolya, Indochine*—all winners—but arguably they had little competition. During this period, the number of submissions stagnated as well, running from thirty-two in 1987 to thirty-nine an entire decade later, even though there was a spike to forty-six in 1995.

It was also a time of the Asian Explosion. India, for instance, was no stranger to international acclaim with the likes of Satyajit Ray, who did submit but was never nominated (although he received a Lifetime Achievement Award in 1992), and Mehboob Khan, whose *Mother Earth* was the first Indian film nominated in 1958. Mira Nair showed her chops in a New Wave–like film *Salaam Bombay!* (1988) and received India's second of three nominations to date.

The People's Republic of China scored big with Zhang Yimou's colorful *Ju Dou* and would follow up twelve years later with *Hero*. Emerging almost consecutively were the only two films submitted by Hong Kong: *Raise the Red Lantern* by Zhang Yimou (yes, the same) and *Farewell My Concubine* by Chen Kaige. Ang Lee from Taiwan also had two back-to-back nominations in *The Wedding Banquet* and *Eat Drink Man Woman*, as well as *Crouching Tiger, Hidden Dragon* sixteen years later.

Iceland, Macedonia, Nepal, Vietnam and Georgia (the country, not the state) had their one-and-only nominations during this period.

What stands out among most of the pictures are their storylines: inventive (*Indochine, Central Station*), at times sentimental (*Kolya, Life Is Beautiful*), historical (*Daens, Four Days in September*) and silly (*Farinelli, Ridicule*). But who has heard of *Hedd Wyn, Strawberry and Chocolate, Children of Heaven* or *Schtonk!*?

You get the picture.

1987

B	*The Assault*	Netherlands
B	*My Sweet Little Village*	Czechoslovakia
B–	*The Decline of the American Empire*	Canada

| C– | *Betty Blue* | France |
| C– | *38: Vienna Before the Fall* | Austria |

At the core of **The Assault** (*De Aanslag*) from Holland, the Academy's 1987 Best Foreign Film, is an old-fashioned whodunit, the kind where the writer obviously has begun with a premise and worked backward to connect the threads. It's also a film in which the protagonist, at first seemingly indifferent to the fact his immediate family was murdered by the Gestapo for no legitimate reason in the final months of World War II, slowly seeks and eventually learns the truth about who was ultimately at fault— a revelational twist that disturbs him even more than the massacre itself. One cannot help but think: Oh, no, not another Nazi film, and there are enough twists and turns in it to rank it as mystery rather than history. Responsible for making it was Fons Rademakers, who also did *Village on the River* (1960) and had three other unselected submissions. *De Aanslag* was not an easy film to locate, but a dubbed VHS copy was found at the University of Washington's Bothell Campus northeast of Seattle. This was not the "masterpiece" some have labeled it, but it was gripping and maintained its basic high quality throughout. Acting appeared to be excellent, but it's difficult to tell in a revoiced version. The score by Jurriaan Andriessen was pretty and romantic but commonplace. The two-hour-and-twenty-four-minute film received a strong B, which while average, still qualified it as a winner, matching the committee's determination in an otherwise lackluster year. It debuted February 6, 1986, and in New York City February 6, 1987. It earned $203,781 in its limited run in America. In the cast was Monique van de Ven, who was also in *Turkish Delight* (1974).

Angst fills Anton Steenwijk, played by Derek de Lint, in *The Assault* (1986), Fons Rademakers' winning film from the Netherlands.

The small Czech comedy *My Sweet Little Village* (*Vesničko má středisková*) is a joy to watch on several levels. The central characters are Mutt and Jeff—Otík, gangly and simple, and his boss Pavek, roly-poly and mouthy. The latter owns a truck in which he hauls dirt to construction projects, while the former, who speaks little but laughs a lot in a Pee Wee Herman kind of way, appears to love his role as Pavek's sidekick. Each morning on the way to work, he keeps in step with his companion-boss and finds amusement even in adversity. Otík owns a small cottage that a city-slicker wants to buy for use as a weekend retreat, and perhaps more. For he also has an attractive secretary who always accompanies him, so you can guess an ulterior motive. Otík lives with his pigeons and a dog and doesn't know much about life beyond the little village or tiny home, but the bureaucrat offers him work in the city if he'll relinquish the cottage, and that sounds fine to him. It would be disingenuous to tell you more; suffice to say the villagers come to his rescue. The hour-and-thirty-eight-minute picture, like the title, is truly "sweet" and has as many sight gags as a Buster Keaton comedy. Director Jiří Menzel, who had three submissions and created the classic and Academy Award-winning *Closely Watched Trains* (1968) as his other nominee, was one of the original members of the Czechoslovak New Wave, which set out during the '60s to ridicule Communist oppression and incompetence. Zdeněk Svěrák from *The Elementary School* (1992) and *Kolya* (1997) has a part. Judged a B, the film premiered August 1, 1985, and opened in America January 9, 1987.

In the 1997-nominated film *Ridicule*, biting wit is a measure of cleverness among the aristocratic class, and the competition, whether successful or not, is fierce. In ***The Decline of the American Empire*** (*Le Déclin de l'empire américain*), Canada's 1987 entry,

(*Clockwise from left*) **Louise Portal, Dominique Michel, Dorothée Berryman and Geneviève Rioux laugh it up in Canada's 1987 entry,** *The Decline of the American Empire* **(1986).**

wit is also paramount, but the subject matter is almost entirely about sex. Eight college professors—four men and four women—discuss the meaning, object and triviality of the carnal arts. The participants talk about their affairs, some of which have been with others present, and two of them, one a homosexual, say they relish engaging in risky activities. This is not a pornography session; this is what Rita Kempley described in her *Washington Post* review as an "intellectual gabfest." At times it can be rather disturbing, but for the most part it's simply a platonic bore. The hour-and-forty-one-minute satire deserved a B–. Director Denys Arcand, with a total of five submissions, scored his first of several Oscar nominations with *Decline....* He also received bids for *Jesus of Montreal* (1990) and *The Barbarian Invasions* (winner 1994). In addition, he was shortlisted in 2008 for *Days of Darkness*. For this film, he had $1.8 million Canadian ($1.3 million U.S.) to work with, and when it opened in the States November 14, 1986, it zoomed to $1,902,706 in ticket sales. The feature premiered June 19 of that year. Two of the cast members were Dominique Michel and Dorothée Berryman, both of whom appeared in *The Barbarian Invasions*.

After viewing France's ***Betty Blue*** (*37°2 le matin*), it was a struggle to understand how a shallow, senseless film like this could ever make it to the Academy Awards, let alone get past the January shortlist and receive a nomination. Unless, of course, mostly male members came to be transfixed by Betty's lissome, fetching body, of which we see a great deal. Her lover—saddled with the unlikely name of Zorg—is also naked a lot and rather striking to those who should notice. Betty, played bravely by Beatrice Dalle in her first film, could be described as a rather wild, perhaps bipolar nymph who latches onto a novelist at a quiet beach resort during the offseason. She's harassed by the licentious and disheveled owner of the beach cabins and isn't afraid to take the oaf to task. "She's a real hellcat!" he exclaims. Before long, she's burned down her lover's cottage and they're forced to move to a small hotel on the outskirts of Paris. From there, things go downhill for her and she sinks into depression, and worse. It was easy to give this erotic French drama a generous C–, having found the show, as did a number of reviewers, empty, repetitive and boring. Even so, the two-hour movie made $2,003,822 when it was released in the United States November 7, 1986, seven months after its premiere. The picture is nicely filmed by director Jean-Jacques Beineix, who had one other submission but no other nominations.

38: Vienna Before the Fall (*'38-Auch das war Wien*) is the only Austrian nomination between 1962 and 2008 for a Best Foreign Language Film award. The hour-and-thirty-seven-minute motion picture is about the days leading to the *Anschluss* that linked Austria with Germany in 1938. The Jews were targeted by the Brown Shirts, and if you were a Jew in good standing, as was Mr. Hoffman, it wasn't easy to figure out what was going on, especially when you've become engaged to a striking blonde named Mrs. Hell who happens to be Aryan. This isn't much of the film; it's hackneyed and not very effective. The ending, at the midpoint of March 1938, is quite abrupt. Hoffman, who's lost his betrothed as well as his passport, skips around Vienna until he finds a cabbie who will take him to and even across the Czech border to safety. He barely avoids the Brown Shirts as they seek out Jews to dispose of in the black hole that was the Gestapo system. Then, finally, he learns Mrs. Hell is okay, in Prague, and all will be well tomorrow once he's escaped. All of that known, he ventures to the street, almost with a skip, and—spoiler alert!—runs smack-dab into two Nazis who quick-march him up the cobbled roadway in a long sequence that telegraphs the end of the film. The hour-and-thirty-seven-minute feature earned a C–. Directed by Wolfgang Glück in his only submission, it opened in Austria in 1986 and had a short run in New York City starting May 6, 1988. Otherwise, it only appeared in both East and West Germany. One of the stars was Sunnyi Melles, a Luxembourg-born actress who later married a real prince, Peter zu Sayn-Wittgenstein-Sayn. She appeared in *The Baader Meinhof Complex* (2009).

1988

A	*Babette's Feast*	**Denmark**
A–	*Au Revoir les Enfants*	France
B	*Pathfinder*	Norway
B	*The Family*	Italy
—	*Course Completed*	Spain

The Danish classic foodie-flick, **Babette's Feast** (*Babettes gæstebud*), is not a film one should watch just once and be satisfied. Its great acting, direction, cinematography, makeup, and, most of all, the great feast Stéphane Audran prepares, demand multiple

Gabriel Axel's Oscar-winning gastronomic film *Babette's Feast* (1987) is not only a scrumptious treat for food fans, but it is also a feast for the eyes, as attested by this closing banquet scene.

viewings. She is Babette, a French immigrant living with two Danish sisters, who conjures the banquet for them and their fellow Danish Puritans living austerely in Jutland during the last quarter of the 19th century. Based on an Isak Dinesen (Karen Blixen) short story, Denmark's 1988 entry figures high in the annals of food-related films—maybe highest—and tempts one to drool for most of the last half of the motion picture as Babette cooks up and serves a seven-course meal consisting, in part, of turtle soup, quail in puff pastry shell with foie gras and truffle sauce, rum sponge cake with figs and candied cherries, buckwheat cakes with caviar and sour cream, endive salad, assorted cheeses and fruits, champagne, cognac, and coffee (according to cookbook author Celeste Heiter). The director was Gabriel Axel, who had two films submitted but only this one winning nomination. It premiered August 28, 1987, and made a killing of $4,398,938 after it opened in America March 4, 1988. The hour-and-forty-two-minute picture consistently garnered an A with each viewing and deserved its Oscar. Dinesen, by the way, wrote the story upon which the 1986 Best Picture *Out of Africa* was based. Audran also appeared in *The Discreet Charm of the Bourgeoisie* (1973) and *Coup de Torchon* (1983).

As frequently noted, films depicting the plight of Jews during World War II are common enough and some even feature the many good Samaritans who came to their aid and protection, situations that present dramatic, suspense-filled stories, often based in fact. *Defiance*, *Schindler's List* and *Black Book* immediately come to mind. The French entry, **Au Revoir les Enfants**, is like that. Director Louis Malle, a Christian, relates the experience he had as a boy at a Carmelite school in occupied France where a priest took in three Jewish boys, gave them Gentile names and did his level best to keep them out of harm's way. The black-and-white film delves into student diversities, behaviors and escapades—a virtual boarding-school tale—as well as how childhood animosities and eventual friendships evolve, adding tensions to the storyline. This A– picture is considered one of the better films of the genre and could easily have won the Oscar almost any other year. It opened October 7, 1987, and did quite well after it debuted in the States February 12, 1988, chalking up $4,542,825 in its first run. The hour-and-forty-four-minute motion picture also garnered a Best Writing Directly to the Screen bid. It was a second nomination, out of three submissions, for Malle, the other being *Lacombe, Lucien* (1975). In the cast was François Berléand, who also was in *Camille Claudel* (1990) and *The Chorus* (2005).

The poster of the film **Pathfinder** (*Ofelaš*), the 2007 American remake of the film of the same title that vied for a Best Foreign Film Oscar in 1988, shows a ripped warrior cutting unmercifully into a giant beast affront a Viking ship's figurehead. This B thriller, which later inspired a graphic novel, was loosely based on the earlier Lapland version. That picture, submitted by Norway, broke ground as the first feature film in Sami—the language of northern Scandinavia—and was drawn from a legend that took place 1,000 years ago. A Lapp family is murdered by the equivalent to foreign terrorists. One young boy escapes and dedicates his survival smarts and hunting skills to avenging the massacre. There's a lot of mystical quality to the hour-and-twenty-six-minute movie, which was written, directed and acted by Laplanders, led by Nils Gaup in his only submission. It's a good film—needless to say much better than its later version—and the filming techniques, including cinematography, were superb. Known also as *Ofelaš* in

Sami and *Veiviseren* in Norwegian, it originally opened September 3, 1987, and came to the United States April 7, 1989.

At the end of the Italian film **The Family** (*La Famiglia*), Carlo asks his old flame and adversary, Adriana, how many family members have gathered in the old house for his 80th birthday photograph. "A lot," she says, then admits she might

Aigin, played by Laplander Mikkel Gaup, must trust his instincts and learned survival skills after his family is massacred in Norway's Sami-language *Pathfinder* (1987).

"know half of them," to which Carlo agrees. This is a big family. The photo will include around thirty-five people, including many children. The feature begins in 1906 when Carlo is an infant and family members have gathered for his baptism. It proceeds through generations—and wends its way along the main corridors of the big Roman house—and the nearly eighty years of social, economic and political ups and downs of Italy during most of the 20th century. The on-again, off-again love affair between Adriana and Carlo is at the core of this film, but not particularly central to its plot. Carlo marries Beatrice, Adriana's sister, and fathers children who go on to have families of their own, and so forth. Perhaps even more telling is the relationship between Carlo, the prosperous "professor" and intellect of the family, and his brother, Giulio, an oft-failed entrepreneur and aspiring writer. On his deathbed earlier, their father asks Carlo to watch over Giulio, but the former fails to do so. In a climactic scene, Carlo admits he actually read a book his brother had written fifty years earlier, his negative criticism of it at that time causing Giulio to drop the notion of being a writer. Carlo has now reread it and admits he found it "beautiful," adding that Giulio showed a sensitivity in his writing that the older brother never expected. Giulio, of course, is nonplussed that he could have achieved his dream and become rich had he only known is brother's true feelings—a greedy notion, Carlo admonishes. This is the extent of the scene: mildly adversarial without being overwrought and passionate, as these characters have been throughout. A slightly grainy VHS was obtained from the Knox County Public Library in Tennessee. It was slow and methodical, with too many characters to keep straight, except for the leads: Vittorio Gassman, who comes into the film about halfway through as the middle-age Carlo, and Fanny Ardant, introduced earlier as the young, stylish, piano virtuoso who had chosen schooling in Paris over Carlo's advances—that, perhaps, because she recognized in their relationship a turbulence that would always haunt them through life. It's a satisfying film, very Italian in a way only Italians can present the family as the central character. It received a B in a year with several excellent films and opened January 20, 1987, and later in the U.S. December 1987, earning in its first run $346,730. The two-hour-and-seven-minute film was directed by Ettore Scola, who had four submissions and three nominees, including *A Special Day* (1978) and *Viva Italia!* (1979). The two chief cast members are accomplished as well: Gassman was also in *Big Deal on Madonna Street* (1959), *The Great War* (1960), *Scent of a Woman* (1976) and *Viva Italia!* (1979). Ardant starred in *Ridicule* (1997). Also in the cast was Giuseppe Cederna from *Mediterraneo* (1992).

    Course Completed (*Asignatura aprobada*), received no critical comment, either by professionals or "users" of IMDb; no copies of the film can be found on Amazon.com or eBay. But we know from brief synopses that it's about a man named José Manuel Alcantara, about 50, who is undergoing a midlife crisis because of a failed marriage and career. He moves from the bustle of Madrid to the peaceful serenity of Gijon (scene of other José Luis Garci films) to find himself—and perhaps love—again. Garci had six submitted for Oscar consideration of which four were nominated and *Begin the Beguine* (1983) won; he also did *Double Feature* (1985) and *The Grandfather* (1999). Jesús Puente acted in this and *Double Feature*. The hour-and-thirty-four-minute film opened in Madrid, Spain, April 23, 1987, but was not distributed in the States. A translation from *El Cine De Ramón*, discovered on Spanish Google, tells us *Course Completed* is a "sentimental" and "emotional" picture, "directed with a slow pace and with a particular and intimate style [that goes] to the heart of the viewer." We'll leave it at that. There is no ranking for this effort.

1989

B+	***Pelle the Conqueror***	**Denmark**
B+	*Women on the Verge of a Nervous Breakdown*	Spain
B+	*Hanussen*	Hungary
B	*Salaam Bombay!*	India
C	*The Music Teacher*	Belgium

    Pelle the Conqueror (*Pelle Erobreren*) not only won the Best Foreign Film award at the 1989 Oscars, it also garnered a Best Actor nomination for Max von Sydow for his strong, emotive portrayal of Lasse Karlsson, who immigrates to Denmark from Sweden with his prepubescent son Pelle only to discover a life of servitude, toil, discrimination and humiliation. Unable initially to find work, the middle-aged Karlsson eventually lands on a farm with an assortment of characters, some good, some bad, some indifferent and some caught up in their own abject misery. This is a spectacular acting job by von Sydow, but not particularly a well-directed tale—perhaps in part because of the epic nature of the storyline that tries, unsuccessfully, to draw away from the slow-but-sure character development and feels compelled by time limitations to skip necessary exposition. The other bright star is Pelle, the boy, played by Pelle Hvenegaard, a novice actor whose parents named him after the fictional character in the 1906 book by Danish writer Martin Andersen Nexø. Nexø begins his story on May 1, 1877, but critics and other sources do not agree on the film's timeline (one source said "late 1850s" and another "the end of the 19th century"). Nexø died in 1954. Another character that stood out was Erik the anti-authoritarian-turned-simpleton, played by veteran Swedish actor Bjørn Granath—*The Ox* (1992) and *Evil* (2004)—and the odd-looking, sympathetic Rud, played by young Troels Asmussen. It was directed by Bille August, who had one other film submitted but not nominated. Despite its flaws, *Pelle ...* was worthy of a B+, which virtually tied the two-hour-and-thirty-seven-minute film with two other contenders. The motion picture brought in $2,053,931 from its first run in the States, opening December 21, 1988; it had premiered in Sweden December 25, 1987.

Pedro Almodóvar's **Women on the Verge of a Nervous Breakdown** (*Mujeres al borde de un ataque de nervios*), his first of five submissions and two nominations, did not garner the Academy Award in 1989, but it was equal to the winner, receiving a B+ rating. Filmed in vivid—dare one say, *intense* "Hispanic"?—colors, *Women ...* is a black comedy, a farce bordering on the absurd, and takes its theme from an austere play and the later fifty-one-minute Jean Cocteau film with Ingrid Bergman called *The Human Voice*. *The New Yorker* magazine's Pauline Kael once described it as "one of the jauntiest of all war-of-the-sexes comedies." The focus is on Pepa, played by longtime Almodóvar muse Carmen Maura, who reacts morbidly to a breakup with her lover—a cad who leaves the bad news on her answering machine—by preparing a suicide cocktail of homemade gazpacho laced with three-dozen Valium. She's interrupted by a fire in her bedding and never gets back to offing herself. The romp continues with her best friend escaping from her terrorist boyfriend and a parade of interlopers, some of whom paradoxically drink her knockout concoction. Five features by this "demonic wit," as one critic described Almodóvar, were submitted for Best Foreign Film contention: two were disregarded, one (*Volver* 2007) was shortlisted, this one was nominated and *All About My Mother* was a winner in 2000. Of note, Maura and Antonio (Zorro) Banderas, who plays the cad's son in *Women ...* had parts in seven of Almodóvar's pictures. Julieta Serrano, who was in *My Dearest Señorita* (1973), was in this film. It opened March 14, 1988, and was a hit in the States, picking up $7,179,298 when it debuted November 11, 1988.

Hanussen from Hungary (in German) is the third of a trilogy that included *Mephisto* (winner 1982) and *Colonel Redl* (1986). The director was István Szabó and featured Klaus Maria Brandauer, who brilliantly starred in all of the films. It's a compelling story about the real-life clairvoyant, hypnotist and occultist and his look into his own future during the rise of the Third Reich. This is the somewhat fictionalized story but basically follows the awakening of Klaus Schneider, an Austrian who, using the stage name Erik Jan Hanussen, became an uncannily accurate mentalist in Berlin during the 1920s and '30s. His incredible skills and accurate predictions of Germany's rise to power, caught the attention of the Nazis and he enjoyed fame and fortune under Hitler's rule. Brandauer's performance is riveting and carries an otherwise lackluster story. The two-hour-and-twenty-minute film arrived from Linfield College in McMinnville, Oregon, but it opened in Hungary October 6, 1988, and in America March 10, 1989. Szabó turned in seven films to the Academy and garnered a total of four nominations and one win. The other nominated film was *Confidence* (1981). Brandauer further distinguished himself as the baron in *Out of Africa*, a multiple award winner in 1986 (eleven nominations, including Best Supporting Actor for Brandauer, and four wins, among them Best Picture). In the *Hanussen* cast were Ingmar Bergman regular

Erland Josephson: *Fanny and Alexander* (1984) and *The Ox* (1992); Ildikó Bánsági and Péter Andorai: *Confidence* (1981) and *Mephisto*; György Cserhalmi: *Hungarian Rhapsody* (1979), *Mephisto* and *Želary* (2004); and Sándor Zsótér: *Son of Saul* (2016). Like the others above, *Hanussen* weighed in with a B+ ranking.

Readily available online with English subtitles and in vivid color, **Salaam Bombay!** is a slice of life (if you can call it that) of street life in the underbelly of Mumbai, India, directed by Mira Nair in her only submission. The street children—Chaipau (Krishna), Manju and Sola the Nepalese girl—are at the heart of the film as they learn to survive as best they can in a nest of prostitutes, a pimp, a sad and tragic dope addict and a gaggle of young orphans of all ages and various stages of sanity. The main character, 11-year-old Krishna, who was sold to and abandoned by a traveling circus, wants desperately to return to his family near Bangalore. His efforts to earn money for the trip home—selling glasses of tea on the street, ripping off foreigners wanting hashish—are thwarted several different ways. He befriends Chillum, the young adult addict who sells "brown" for pimp Baba until he's fired for no reason of his own and left to fend for himself with dire consequences. He tries to help Sola, a 16-year-old "virgin" forced by Baba's employer into prostitution. He takes care of Baba's daughter, little Manju, until the police nab the two walking home from a "job" serving food at a wedding. It's a film about struggle and endurance, becoming streetwise and smart, and remaining true to friends and those who show you kindness. There were as many tender moments in this film as there were scenes of repression, depravity and absolute paucity. Western filming

Shafiq Syed as Krishna (*right*) assists Raghubir Yadav's Chillum—a thief, drug pusher and Krishna's mentor—in Mira Nair's *Salaam Bombay!* (1988).

techniques were key to the film's success outside the Bollywood circuit (a soprano sax replaces usually pervasive sitar and tabla music, for example) and anticipated another Mumbai-based movie that won the Oscar in 2009—not for the Best *Foreign* Film but the big prize—*Slumdog Millionaire*. For some, Indian films are difficult to watch. This one, at an hour and fifty-three minutes long, is no different, but not because of the overachieving, sometimes strident ethnicity of the subject matter, but mostly because of the nature of life on the streets, which can be harsh, cruel, desperate and dangerous. This B film was popular among American viewers, earning $2,880,046 in its first run when it arrived October 7, 1988. It premiered August 24, 1988, in France.

Little Belgium has produced several fine films for consideration over the years, less notably perhaps *Farinelli* (1994). The same director, Gérard Corbiau, also created **The Music Teacher** (*Le maître de musique*). Little external information is available about this colorful period piece about an aging opera singer who retires to the countryside and takes on two students, a fetching young woman named Sophie and a petty thief named Jean. Sophie's soprano voice is beautiful to listen to; Jean's rough-around-the-edges tenor not so. And the baritone of teacher Joachim also delights. But paraphrasing what one reviewer said: While the music is great, when they begin to talk, the movie falls flat. It's a pretty movie—countryside, chateau, men, women, music—but a C picture at best. Difficult to locate, it was viewed streaming online. It opened February 1, 1989, and sold $1,086,894 worth of tickets in New York City after it arrived there July 1, 1989. Among the cast was Philippe Volter, who appears in five-times-Oscar-nominated, including BFF, *Cyrano de Bergerac* (1991). Corbiau also directed the insufferable *Farinelli* (1995).

1990

A–	*Cinema Paradiso*	Italy
B	*Camille Claudel*	France
B	*What Happened to Santiago*	Puerto Rico
C+	*Memories of a Marriage*	Denmark
C–	*Jesus of Montreal*	Canada

A small-town movie house in Sicily becomes the allegorical backdrop for **Cinema Paradiso**, a heartwarming nostalgia film by Giuseppe Tornatore, which won the 1990 Best Foreign Film for Italy. At the time it appeared in American theaters, it was *the* film to attend; people talked about it for weeks and, for the most part, raved. If you were a cinema buff, you went to see it. In extended flashbacks, the theater's aging projectionist, played by Philippe Noiret, shuns and then "adopts" a young boy who is enamored by motion pictures of all kinds. A critic sagely viewed the old man as the boy's surrogate "father," while the movies themselves were the "mother." It's a coming-of-age movie, a magical, some would say "sentimental," film about friendship and mutual respect and admiration. With it, Tornatore—only 32 when he made this his second feature—helped relaunch a straggling, once-vibrant Italian film industry struggling against the competition of television. It garnered an A–. Noiret had an outstanding career including appearances in nominated films *Three Brothers* (1982), *Coup de Torchon* (1983), *The*

Family (1988), as well as a bit part in *Gigi* (Best Picture, 1959) and *Il Postino: The Postman* (Best Picture nominee 1994). Antonella Attili—*The Star Maker* (1996)—and Brigitte Fossey—*Forbidden Games* (1953)—also appeared in the cast. It cost Tornatore, who made *The Star Maker* and had two other films submitted without nomination, an estimated $5 million to create this film, which opened November 17, 1988. It was a good investment in America, arriving there February 23, 1990; the box office exploded to $11,990,401!

Anytime Gérard Depardieu is in a film, it's worth the trip to see it. A B picture, **Camille Claudel**, in which Depardieu stars as 19th-century sculptor Auguste Rodin, is no exception. The title role, played by the picture's producer Isabelle Adjani, is a snapshot of the famous French female artist who became his mistress. Rodin, famous for *The Kiss* and *The Thinker*, was a bit of a cad, however, and it drove Claudel mad, literally. As critic Roger Ebert pointed out: "The film … is more concerned with her personality and passions than with her art." And she displays lots of passion throughout this lengthy, two-hour-and-fifty-five-minute picture, which led to Adjani's second Oscar nomination for Best Actress in a Leading Role. (She was nominated in François Truffaut's unsubmitted *The Story of Adele H.* in 1976.) By the way, Depardieu was at this time at the height of his cinematic prowess; indeed, he scored big the following year with another BFF nominee, *Cyrano de Bergerac*, for which he received a Best Actor bid. Also in the cast was Madeleine Robinson, who played the mother in *A Simple Story* (1980). *Camille Claudel* opened December 7, 1988, and came to the States in December 21, 1989, where it earned a mere $201,055 in its initial run. It was director Bruno Nuyt-

In *Camille Claudel* (1988), Police haul off French artist Camille, played by Isabelle Adjani, in Bruno Nuytten's biopic of the troubled lover of sculptor Auguste Rodin.

ten's only submission. Also in the cast was François Berléand of *Au Revoir les Enfants* (1988) and *The Chorus* (2005).

Puerto Rico, not a country but a territory, was permitted to enter its only nomination out of twelve submissions since 1987, **What Happened to Santiago** (*Lo que le pasó a Santiago* or *Santiago, the Story of His New Life*), for Oscar contention in 1990. Directed by Jacobo Morales, it starred Tommy Muñiz, who for many years owned the Ponce television station WSTE, which helped fund the film. He plays a stubby, tonsured and bespectacled accountant who has just retired to a life of boredom, but it's a routine he can deal with. He's a widower, and one of his pleasures is to walk around San Juan's Old Town enjoying the sunshine, trees and people who come and go. He has grown children, but they are involved in their own lives and indeed have disputes he doesn't particularly want to be part of. His only great pleasure in the family is his grandson of about 10. Walking in the park one day, he casually meets an attractive older woman named Angelina. She likes to sit on the bench and read. They strike up a conversation, which leads inevitably to a relationship that seems a bit out of kilter—he being a frumpy man with thick glasses and she a stylish younger woman who dresses immaculately in summery dresses and hats. In any event, she eventually leads him to "mi casa" out in the wilderness where they make love. On the way home, Santiago gets his Chevrolet Impala stuck in the mud during a tropical storm, and although he gets out of it (how, we do not see), he contracts a fever and nearly dies in hospital. While recuperating, Angelina comes to the park hoping to find him and is nonplussed that he isn't around. One morning, she awakes in her house, bathes, dresses and heads to town to find Santiago standing in the road waiting for her. Life is good. And that's what happened to Santiago. There's a Buñuelesque quality to this film: what's with the nun carrying the lamb? She pops up at unexpected times and places. Santiago sees his own mortality in her, as well as in a funeral procession scene in which his Impala is unable to move through the masses. The hour-and-forty-five-minute print came from Elgin (Illinois) Community College via the local library. It merited a B. Morales had one other submission, but this was the only nomination. Oddly, there were no release dates, budgets or box office information immediately available, but then, it was a hard film to find, too.

A memoir, study of marital philosophy, a love story?—all of them, and perhaps more—may describe **Memories of a Marriage** (*Dansen med Regitze* or *Waltzing Regitze*) from Denmark. It's an examination of a marriage, warts and all, from the beginnings to the present day with several stops in between, as seen from the husband's perspective. Regitze is a vibrant, no-holds-barred woman who is courted by romantic but reserved Karl. In their twilight years, they hold a summer garden party and invite all their neighbors and son, John, and his family. Rather than jump enthusiastically into the festivities, a detached Karl begins a series of flashbacks about how the two met, some of the good and bad times they shared, and what their marriage has come to signify. One reviewer called it "an ode to an ordinary life for two ordinary persons." In an interesting sidelight to the casting of the hour-and-a-half film, director Kaspar Rostrup used the actual sons and daughters of the older stars to maintain resemblances in flashback sequences. A C+ film, it opened November 17, 1989, and came to New York City January 28, 1991. It included in its cast Ghita Nørby, the narrator in *Babette's Feast* (1988).

When *Birdman* deservedly won the Academy Award for Best Picture in 2015, questions immediately arose among critics about its hidden meanings. Was it allegory or just an egotistical actor's struggle with delusions? This—actors staging a tale to the point of actually living it—can be construed as inherent in the pseudo-religious French Canadian picture *Jesus of Montreal*. It's directed by Denys Arcand, responsible also for four submissions including the satires *The Decline of the American Empire* (1987) and *The Barbarian Invasions* (2004)—and features an actor, Daniel, who's selected to play Jesus in a church Passion play in desperate need of revitalization. This is done, but as the lead character and his players quickly begin to "live" the story they are telling, they run into serious opposition from church leaders who, believing their unorthodox biblical interpretations are offensive, stop the performances. As critic Roger Ebert put it: "Filled with a vision they believe in, nourished by the courage to carry on in the face of the authorities, these actors persist in presenting their play even in the face of religious and legal opposition." This is not a Christian film but one that explores the reality of what might happen if Christ's ordeals took place on today's stage. There are multiple parallels between the Gospel teachings and today's reality. A few examples: Daniel angrily disrupts a casting session when he discovers the director is humiliating auditionees, a reference to Jesus and the money-lenders of the Temple; he is arrested and brought before a judge whose indecisive reaction is similar to that of Pontius Pilate, who turned Jesus over to Jewish leaders; and in the end—spoiler alert!—Daniel dies in a Jewish hospital and his organs are "resurrected" to heal others. Rated as a C– picture, it originally opened in France May 17, 1989, and made $1,601,612 in its first U.S. run starting May 25, 1990. It's two hours long. Also in the cast was Johanne-Marie Tremblay from *The Barbarian Invasions* (2004).

Lothaire Bluteau plays the lead in *Jesus of Montreal* (1989), a French Canadian film by Denys Arcand.

1991

A	*Journey of Hope*	Switzerland
B+	*Cyrano de Bergerac*	France
B	*Ju Dou*	China
C+	*The Nasty Girl*	Germany
C	*Open Doors*	Italy

The 1991-winning Swiss picture *Journey of Hope* (*Reise der Hoffnung*) will bring to mind the recent, cataclysmic exodus of Middle Eastern, Afghani and Libyan refugees to Western Europe. The Turkish-language film is a moving testament to the struggles and hardships of displaced peoples seeking what they believe will be a better life in the affluent, picture-postcard West and of the predators who prey on them. Swiss filmmaker Xavier Koller painted not a picture of hope, as the title implies, but of despair, as the focus family—a 35-year-old Kurdish farmer, his wife and 7-year-old son—leave six children behind and work their way from eastern Turkey to Switzerland by train, boat, automobile, lorry and finally foot, hoping to reach their illusory goal. It's a heart-rending story that's well told and honest, and a little ironic given the more recent journeys of war-weary immigrants. This hour-and-fifty-minute film garnered an A. Koller had three films submitted, but this was the only nomination—and a winner! It opened in Locarno, Italy, in August 1990, in West Germany April 4, 1991, and in the U.S. three weeks later. It earned $261,718 in its first American exposure.

Gérard Depardieu has a prodigious nose. A perfect match to play the Edmond Rostand iconic swashbuckler ***Cyrano de Bergerac***, you might say. Well, in France's entry by that title, Depardieu *is* the eloquent romantic head of the Gascony Cadets who ghostwrites love notes for hapless Christian de Neuvillette in the latter's efforts to woo the naïve Roxane to his love nest. The problem is, Cyrano also loves Roxane but is self-conscious about his schnoz. "'Tis a rock! A peak! A cape! No, it's a peninsula!" the 17th-century soldier shouts in his famous, descriptive nasal soliloquy. The International Movie Database (IMDb) lists thirty-eight performances of various kinds involving Rostand's beak-nosed character of unrequited love, going back to original actor Benoit Constant Coquelin's 1900 cylinder recording, made just three years after the play opened in Paris. This two-hour-and-seventeen-minute, B+ melodrama was well received by critics but failed to win Best Foreign Film. Even so, it did well otherwise, with four other nominations, including Best Actor for Depardieu and a win in Costume Design (the others were Best Art Direction-Set Decoration and Makeup). It was also highly popular when it arrived in the United States December 1, 1990, accumulating a gate of $15,140,007. It was director Jean-Paul Rappeneau's only nomination of two submitted films. Depardieu, with at least 225 acting credits, was in *Camille Claudel* the previous year. Also in the cast were Vincent Perez from *Indochine* (1993) and Philippe Volter of *The Music Teacher* (1989).

"Colorful" and "controversial": These are the terms that best describe China's entry to the 1991 Oscar completion, ***Ju Dou***. Using a three-strip coloring process abandoned by Hollywood, director Zhang Yimou painted his canvas brilliantly. A cinematographer by trade and one of the so-called Fifth Generation of Chinese filmmakers, he employed the dyeing of broad textile sheets to convey the passion of the play, which the Chinese government considered too sexy to rate a thumbs up; indeed, paramount leader Deng Xiaoping and his cohorts even fought the Academy over the movie's acceptance for Oscar consideration. The title figure, played excellently by Gong Li—*Raise the Red Lantern* (1992) and *Farewell My Concubine* (1994)—marries an impotent old sadist (the dyer) and has a child by the codger's live-in nephew. The child grows up and discovers the subterfuge, which results in a violent finale. (It is believed the Chinese also viewed the picture as an allegory for China's Maoist struggles with the young revolutionaries of the Cultural Revolution, despite the fact the film is set in the 1920s.) The hour-and-thirty-five-minute feature warranted a B. Zhang's seven-submission output is prodigious, and *Raise the Red Lantern*, which he submitted from Hong Kong, also garnered a BFF nomination. The other nominee was *Hero* (2003). In this one, he had a co-director: Fengliang Yang, who had no other submission. One uncredited cast member, Baotian Li, was in *Raise the Red Lantern*. *Ju Dou* opened in Japan April 21, 1990, and never achieved distribution in Mainland China. It came to America in April 1991 where it enjoyed a box office of $1,986,433.

Mel Brooks' *The Producers* makes a screamingly funny mockery of the Third Reich in the ironically themed musical *Springtime for Hitler*, produced purposefully as a means of *losing* an audience in order to benefit from advance ticket sales, a plan that incidentally backfires. ***The Nasty Girl*** (*Das schreckliche Mädchen*), from Germany, appears to strive for the same effect, but unsuccessfully. It's about Sonja, an overly exuberant young woman, who as a pigtailed coed is bent on winning an essay contest by writing about buried secrets involving Nazi collaboration in her hometown several decades earlier. It's based on a true story, about

Li Gong, as the title character in Zhang Yimou's *Ju Dou* (1990), mysteriously peers out from behind colorful sheets of cloth she has dyed for her sadist husband.

Anna Rosmus, who did the same thing with dire results in her German hometown of Passau near the Austrian border, where this picture was made; she eventually emigrated to America to avoid harassment. Writer-director Michael Verhoeven attempted to keep the picture lighthearted, but critics thought the tale would be better told in a more serious vein. After failing to enter her second essay and then marrying and having children, Sonja feels compelled to rekindle her research project. She digs up information about sending a Jew to his death, incurs the wrath of neo–Nazis and other townsfolk, and nearly gets her husband killed in a bomb attack. Through all this, she remains perky and unwavering in her mission. Verhoeven, meanwhile—as *Washington Post* critic Desson Howe wrote—"tells this story with a surreal, ironic sense of humor and in a grab bag of styles, ranging from TV documentary to Federico Fellini–like comedy." The hour-and-thirty-two-minute film scored a C+. Verhoeven, no relation to Peter Verhoeven of the Netherlands, had submitted a film two decades earlier that never made it to nomination. The movie opened February 15, 1990, and did well in the United States—$2,281,569—on its first run starting October 26, 1990.

Open Doors (*Porte aperte*), Italy's submission, is a character study of a mass murderer, who is no doubt guilty of his crimes and wants to die for them, and the judge, who far beyond the aspirations of his court and the general population searches for a reason to sentence him to life imprisonment. The action, slow as it is, takes place in

Palermo, capital of Sicily, in 1937–38 when the controlling Fascists demanded quick and lethal retribution for capital crimes. Judge Vito di Francesco does not believe in the death sentence and works in convoluted ways to find another solution, though the criminal, known as the "Monster of Palermo," has admitted brutally killing his boss, a colleague and his wife. The hour-and-forty-eight-minute picture is directed by Gianni Amelio in a plodding, introspective manner, as though encouraging us to get into the characters' heads. It didn't work so well and received a C. Four of Amelio's films were submitted for consideration, but only *Open Doors* was able to make the cut. It premiered March 29, 1990, and in New York City March 8, 1991, where it had a paltry $124,470 run. Playing the judge was Gian Maria Volontè, star of *Investigation of a Citizen Above Suspicion* (winner 1972), *Letters from Marusia* (1976) and Sergio Leone "Westerns" like *A Fistful of Dollars* or *For a Few Dollars More* from the mid–1960s.

1992

A	*Mediterraneo*	**Italy**
A–	*Raise the Red Lantern*	Hong Kong
A–	*The Elementary School*	Czechoslovakia
B	*The Ox*	Sweden
B–	*Children of Nature*	Iceland

"*Mediterraneo* isn't much of a movie," wrote *Washington Post* critic Hal Hinson about Italy's 1992 winning Best Foreign Film. Many will disagree and say it's a delightful comedy, more like *South Pacific* meets *Shangri-La* meets the Marx Brothers. Here's the gist: A motley squad of eight Italian sailors are sent to hold a remote, strategically unimportant Greek Island during the early stages of World War II and find all the able-bodied men gone, captured by the Germans. The islanders have left their desperate wives and a few others behind. To make matters worse—or better, depending on your point of view—enemy fire sinks the ship of the rescue crew and one of the visiting misfits smashes their only

Part of the fun of *Mediterraneo* (1991) is the interaction between female inhabitants of an isolated Greek isle and the men who come to rescue them, including Vana Barba and Giuseppe Cederna, shown here.

radio in a fit of pique, leaving the team totally isolated. Indeed, they're stuck in a secret paradise of beautiful, lonesome women, a priest and a couple of old geezers, as well as a gifted prostitute named Vassilissa, a variation on the Greek name for "queen." Needless to say, the bumbling seamen enjoy the good life in this Aegean utopia until liberated by the British at the close of the war. Some critics described Gabriele Salvatores' hour-and-thirty-six-minute dramedy as "schmaltzy," "pandering," "breezy," a "cloying day-dream." Joining Academy members and tens of thousands who spent $4,532,791 to see it in American theaters, the author thought the colorful fantasy rather charming and gave it an A. It opened January 31, 1991, and came to New York City March 22, 1992. Salvatores had one other film submitted, but it wasn't nominated. In the cast was Giuseppe Cederna, who was in *The Family* (1988).

Set in the 1920s during the last decades of the Warlord Period of China, Zhang Yimou's **Raise the Red Lantern** (*Da hong deng long gao gao gua*) is another of his lush, Technicolor films, like *Ju Dou*, among last year's nominees, which was accepted and then banned by the People's Republic. It's about sexual enslavement; about Songlian, played by favorite film star Gong Li, a partially educated teenager who becomes the fourth concubine in the home of the rarely seen master; and about how day-to-day interactions, including conspiracies and jealousies, govern the small world in which the participants live. Each concubine has a role to play in the sprawling mansion. Each night, a red lantern is lit at the chosen woman's doorway, summoning her to the lord's bed. Many intrigues take place during the course of the two-hour-and-five-minute film, shot using the same three-color-strip process as *Ju Dou*, which allowed for a rich, opulent color saturation that dazzled the senses. It was judged an A− picture. It opened in Italy December 18, 1991, and came to Los Angeles March 13, 1992. During its first run in the United States it grossed $2,603,061. Zhang also made *Hero* (2003). Gong Li starred in *Ju Dou* and *Farewell My Concubine* (1984).

Character-driven ensemble motion pictures, especially those concerning kids, can always make a viewer's day. *My Life As a Dog*, Lasse Halström's classic, comes to mind, as do a number of the better foreign-language nominees such as Jiří Menzel's *My Sweet Little Village* (1987) and *Kolya* (1997), which won top prize for Jan Svěrák. Both of those films were Czech, the first produced under communism and the second when Czechoslovakia had become the free Czech Republic. Another of Svěrák's Oscar submissions (he had three in total) was **The Elementary School** (*Obecná skola*), a candidate for this year. Eda is a 10-year-old, overactive rascal who attends a boys' school in suburban Prague shortly after World War II. He and his classmates are so out of control they cause their teacher to go insane and another instructor—a war hero wearing knee boots, jodhpurs and a pistol and concealing a questionable past—is hired to rein in the boys. When external matters turn against the new teacher, the youths come to his defense. The hour-and-forty-minute film is populated with colorful, eccentric characters, both young and old, and there's a great deal of humor in Svěrák's tale (his father, Zdeněk, actually wrote the screenplay and helped write and played in *My Sweet Little Village* and acted in *Kolya*). Also in the cast of this movie was Jan Tříska who appeared in multiple-Oscar-winning American films *Ragtime* (1982), with twelve nominations and three wins including Best Picture, and *Reds* (1983), with eight including the top prize. Despite mixed reviews, the film deserved an A−. Also in the cast was Bolek Polívka of *Divided We Fall* (2001).

How far will a man go to feed his starving family? One answer lies in Sweden's entry, **The Ox** (*Oxen*), when farm laborer Helge Roos, after two failed harvests in a row, butchers his employer's prized ox for food. He knows his indiscretion will garner him forty lashes and life in prison, but it's wintertime during the mid–1860s in southern Sweden's Småland and his family is starving. Helge and his wife Elfrida, who's shocked by her husband's devious work, try to hide the carcass, but how do you accomplish that in a small Calvinist community where everyone knows neighbor's business? Enter the priest, played by Max von Sydow, who convinces Helge, played by Stellan Skarsgård, to turn himself in and potentially escape with a lighter sentence. This does not turn out to be the case, however, and his imprisonment places his wife and their infant daughter in dire straits. The film is directed by Sven Nykvist, Ingmar Bergman's cinematographer, in his only directorial Best Foreign Language Film contender. Liv Ullmann also has a part playing von Sydow's wife. Quite a cast! Considered "good but bleak," the picture received a grade of B. It opened November 22, 1991, and then made it to the United Kingdom and New York City August 21, 1992, but apparently nowhere else before it went to VCR. The rest of the cast was venerable enough: Ewa Fröling and Erland Josephson from *Fanny and Alexander* (winner 1984 and recipient of five other nominations) and *Hanussen* (1989), as well as Skarsgård, who appeared in multiple-Oscar contenders *Goodwill Hunting* (1998) with nine nominations including Best Picture and two wins, *Amistad* (1998) with four and *The Girl with the Dragon Tattoo* (2012) with five including a win. Another actor with BFF chops was Bjørn Granath of *Pelle the Conqueror* (1989) and *Evil* (2004).

Iceland's only nominated Best Foreign Film contender since its first entry in 1981, **Children of Nature** (*Börn náttúrunnar*) tells the peripatetic story of a geriatric couple, reconnected after decades apart, who steal away from their nursing home on a harrowing adventure to rediscover the land where they grew up on the island country's remote western fjords. Thorgeir is a crusty farmer who reluctantly moves into his daughter and grandchildren's tiny apartment in Reykjavik, the capital, only to find it too small for the four of them. He lands in a rest home where he meets Stella, an old flame, who can't stand living there, and the two of them pack up, withdraw their savings, don tennis shoes, hotwire a Jeep and head west. The trip is not for the faint of heart, and despite all its cinematic splendor, the drama—by filmmaker Fridrik Thor Fridriksson, who had six submissions but only this one nomination—trails off to a tragic but logical conclusion. *New York Times* critic Vincent Canby summed up the feature this way: "'Children of Nature' is an intelligent film, not easily categorized. Neither [Thorgeir] nor Stella is a character in a conventional sense. They are representations, figures in a modern myth that is dramatized in settings of spectacular, chilly beauty. Mr. Fridriksson has directed 'Children of Nature' with a notable rigor, but it prompts rather more awe than passionate interest." The hour-and-twenty-two-minute movie warranted a B–. It opened August 1, 1991, and appeared in a film festival in New York City April 2, 1992, its only known U.S. presence.

1993

A–	*Indochine*	France
B+	*Daens*	Belgium

B	*Close to Eden*	Russia
B	*Schtonk!*	Germany
—	*A Place in the World* (scratched)	Uruguay

Indochine is a lavish and longish film set mostly in Vietnam prior to the French-Indochina and, of course, Vietnam wars. The French drama, winner of the Best Foreign Film in 1993, stars Catherine Deneuve as a rubber plantation operator who adopts an orphan girl played by Linh Dan Pham, who becomes embroiled in a love affair with Deneuve's young beau, creating a love triangle with melodramatic consequences. The gorgeously filmed masterpiece requires a certain amount of patience because of an elaborate storyline and side plots involving the growing communist revolution that make its two hours and thirty-nine minutes drag on a bit. But it's a feast for the eyes, not only for the exquisite landscapes but also the beauty of its main characters. Deneuve also received an Oscar nomination for Best Actress for her part as the plantation owner. The film received an A–. The director was Régis Wargnier, a twice-submitted and – nominated filmmaker, whose *East/West* (2000) also got a bid. Deneuve—perhaps best known for Luis Buñuel's *Belle de Jour* and Roman Polanski's *Repulsion* of the mid–1960s, which were never submitted—did appear in best foreign-language nominees *The Umbrellas of Cherbourg* (1965), Buñuel's *Tristana* (1971), *The Last Metro* (1981) and *East/West*. Vincent Perez, also in the cast, appeared in *Cyrano de Bergerac* (1991). *Indochine* opened April 15, 1992, and came to America December 23, 1992, where it had an outstanding first-run box office, likely due in part to its Oscar win, of $5,734,232.

Adolf Daens was a Catholic priest in the Belgian province of East Flanders. The area was known for its textile manufacturing industry, which for centuries employed whomever they could exploit for cheap labor.

Poster art features Catherine Deneuve as Eliane, the rubber plantation operator, from the 1993 winning film *Indochine* (1992), directed by Régis Wargnier.

In 1890, Daens returns to his hometown to discover how poor the working conditions are. The capitalists who own the mills have laid off the men and hired the women and children for reduced wages and kept them laboring long, tedious hours. Accidents, some fatal, are commonplace. The film **Daens**, a Belgian contender, was a biopic about the historic priest, who later became a firebrand politician seeking relief for the poor workers. Indeed, the pope at the time, Leo XIII, urged him to quit the priesthood and become a political official, but he carried on until the Bishop of Rome had had enough and defrocked him. Several years ago, *Priest*, as the film was also known, could be viewed online without subtitles, but that was it. There was also a dearth of critical comment available, unless one was willing to explore foreign websites or peruse nonprofessional "user" reviews. One user from Belgium gushed, "This is … undoubtedly the most important Belgian film ever made, a cinematic event in its home country when it came out. People flocked to see it, awards were bestowed on it, students wrote term papers about it, everybody talked about it, every school showed it to its students … and its director, Stijn Coninx, even got made a baron on the strength of it." So why is this film so difficult to find? Who knows! It opened February 25, 1993, and appeared in the States at the Chicago International Film Festival in October of the previous year. Coninx had two submissions but only this one nomination. The two-hour-and-eighteen-minute picture, which received a B+ despite its unavailability, starred Jan Decleir, who was in BFF winners *Antonia's Line* (1996) and *Character* (1998), and Matthias Schoenaerts, who played in *Bullhead* (2012) as well as *The Danish Girl* (2016), which garnered four nominations and one win for Swedish actress Alicia Vikander in a Best Supporting role.

 Close to Eden (*Urga*), filmed on the steppes of Inner Mongolia, is a little film with a big heart and an immense landscape. It's about a family of present-day Mongols who live in a yurt, raise cattle and sheep and love one another. They don't have television or electricity, both situations that can and will be rectified. The picture, Russia's entry with an indigenous cast and a Russian truck driver, could have been submitted for Best Documentary, so matter-of-factly so was it produced. Directed and co-written by Nikita Mikhalkov—whose *Burnt by the Sun* (1995) won the Oscar—*Close to Eden* was the first submission after the breakup of the Soviet Union, and perhaps because of that was less invasive and free of the propaganda you'd normally find in films made under communism. The only political statement—and it's a dandy—concerns the encroachment of civilization and how it affects the simply life of these nomadic peoples. "It's a saga of cultures clashing together," says the trailer narrator. This colorful film with its sweeping cinematography rated a B. The post–Soviet filmmaking of Mikhalkov has been prolific. As of this writing, he has had six films submitted, received three nominations (*12* in 2008 being the other), won one and directed another that was disqualified by the Academy because the print failed to arrive on time. This motion picture runs a minute short of two hours and opened in France September 25, 1991. America saw a run beginning October 30, 1992.

 In 1983, *Stern* magazine in Germany published what was purported to be Adolf Hitler's diaries, later proven to be obvious forgeries. A decade later we have **Schtonk! The Film Accompanying the Führer's Book**, which lampooned the whole incident. The film—a DVD from Wellesley College (Massachusetts) Library, via the local library—

was a good print, replete with a score that included Wagner music, but it came without subtitles. What "schtonk" means has been debated, but the most logical explanation is that it's a made-up German word Charlie Chaplin employed a number of times during his famous speech in *The Great Dictator*, nominated for five Oscars, including Best Picture, in 1941. *Schtonk!* is a good little caper film, reminiscent of *The Italian Job* or even *Ocean's 11*—both versions—full of humor and good fun. Apparently it isn't seen as such by the world at large, since there exist but four reviews posted on IMDb.com (one in Dutch and three in German). The hour-and-fifty-five-minute film, which cost approximately $10 million to make, warranted a B. It was directed by Helmut Dietl, his only submission, and it opened March 12, 1992, but was not distributed in the United States. Indeed, it only made it to Germany, Canada, the United Kingdom and France. In the cast was Ulrich Mühe, who was in *The Lives of Others* (2007). Uwe Ochsenknecht also had a part; he was also in *Das Boot* (1983), which garnered six nominations but not one for foreign language.

(This singular year excluded a fifth nominee. The Uruguayan feature **A Place in the World** was submitted but withdrawn when the committee overseeing nominations determined it was really an Argentine film, both in cast and crew, and therefore not acceptable. By then it was too late to submit a replacement and Argentina had already proffered a film, which did not get past the nomination process. Consequently, only four selections were honored.)

1994

B+	*The Wedding Banquet*	Taiwan
B	***Belle Époque***	**Spain**
B	*The Scent of Green Papaya*	Vietnam
C	*Farewell My Concubine*	Hong Kong
C–	*Hedd Wyn*	United Kingdom

There exists a definite tone shift from madcap comedy to dramedy to drama and back again in Ang Lee's **The Wedding Banquet** (*Xi yan*), Taiwan's mostly Mandarin submission for the 1994 Best Foreign Film. Set in New York, it's about a closeted gay man faced with reality when his aging parents push him to marry and sire children. His partner suggests hitching with a tenant, a young Chinese woman in search of a green card—a marriage of convenience that all accept. Things go awry, however, when the parents fly in with $30,000 to fund an elaborate and traditional wedding feast following the civil ceremony and discover the true facts. Needless to say, being principally a comedy, all comes out well in the end. This film—Ang's first among three Best Foreign Film nominations, one of which (*Crouching Tiger, Hidden Dragon*) won in 2001—has been compared to *La Cage aux Folles/The Birdcage* as well as *Eat Drink Man Woman* (1995), the next film up for Ang, which garnered him the other BFF nomination. *The Wedding Banquet* earned a B+, putting it ahead of all of the other foreign films nominated, including the winner. Ang spent $1 million on this hour-and-forty-six-minute feature, but in the United States alone, where it opened August 4, 1993, it got back $6,933,459 during a first run. After two decades, it finally made it to Taiwan

May Chin, as Wei-Wei Gu, receives an insincere peck on the cheek from Winston Chao, as Wai-Tung Gao, a gay man entering into a marriage of convenience to please his parents in *The Wedding Banquet* (1993).

for a limited run March 1, 2013! The cast included Winston Chao and Grace Gua Ah-lei of *Eat Drink Man Woman*.

This unlikely scenario seems kind of familiar: Boy meets four girls, samples each in turn, chooses the least likely and they live happily ever after. Not quite. The setting for **Belle Époque** is 1931 Spain, just before the Spanish Civil War when people, unaware of the consequences, were choosing among fascism, communism, democracy or indifference. A Matt Damon lookalike, Fernando, is on the lam from the Republican army and is befriended by Manolo, an older anarchist artist who just happens to have four lovely daughters who join him during a sunbathed summer at his country home. Fernando is welcomed there as a (potential) member of the family, and the stage is set. He dallies with the young women, each of whom has a charm unlike the others. All of this takes place while his patron, a man of the times—the quiescent *Belle Époque*—looks the other way. In the end he selects the youngest of the quartet, Luz, played artfully by 18-year-old Penélope Cruz. This colorful, joyful Spanish picture, directed by Fernando Trueba who had one other submission, won in this year, a year of exceptional competitors. Was it the Best Foreign Film for 1994? It rated a B, just below *The Wedding Banquet*, which coincidentally was viewed the same day. The movie runs an hour and forty-nine minutes and opened December 4, 1992, and later in the United States February 25, 1994, where it garnered $5,971,369. Prolific actor Fernando Fernán-Gómez starred, as he did in *Mama Turns 100* (1980), *The Grandfather* (1999) and *All About My Mother* (2000). In the cast as well was Adriana Gil, who appeared later in *Pan's Labyrinth*

(2007). Cruz also was in *All About My Mother* and eventually won a Best Supporting Actress award for Woody Allen's *Vicky Cristina Barcelona* (2008) after a Best Actress nomination for *Volver* two years earlier. Trueba's brother, David, also had two films submitted for BFF consideration but no nomination.

Another B film for the year, **The Scent of Green Papaya** (*Mùi du du xanh*), has a Zen quality to it that mesmerizes the viewer like few other films. The country submitting the nominee was postwar Vietnam, but its entire production was filmed on a soundstage in Paris by Tràn Anh Hung, who had no other nomination but one other submission. It's a picture, as Roger Ebert said, "of great visual beauty," with details that recall tranquil scenes of nature, meditation and mental acuity. It's about a young girl who grows up as a servant in the house of a well-to-do Vietnamese family during the 1940s and '50s. When the family falls on hard times, she's handed over to a young man whom she had played with as a child. She falls in love with him, but her advances are unrequited. What happens next should not be much of a surprise. It runs an hour and forty-four minutes and opened in France June 8, 1993, but not in Vietnam. When it came to the States January 28, 1994, it made $1,910,763 on the first run.

A Chinese saga about life backstage at the Peking Opera, juxtaposed with modern-day history of the People's Republic in eight "chapters," the highly respected and award-winning **Farewell My Concubine** (*Ba wang bie ji*) was Hong Kong's 1994 nominee for Oscar. This complex, two-hour-and-fifty-one-minute drama, which also was nominated for Best Cinematography, features two boys who are trained in the theatrical arts and grow to become stars in the stylized and traditional opera begun in the 18th century.

Leslie Cheung plays the gay, transvestite actor in Kaige Chen's controversial *Farewell My Concubine* (1993), a colorful taste of the 53 years of Chinese opera that progresses well into the communist era.

One of them is gay and plays a transvestite opposite the one he loves, who eventually marries a prostitute played by China's number-one box-office star, Gong Li—*Ju Dou* (1991) and *Raise the Red Lantern* (1992). The drama takes us from 1924 warlord rule, through the Japanese occupation, World War II, the 1949 Communist Revolution and the Cultural Revolution of the 1960s and '70s, ending in melodramatic fashion in 1977. Director Chen Kaige took liberties with this film and found the final cut (originally nine minutes short of three hours long) banned in China—twice—in part because of the homosexual theme. Even so, the film is a feast for the eyes and ranks high as a tutorial for those interested in latter-day Chinese history. Ironically, the picture was up against another Chinese nominee, Ang Lee's *The Wedding Banquet* from Taiwan. This one garnered a lackluster C in an otherwise mediocre year. Kaige—a member with Zhang Yimou of the Fifth Generation group of Chinese moviemakers opposed to the ideological purity of the Cultural Revolution—had four submissions but only this one nomination; two of the submissions were from Mainland China. The film opened January 1, 1993, and in the U.S. October 15, 1993, where it reached $5,216,888 in its initial run.

To date and since 1991, the United Kingdom has sent more than a dozen films to the Academy for Best Foreign Film consideration. Of these, ten were predominately in Welsh and two, **Hedd Wyn** and *Solomon and Gaenor* (2000), received nominations. The former is an antiwar motion picture based on the life of Ellis Humphrey Evans, a critically acclaimed Welsh poet whose short life ended at the Battle of Passchendaele near Ypres during World War I. The emphasis of the story, beautifully filmed in color near the poet's native Meirionnydd in North Wales, is about Evans' gifts as a poet and the coveted chair of the National Eisteddfod of Wales, a grand festival started in 1861 and still going strong. This was not a praiseworthy contender for Oscar. Indeed, it rated only a C–, but the nationalism that surrounded the epic on two levels—that of Wales and its preservation of the Welsh language, as well as the fervent patriotism of Britain during the war—is worth noting. Directed by Paul Turner, his only submission, the two-hour-and-three-minute drama appeared first at the Edinburgh International Film Festival in 1992 and arrived in the United States January 12, 1996.

1995

A–	*Burnt by the Sun*	**Russia**
B	*Eat Drink Man Woman*	Taiwan
C–	*Before the Rain*	Macedonia
D	*Farinelli: Il Castrato*	Belgium
D	*Strawberry and Chocolate*	Cuba

Three years and two months after the dissolution of the Soviet Union, Russians flocked to their theaters to see a political film, **Burnt by the Sun** (*Utomlennye solntsem*), which won the Best Foreign Film award in 1995. Directed by Nikita Mikhalkov, who also stars as a Russian revolutionary hero, the two-hour-and-fifteen-minute motion picture takes place in 1936 at the start of Joseph Stalin's Great Purge of counterrevolutionaries. There is a love triangle in which Mikhalkov's character, Kotov, a fervent believer in the ruthless dictator, is approached by the secret police over a minuscule complaint. The leader of the goon squad, Mitya, happens to be the former lover of Kotov's wife, Nadia, causing the conflict. Much of this has been seen, as Roger Ebert put it, "as a parable about the approaching change in Soviet direction" within the shadow of Nazi Germany's rise to power. While an A– was proffered to this political drama, critics thought the film lacked originality and preferred other nominations for the year. Ebert, for instance, opined boldly that *Before the Rain* from Macedonia should have won. Ironically, *Burnt by the Sun* wasn't even properly released in the United States to qualify, but since it had been viewed by Academy members in a preview screening, it was allowed to receive votes. The movie is beautifully filmed in pastoral settings utilizing a leisurely—some say "too leisurely"—style of filmmaking. It ends on a sad note, with the final written comment (in the English release): "This film is dedicated to all who were Burnt by the Sun of the Revolution." The film opened in the States April 21, 1995. Of the five submissions attributed to Mikhalkov films, three resulted in nominations, including—*Close to Eden* (1993) and *12* (2008) and another was late getting to the Academy in time. Mikhalkov, as an actor, appeared uncredited in Bondarchuk's double Oscar-winning *War and Peace* and his own *Close to Eden*. He also was one of the *12* in that Russian movie. Oleg Menshikov also appeared in *Burnt by the Sun* as Mitya; his credits include *Prisoner of the Mountains* (1997) and *East/West* (2000).

Confucius say, "Greatest desires of mankind are found in meat, drink and sexual pleasure"—in other words: **Eat Drink Man Woman** (*Yin shi nan nu*), the name of Taiwan's 1995 entry for consideration. This marvelous food flick—with incidental nods to *Babette's Feast, Tampopo, Big Night, Like Water for Chocolate, Julie & Juli*a, *Le Chef, A Chef in Love, Vatel*, even *Ratatouille*—revolves around a talented but aging Chinese chef who cooks a spectacular dinner every Sunday for his three beautiful but spinster daughters, all diverse and unlucky in love. The stories they impart over these lavish weekly feasts, even during tense dinner-table discussions, moves this film by Ang Lee forward at an entertaining clip. There is a great deal of irony (the father has lost his sense of taste, for example), poignancy and humor in all of this. This sumptuously edited, two-hour-and-four-minute color motion picture qualified for a well-considered B. It had its premiere in America August 3, 1994, where it earned $7,294,403 in its first run; it opened in Taiwan nearly twenty years later, March 1, 2013, when it had a limited run in the Nationalist Chinese capital. Among the cast were Grace Gua Ah-lei and Sihung Lung of Lee's *The Wedding Banquet* (1984). Lung also was in *Crouching Tiger, Hidden Dragon* (winner 2001), with ten Oscar nominations including Best Picture and four wins. Other Lee pictures garnered multiple Oscar wins and nominations. Three of those with Best Picture nominations were *Sense and Sensibility* (1996), *Brokeback Mountain* (2006) and *The Life of Pi* (2013).

The Balkans have always been a tinderbox, and Macedonia, formerly part of the Yugoslav Federation, tried and failed to stay out of the frays, not the least being the Bosnian conflict of the 1990s. That war raged practically next door at the time **Before the Rain** (*Pred dozhdot*) was made by Milcho Manchevski, his only nomination among three submissions for Macedonia, France and the United Kingdom. It's a thoughtful, symbolic, multilayered motion picture centered on one man, a Pulitzer Prize-winning photographer named Aleksandar, who witnesses more than his share of the internecine warfare, in which loved ones are sacrificed in the name of fervent nationalism, and then goes to Britain. In a third segment, he returns to his homeland and finds life there more hostile than ever. Manchevski uses the symbol of circles throughout his film, exploring the vicious cycle of violence so prevalent in the Balkan region. Before the opening credits are over, we see a wheel of fire, the halo around the figure of Christ and the round moon high in the sky. Critics—and there are few to draw on—thought very highly of this picture, in part because it's so well made, but also because it sheds light on

In Macedonia's first Oscar entry, *Before the Rain* (1994), Aleksandar (Rade Šerbedžija) witnesses plenty of warfare in Bosnia, where loved ones were sacrificed in the name of fervent nationalism.

a remote area that has suffered so much going back to a time before World War II, a region with which few Westerners are all that familiar. Some might find the hour-and-fifty-three-minute movie too plodding, overly symbolic and in your face, but it does illustrate how tribal and ethnic bloodshed is not always rooted in any one, backward locality, but has the ability to spread to "more civilized" areas of the world. A C– was justified. The film cost $1.9 million and opened in Italy October 26, 1994, and in the U.S. February 24, 1995, with a box office of $763,847. Starring was Katrin Cartlidge of *No Man's Land* (2002). This was the first time since the initial years in which two countries had debut films nominated by the committee. Macedonia was one and Cuba, coming up, was the other. It wouldn't be until 2015 that this happened again with the advent of films from Estonia and Mauritania.

The lavish Belgium production of ***Farinelli*** elicited some fine quips from critics when it came out. But first: Carlo Maria Broschi, who changed his name to Farinelli, was an 18th-century aria singer who was castrated before puberty to preserve his high voice, a common practice back then. Farinelli had a brother who wrote tunes—rather poorly, it might be added—and there's a side story about his feud with George Frideric Handel, who wrote sublime music. The soprano/mezzo/contralto Farinelli was employed by Philip V of Spain but quickly became the toast of Europe. His voice is said to have caused ladies to swoon and, indeed, the film propounds the myth that he'd engage women up to the point of lovemaking and then turn them over to his normally endowed brother. Actually, the film, directed by Gérard Corbiau, provides little in the way of reality and should not be considered a legitimate biopic. Desson Howe of the *Washington Post* ironically wrote, "'Farinelli' reaches rather too grandiosely for the high notes of life.... The movie unwittingly puts itself in the Monty Pythonesque position of celebrating the world's first karaoke artist." Edward Guthmann of the *San Francisco Chronicle* opined: "...bubble gum masquerading as art, [the film is] an absurd Italian import that wants to say something about the price of fame and of being different, but instead exploits its subject for cheap titillation." Barbara Shulgasser of the *San Francisco Examiner* added that "even the music is boring." Colorful, yes; well costumed, maybe. But this hour-and-fifty-one-minute movie deserved no more than an unmitigated D. By the way, Corbiau also directed *The Music Teacher* (1989), his only other submission. *Farinelli* opened in France December 7, 1994, and in the U.S. March 17, 1995, where it earned $2,122,948.

Say what you will about **Strawberry and Chocolate** (*Fresa y chocolate*), Cuba's only nominee to date warranted a mere D. This sociopolitical spy thriller with homosexual overtones takes place in 1979 when the Castro regime was on the warpath against decadent Western mores in general and the LGBTQ community in particular. David, who is straight, meets a flamboyant Diego in a park one day. The latter eats strawberry ice cream, an apparent stereotyped reference to what a gay man prefers over chocolate. The movie could end here with a rebuff; after all, David is not interested in Diego sexually, albeit he's fascinated by his lifestyle and artistic background. But he's recruited by a Marxist friend, a bureaucrat, to befriend the gay guy and find out more about his subversive intentions. This sets the stage for some interesting interaction. Though done by the pro-revolutionary filmmaker Tomás Gutiérrez Alea with help from Juan Carlos Tabío, the hour-and-forty-eight-minute picture is oddly critical of Castro's Cuba and employs that country's taboo themes of homosexuality, dissident politics and the use of hard liquor. Some say this was a ruse on Gutiérrez Alea's part, that he was trying to send the West a message—call it propaganda—that Cuba was freer than it actually was at the time. It was one of the director's two submissions, but only nomination. The movie has an interesting life span: It started at the Havana Film Festival December 1993 and went on to open in Portugal August 19, 1994, then in the States January 20, 1995, where it had a surprising gate of $2,080,805.

1996

A	*Antonia's Line*	**Netherlands**
B+	*All Things Fair*	Sweden
B	*The Star Maker*	Italy
B−	*O Quatrilho*	Brazil
B−	*Dust of Life*	Algeria

Antonia's Line (*Antonia*), the Netherlands' winning entry in the 1996 Oscar ceremony, is a chronicle of one strong woman's "line" of descendants, spanning half a century in a small, anonymous Dutch village of milch cows and muddy cart roads. It begins with the great-granddaughter's narration on the day of Antonia's death and ends with the moment Oma's eyes finally close. In the meantime, we meet a menagerie of village folk—most good, some bad—starting when the woman arrives in town with her shy, imaginative and artistic teenage daughter, Danielle, to bury Antonia's demented mother. Danielle has sex with a chosen sperm donor, which results in the birth of superintelligent and spirited Thérèse, who grows up to have Sarah, the narrator. Got that? This is a feminist movie; although numerous men people the play, few speak more than a few lines and some are downright despicable (including a man who rapes Thérèse—having

Enjoying each other's company in Marleen Gorris's *Antonia's Line* (1995) are (from left) Reinout Bussemaker, Jan Decleir and Willeke van Ammelrooy.

already done so to his mentally disabled sister—and gets his just desserts via a pitchfork where it most hurts). Antonia is a tower of strength and wisdom, cheerful and easygoing and remarkably self-sufficient. The picture, an hour and forty-two minutes long, was directed by Marleen Gorris in her only submission. It opened September 21, 1995, and in the United States February 2, 1996. This is an A movie. In the cast was Johan Heldenbergh, who performed in *The Broken Circle Breakdown* (2014), and Jan Decleir, star of *Daens* (1993) and *Character* (1998).

The year is 1943, and blond, blue-eyed Stig is falling in lust with his teacher, a strawberry-blonde, Mary Kay Letourneau-lookalike named Viola. He's 15; she 37. One might label ***All Things Fair*** (*Lust och fägring stor*) perverse. But critics were more intent on calling the Swedish entry a well-directed, well-acted coming-of-age story, and it earned a B+. The director was Bo Widerberg, a master filmmaker particularly active between 1963 and 1976, making him a late contemporary of Ingmar Bergman, but despite the long layover, he resurrected himself for this film. Stig, by the way, was played by Johan Widerberg, the director's son, who was actually 21 at the time. In the film, Stig and Viola have a torrid love affair right under the nose of the teacher's hard-drinking husband, a wool-stockings salesman, and indeed he and Stig strike up a decent relationship despite the suspicious activities. The boy eventually tires of his adult friends and she, having taken up the bottle herself, throws a fit, ending the partnership. The story was not so far removed from that of Letourneau, a Seattle, Washington, teacher convicted of having sex with a 12-year-old, whom she later married. The two-hour-and-ten-minute movie opened November 3, 1995, and in the U.S. March 8, 1996. Widerberg, best known for the diaphanous art-house film *Elvira Madigan* that made the 2nd Movement of Mozart's C Major Piano Concerto No. 21 popular for a while, also directed *Raven's End* (1965) and *Adalen 31* (1970), as well as one other that was submitted but didn't make the cut. Young Widerberg went on to act in a number of other good nominated films including *Under the Sun* (2000) and *A Man Called Ove* (2017).

Some people are compelled to perform a service for others. Look no farther than the grim letter writer in *Central Station* (1999) from Brazil, who helps illiterates compose their various missives. So it is that we have Joe Morelli, the self-aware imposter who charges local rubes a fee of 1,500 lire to take their phony screen tests in ***The Star Maker*** (*L'Uomo delle stelle*), Italy's contribution to Oscar contention. Morelli is a sort of magician, too. He can enliven a town with his promises by tossing sheets of paper in the air—pink for women, blue for men—purportedly containing lines from *Gone with the Wind*. The people begin to memorize their lines, pacing through squares, sitting in outdoor cafés, even hanging in the local barbershop while Hoagy Carmichael's "Stardust" plays in the background. When they get their chance before the camera, they give their best, which isn't saying much since none has a clue about acting. When he's confronted by a policeman along the road, Morelli finds the cop isn't chasing him for the fraud that he is but seeking a screen test of his own. He's even able to inveigle the local anarchists, set to rob him of all his money, to pose for the camera and actually pay him his fee. As critic Roger Ebert put it: "He may not be seriously filming his subjects—but he's seriously looking at them. Through the camera, he sees their souls." Another side to the story is that of Beata, a young girl who makes a few coins exposing her body parts to men. She latches onto Joe and then goes mildly insane when he's eventually arrested. There's more, but as Scarlet says in *Gone with the Wind*: "After all, tomorrow is another day." The film is the product of Giuseppe Tornatore, who also made the 1990 winning film *Cinema Paradiso* and later saw two other submissions fall short. This small gem deserved a B. It runs an hour and fifty-three minutes and opened September 21, 1995, and then for a short run in America March 8, 1996. It includes in the cast Sergio Castellitto, an uncredited terrorist in *Three Brothers* (1982) who also acted in *The Family* (1988), and Antonella Attili from *Cinema Paradiso*.

Quatrilho is a kind of "screw your buddy" card game that serves as a metaphor for a Brazilian film about Italian immigrants in the rural south of that country about 100 years ago. Two men marry very different women and then become associates in business. Over time, it's discovered each woman married the wrong partner, in both literal senses, and one by one yield to the other's spouse. ***O Quatrilho***—as the name infers—here means that in order to win, the men must defeat the other in the game of love, and each succeeds in different ways. But the film is really about mismatched love, business and ultimate success. It's about cultural behavior, how the church views adultery—in this case between two separate Catholic societies—as well as forgiveness in sin. Filmed in beautiful color with broad cinematography of the rolling landscape of southern Brazil, this movie received only one review in the International Movie Database (IMDb.com), but at least one whole academic dissertation has been ascribed to it in Portuguese [if interested, see: http://geografias.net.br/papers/9_JamileDalpiaz.pdf]. Some of the more pertinent dialogue appears in this article, including a woman's rebuke of the village priest during a church service for the way Catholics view sin. Viewed in

Portuguese online, the hour-and-thirty-two-minute film received a B–. It was directed by Fábio Barreto—brother of Bruno Barreto—and was the only film of two submitted that was nominated. It opened October 20, 1995, but did not have a first run in the States. It's one of the harder-to-find pictures in the catalog.

Rachid Bouchareb, a French-Algerian, directed three films submitted by Algeria and nominated by the Academy. One was *Days of Glory* (2007), another *Outside the Law* (2011) and the first one **Dust of Life** (*Poussières de vie*), all based on war themes. The latter tackles the sad tale of an Amerasian 13-year-old swept up off the streets of Saigon and taken to a rehabilitation camp just after the United States abandoned the war in 1973. Son has a black American father, long gone, and a Vietnamese mother, whom he desperately hopes to contact. Despite the physical and mental brutality at Fanta Hill camp, Son ingratiates himself with an adult camp guard by proving to be more educated than the camp's "dust-specs of life," street kids who run the gamut of minor criminals and young grifters. In fact, the film's storyline recalls the Academy Award's first honorary foreign winner, *Shoeshine* (1948), in many ways. Son also befriends teen Bob and 9-year-old Paul, who goes under the protective pseudonym of "Little Haï," and these three attempt an escape that fails, landing them in the horrific "tiger cage." Son's second attempt, however, succeeds, and that's where the film leaves us, him free on the Mekong River headed for home and possibly, someday, America to be with his dad. Director of photography Youcef Sahraoui's cinematography in the jungle camp and occasional landscapes is a highlight of this nominee. Among the harder-to-find films, it was viewed at the Newton Branch of the Surrey (British Columbia) Public Library and warranted a B–. The movie, one of five Bouchareb submissions, opened in France January 18, 1995, and runs an hour and twenty-seven minutes. It did not appear in the United States, but did in Germany and the Czech Republic and apparently nowhere else.

1997

A+	*Kolya*	**Czech Republic**
B+	*A Chef in Love*	Georgia
B	*The Other Side of Sunday*	Norway
C	*Prisoner of the Mountains*	Russia
D	*Ridicule*	France

Only a handful of foreign films have garnered this study's highest praise. One of them is the Czech gem **Kolya**, which won the Oscar (and most of the other top foreign film prizes) in 1997, and earned an exceedingly rare A+. This is a picture of perspective, principally 5-year-old Kolya's—what he sees, how he reacts to it, what it might mean later. He's Russian in the turbulent time of the 1968 Velvet Revolution in Prague, Czechoslovakia, when the Soviet Union cracked down on dissidents. The boy doesn't know about this but he does knows about *Russkie Soldati*, Russian Soldiers, whom he idolizes and at one point fraternizes with against the wishes of his guardian. Who is the guardian? A curmudgeon cellist who dallies with his female students and co-musicians. The last thing he wants in his life is a little boy to care for, but you play the cards you're dealt. The boy's Russian mother hires the cellist, Louka—played so beautifully well by Zdeněk Svěrák—to enter into a marriage of convenience so she can become a Czech citizen, the only way she can get to West Germany to join her true lover. Louka does so because he covets a car, an East German Trabant, which his mercenary stipend will buy. Immediately after the wedding, she departs for points west, leaving little Kolya

Outstanding Czech film *Kolya* (1996), the Oscar winner in 1997, features little Andrej Chalimon in the title role and Zdeněk Svěrák as Louka, his surrogate father.

in her surrogate husband's charge. It's through Kolya's perspective that this motion picture truly works. To achieve this, the director—Svěrák's son, Jan, in his only nomination amid two submissions—uses various low or high camera angles focused on images of a church angel and bells; pigeons on the window cell, a hawk on an electric wire, clouds; a puppet; coffins sliding jerkily into a crematory; the boy looking upward and askance at his guardian; and a crush of people on a subway car. The film is not terribly long, not particularly sentimental, but hits all the right marks to its abrupt conclusion, perhaps the only downer. The film opened May 15, 1996, and in America January 24 of the next year. By July 11, it had grossed $5,739,711 in U.S. ticket sales. Svěrák was also in *My Sweet Little Village* (1987).

Several sumptuous culinary films have made us drool over the years—think of four Best Foreign Language Film nominees: *Babette's Feast* (1988), *The Wedding Banquet* and *The Scent of Green Papaya* (both 1994) and *Eat Drink Man Woman* (1995)—and a fifth candidate, **A Chef in Love** (*Shekvarebuli kulinaris ataserti retsepti*), is no exception. This first and only nomination from the republic of Georgia between the Black and Caspian seas is a seriocomedy by filmmaker Nana Dzhordzhadze (or Jorjadze). It features a multitalented French chef named Pascal who, in the early 20th century, travels to a Eurasian country on a search for new cuisines and meets and falls in love with a woman thirty years his junior. They start a restaurant in the Georgian capital of Tbilisi that quickly gains fame far and wide. But in 1921, the Red Army of the Caucasus captures the country, steals his restaurant, relegates the poor chef to a tiny room above the eatery, assigns his lover to a soldier and hires an illiterate to run the bistro, now a hair above being a greasy spoon. There is much to love about this film: grape stomping, a duel with bricks, a bomb in the opera house and platters of savory food you can almost smell and taste as you observe. The BFF candidate also stands out as a political statement, particularly the way Pascal and the Georgians are treated by the Soviets. One great line proffered by the hero says it all: "Marxism will pass away, but great cuisine will live forever." It was Dzhordzhadze's only nomination between two submitted films and cost an estimated $3.56 million to make. It brought in $603,957 in its first run in the United States, starting April 23, 1997, a year after it opened in Georgia. This hour-and-forty-minute, French-Russian-Georgian movie earned a B+, which placed it second for the year. (How can you top *Kolya*?)

A rebellious teenage girl, Maria, is brought up in the late 1950s by her preacher father but wants more out of life in Norway's contribution **The Other Side of Sunday** (*Søndagsengler*). The title says it all. Raised in orthodox Christianity at a small town in southeastern Norway, Maria yearns for freedom. This is especially relevant after her mother is hauled off in an ambulance leaving her to toe the line with her overly pious father. She's chastised for wanting to have a Coca-Cola with her friends and dabbling in other worldly "sins." But uppermost, she fears turning into a "church crone." She finds solace in Mrs. Tunheim, whom she happens across one day swimming nude in a lake. Mrs. Tunheim, who works at the church and obviously fancies the pastor, counsels the child that she can obtain peace through swimming, and the girl discovers this to be true. Described as "beautiful," "humorous," "warm" and "serious," the hour-and-forty-three-minute motion picture is a rare coming-of-age film involving a young woman and it doesn't disappoint. Directed by Berit Nesheim in her only nomination of two submissions, it opened February 9, 1996, and eventually made it to the States May 1, 1998. This difficult-to-find film was reviewed online and deserved a B.

An age-old story, **Prisoner of the Mountains** (*Kavkazskiy plennik*), the Russian entry for the 1997 ceremony, is about two sides at war and the individuals who fall victim to it. In this case, it takes place near the north Caucasus Mountains where bitter conflict between Russia and the Chechen rebels was raging in the 1990s. Two lone survivors of a Moslem rebel ambush are taken prisoner and kept chained together at a mountain hideout. One Russian is a tough, never-say-die sergeant; the other a young, impressionable kid. Their captor is a fierce, determined village chief who schemes to use the prisoners in negotiating for the release of his son. Adding to the humanistic side, the younger captive's mother enters into face-to-face negotiations with the rebel leader to get her own son back. This also highlights conflict between cultures: Chechen rebels believe dying is glorious, while Russians, particularly younger ones, are fearful of death. The story is based on Leo Tolstoy's novella *The Prisoner of the Caucasus*, written in 1872, long before Chechnya declared itself independent or, for that matter, Russia adopted communism. The picture was filmed in the north Caucasus not far from the warzone by Sergei Bodrov, who also made *Mongol* (2008) for Kazakhstan. It has its amusing moments, a kind of love story, and the opposing ideologies expected in such a motion picture. And it has exceptional cinematography. This C film runs an hour and thirty-nine minutes and premiered March 15, 1996, coming to the U.S. January 31, 1997, where it garnered $661,361 in two months. Among its cast were Oleg Menshikov, in *Burnt by the Sun* (winner 1995) and *East/West* (2000), and Sergei Bodrov, Jr., son of the director, with a credit in *East/West*.

Ridicule is about purposefully mean-spirited aristocrats chasing favoritism among the peers surrounding the court of the hapless last king of France, Louis XVI. It's a hard film to fathom, or understand why some critics considered it one of the better flicks of the year. The hour-and-forty-two-minute picture, made by director Patrice Leconte

"Wit was king" in the years before the French Revolution, and here a crowd of aristocrats march to their own tambours in *Ridicule* (1996), by Patrice Leconte.

and submitted by France, begins by stating that "wit was king" in the years preceding the French Revolution, but it was biting, rude, malicious humor that took center stage. The movie explores how various characters sharpened and used their cutting verbal skills to gain favors or sexual partners. Sometimes the waggishness backfired. Take the opening sequence when a courtier, nicknamed "stumblebum" after tripping at a masquerade ball, arrives years later at the home of the infirm old aristocrat who gave him the rude sobriquet and extracts his revenge by urinating on him. Pretty funny stuff? If one sees art in acts of humiliation and the ability to score points by being malevolent in the name of jocularity, then perhaps this picture succeeds. It is, after all, well titled and perhaps a glimpse into the why of the Reign of Terror that took hold a few years later. As the old man's wife, played by Fanny Ardant—*The Family* (1988) and Best Picture nominee *Elizabeth* (1999) with seven nominations—states: "The soul of wit is to know one's place." The movie—it got the study's lowest score of D—was made for $10.5 million, debuted May 9, 1996, and arrived in the States November 22, 1996.

1998

B+	*Beyond Silence*	Germany
B	*Secrets of the Heart*	Spain
B	***Character***	**Netherlands**
B	*The Thief*	Russia
C	*Four Days in September*	Brazil

The theme of ***Beyond Silence*** (*Jenseits der Stille*) is simple and direct: When you've got talent, use it or lose it. The 1998 Germany nominee is about music and deafness, two contrary elements that don't mesh easily in the best of times. Lara is the first of two daughters of deaf parents. The family is close and tranquil and the girl becomes a parental surrogate because she can sign and translate for them as needed. Her aunt, her father's sister and a professional musician, gives her a clarinet for Christmas and, as it turns out, she has the gift of music. When the mother is killed in a bicycle accident, the father becomes more dependent than ever on Lara, but now as an 18-year-old, she's drawn to study music in Berlin, a decision that leads the father, who signs with difficulty, to become anxious and frustrated. The communications gap that results turns into a potent metaphor that runs through the second half of the hour-and-forty-nine-minute picture. It was directed by Caroline Link, honored by the Academy with a win five years later for *Nowhere in Africa*. It deserved a B+, a better grade than the winning entry received, according to the survey. It opened December 19, 1996, and came to the U.S. June 5, 1998, where it made $171,334 in a first run.

The Spanish contender ***Secrets of the Heart*** (*Secretos del corazón*) is not exactly a coming-of-age film, yet the 9-year-old protagonist, Javi, does find his way to maturity through interactions, understood or not, with the adult world. Critics are uniform in praising Montxo Armendáriz's movie as "delicate," "insightful," "sweet" and "sensitive." It doesn't start that way. Javi's father commits suicide in his home with a gun. Javi's slightly older brother, Juan, talks him into sitting in the dead man's chair where he hears what he believes to be his father's moans (secrets), when in fact it's something quite different. Indeed, these "interactions" involve sex, alcoholism, depression and a host of other problems. Said Stephen Holden of the *New York Times*: "...this tenderhearted film does a fine job of evoking the mixture of curiosity and fear experienced by an innocent child confronting grown-up sorrows." And there you are. Technically, the director can be criticized for overdoing the emotions the picture tries to convey. Michael Thomson of the BBC wrote: "Armendáriz certainly knows how to sustain a gentle, somber mood and how to light and frame his film ... but he gives us far too many examples of the boy's inexperience." The hour-and-forty-five-minute motion picture merited a B. It opened March 12, 1997, but apparently only received film festival notice in the United States. Another picture by the director was submitted for the 2006 ceremony but not chosen.

Power. Aggression. Anger. Not always associated with a father-son relationship. But it's sorely true in the Netherlands' winning submission to the 1998 Best Foreign Language Film contest, ***Character*** (*Karakter*). The title stems from the molding of the young man, Katadreuffe, the bastard son of a mean, recalcitrant bailiff named Drever-haven and his housekeeper, Joba. Dreverhaven is not a likable fellow—so bad, is he, that he can evict a dying woman from her home into the snow—and his son grows up fearing he's turning into his old man. The two-hour-and-two-minute picture begins with the murder of Dreverhaven and we are to believe the knife-wielding Katadreuffe did it. The finale, with a double surprise ending, will answer the question. Most of the movie takes place in the past—in this case, early 20th-century Rotterdam. Director Mike van Diem, in his only submission, created a sweeping drama with strongly etched characters, Dickensian and Kafkaesque street scenes, and rough-hewn interiors. Even so, it received only a B and seated two other films ahead of it. The picture cost an estimated $4.5 million and opened April 17, 1997, and when it came to the United States March 27, 1998, it garnered $713,413 in its first run. Among the cast was Belgian actor Jan Decleir of *Daens* (1993) and *Antonia's Line* (winner 1996).

As has been the case in recent times with German anti–Nazi films, Russia has proffered its share of post–Soviet pictures that depict Stalinism in a negative light. So it goes with **The Thief** (*Vor*). It's about Sanja, a young boy (engagingly played by 9-year-old Mikhail Filipchuk or Misha Philipchuk depending on whom you read), and his mother, who falls for an Army officer named Tolyan who may or may not be a real soldier. He is, however, a thief, and the tale revolves around Sanja's tough-love education to become an apprentice thief and a rough-and-tumble kid. Tolyan eventually goes to prison and forgets about the boy and mother, that is until the adolescent Sanja, now alone in the world, serendipitously finds him again. What transpires in the next series of scenes, which include Sanja as an adult and Army officer himself, brings the film full circle. "It is clear fairly early in 'The Thief' that the title character [Tolyan] represents Stalin," wrote Roger Ebert in his 1998 review. And following the story from beginning to end, anyone knowing how the Soviet Union suffered under the paranoid, tough-guy dictator, can see how true this is. The hour-and-thirty-six-minute, B motion picture cost $2 million to make by director Pavel Chukhray in his only submission. It opened October 13, 1997, and later in the United States July 17, 1998, where it turned $1,126,115 in gross sales the first run.

Sometimes things become clearer in retrospect years later, and sometimes not. Bruno Barreto's **Four Days in September** (*O Que é isso, companheiro?*), from Brazil, is based on a memoir by a member of the October 8 Revolutionary Movement in which a guerrilla group, in 1969, kidnaps the American ambassador Charles Burke Elbrick, played by American Oscar winner Alan Arkin. The action isn't so much an attempt by young radicals to bring the country's military dictatorship to its knees as it is to raise worldwide awareness of their Marxist-Leninist cause and demand the release of political prisoners. They are, after all, idealistic students. The picture, attempting to balance both sides' points of view, is not judgmental; rather, it makes an awkward attempt to humanize both the naïve revolutionaries and the police, who nevertheless torture the terrorists once caught. It's a not-so-stirring political thriller that garnered a C. Barreto, brother of filmmaker Fábio, had two other unrequited submissions. This one runs an hour and fifty minutes and opened April 19, 1997, and in America January 30, 1998.

1999

A	*Central Station*	Brazil
A–	*Children of Heaven*	Iran
B	***Life Is Beautiful***	**Italy**
C–	*The Grandfather*	Spain
D	*Tango*	Argentina

Brazil's overt preparations for the 2016 Summer Olympics shined a light on the country's impoverished classes, notably in Rio de Janeiro. So did *Black Orpheus*, the

1960 Oscar-winning film, and *City of God*, nominated in four categories but not Best Foreign Film. **Central Station** (*Central do Brasil*), a nominee for 1999, has some similar elements on a highly personal level. It's about a cynical older woman who makes her living at Rio's central train station writing letters for illiterates. Because of unfortunate circumstances, the 10-year-old son of one of her clients becomes enmeshed in her life. At first she's quick to capitalize on the situation by selling the foundling for enough money to buy a television set, but this act of narcissism and the sudden understanding of what dangerous things might happen to the boy bring her around. The rest of the story is one of discovery, of bonding, of companionship, of transitional love. Critics point to the powerful acting of Fernanda Montenegro, who played the letter writer, for the film's huge success; she was nominated for Best Actress. The young actor, Vinícius de Oliveira, in reality a shoeshine boy from the slums, received kudos for his natural acting ability as well. The hour-and-fifty-three-minute movie was not the winning entry, but it warranted a well-reasoned A. Director Walter Salles, with one other unselected submission, used the $2.9 million it took to make the film wisely and it paid off. After it opened in the United States November 20, 1998, it sold $5,595,428 worth of tickets. It first opened in Switzerland January 16, 1998, and in Brazil April 3, 1998.

The trailer evokes the names *Kolya* and *Cinema Paradiso* in comparison with ***Children of Heaven*** (*Bacheha-Ye aseman*), a heartwarming film by Iranian director Majid Majidi about a wide-eyed boy of 9 and his younger sister and their strife and triumphs over a pair of lost shoes. So simple and complaisant is this feature that critics have

Boys race to win a pair of shoes in the child-driven Iranian contender *Children of Heaven* (1999).

deemed it suitable for children to see, subtitles and all (indeed, some public libraries place the DVD in the children section). In addition, it passed the stringent censorship of the Islamic Republic of Iran as an apolitical film worthy of international attention. The motion picture—Majidi's only nomination among five submissions—takes place in a poorer section of Tehran, the capital. Ali has lost his sister's prized possession, her shoes, but promises Zahra he will find them. They conspire to keep this tragic news from their parents, since replacing the footwear would be a financial burden to them. The shoes are discovered, on a ragpicker's daughter, presenting yet another obstacle. Ali enters a footrace to win a new pair of shoes for his sister, which is a set piece to the film's conclusion. The hour-and-twenty-nine-minute picture may not have won the 1999 Oscar, but it was better than the Italian winner, if not as good as the Brazilian runner-up, and deserved an A–. It cost Iran a mere $180,000 to make but garnered $925,402 in its first run in the States, starting January 22, 1999. It opened at the Fajr International Film Festival in Tehran in February 1997. Incidentally, the two films it was compared to both won Oscars in 1997 and 1990 respectively.

Rarely does a foreign film garner so many Oscar nominations in one year as did **Life Is Beautiful** (*La vita è bella*). The Italian winner was written (in part), directed and acted by Roberto Benigni, a natural clown who managed to fit in both genres: drama and tragedy. The hour-and-fifty-six-minute film also won for Best Actor and Best Original Dramatic Score and was nominated for Best Picture, Director, Editor and Screenplay Written Directly for Film. Not bad for a cut-up who, upon his announcement as Best Actor got up on the backs of the seats in the Dorothy Chandler Pavilion to whoop and holler like an overly stimulated Flying Wallenda. The first part of the film is strictly comedy à la Chaplin or Jacques Tati, about how a beanpole Jewish waiter named Guido inveigles Dora (Benigni's real wife, Nicoletta Braschi) into marrying him. The second part begins with the couple and their 5-year-old son Giosuè (Joshua), who becomes the focus of the story, at the close of World War II. The Nazis round up the Jews and send them to an extermination camp where Guido tries to protect his child from the pathos of their circumstances by using comedy to make everything appear a big elaborate game. There's no doubt the film lives up to what the *Los Angeles Daily News* called "a masterpiece of tremendous power and beauty!" Even so, this was a B movie, regardless of sentimentality. It cost $20 million to make and opened December 20, 1997, and in the United States February 12, 1999, where it earned a whopping $57,598,247! Also in the cast were Marisa Paredes (*All About My Mother* 2000) and Giorgio Cantarini, who played the 5-year-old and two years later was cast as Russell Crowe's son in *Gladiator*, the 2001 Best Picture and recipient of five Oscars and seven other nominations. Benigni had one other submission, but only this one nomination.

A proud but impoverished aristocrat returns home to northern Spain from South America around 1900 to discover that his daughter-in-law has taken over his estate after her husband has passed away. It's brought to the old man's attention that his son may have died of a broken heart after learning that his wife had cheated on him. Everyone is against Rodrigo, the old count played by Fernando Fernán-Gómez, except his teenage granddaughters Dolly and Netty, one of whom, he hears, was the product of infidelity. The don delves into the question of which granddaughter shares his bloodline for the purpose of inheritance. This is the crux of **The Grandfather** (*El abuelo*) from

Spain, directed by director José Luis Garci, who received four nominations including one win (*Begin the Beguine* in 1983) out of six submissions. The two-hour-and-thirty-one-minute film received a C–. The film cost $2.65 million and grossed $50,037 in its first run in America. Note: Garci's two other nominations, *Double Feature* (1985) and *Course Completed* (1988), are among the most difficult BFF films to locate. Meanwhile, cast members Cayetana Guillén Cuervo was in *All About My Mother* (winner 2000) and Fernán-Gómez starred in *Mama Turns 100* (1980), *Belle Époque* (winner 1994) and *All About My Mother*. Ironically, another actor, Rafael Alonso, died a week before opening day October 30, 1998.

Red is for passion, and Carlos Saura's ***Tango***, the Argentine entry, has plenty of both. The dance aficionado and filmmaker—and mentor of Luis Buñuel—has been to the Oscars before, with the enigmatic, difficult-to-find *El Amor Brujo* (1967), which he wrote, directed and choreographed, as well as *Mama Turns 100* (1980) and *Carmen* (1984), another dance movie. *Tango* has been described as a multilayered film, a kind of fictional documentary (the audience occasionally sees the cameras), surreal in its dream constructions, thin of plot, but always centered on the music, as well as the theme of sensual love and the heat of the dance, both reflected by the red tinting of the film. One outstanding characteristic is the photography by three-time Oscar winner Vittorio Storaro (*Apocalypse Now* 1979, *Reds* 1981 and *The Last Emperor* 1987). This hour-and-fifty-five-minute motion picture is not for everybody; it often drags, is rife with pensiveness, and you have to love the omnipresent music and intermittent dance sequences to enjoy it. It's a D film. It cost $4.91 million to make and opened in Argentina August 6, 1998, and in the United States February 12, 1999, where it picked up

Carlos Saura's *Tango* (1998) features a multitude of dancers, including Juan Carlos Copes and Cecilia Narova.

$1,687,311. In the cast was Mía Maestro, who was in two Oscar contenders (not BFFs): *Frida* (2003), with six nominations and two wins, and *The Motorcycle Diaries* (2005), with two nominations and one win.

2000

B+	*All About My Mother*	**Spain**
B+	*East/West*	France
B–	*Under the Sun*	Sweden
C	*Solomon and Gaenor*	United Kingdom
C–	*Himalaya / Caravan*	Nepal

As of its release in 1999 the most honored film in Spain's rich cinematic history, **All About My Mother** (*Todo sobre mi madre*), capitalizes on writer-director Pedro Almodóvar's sense of irony to tell a story that can't make up its mind whether it's a tragedy or comedy. The colorful film, the 2000 Best Foreign Film, takes us on a curious ride through the emotions of death and redemption with Manuela, a Madrilenian medical worker and would-be thespian who oversees donor organ transplants. Her teenage son is struck and killed by a car while chasing after an actress for an autograph. Manuela, with trepidation, signs over his heart to the donor program. From there, the film makes a broad leap as she travels to Barcelona to seek out the boy's father to relate the bad news, despite the fact that he, now a transvestite prostitute, did not know the boy even

Cecilia Roth, as Manuela, gives consultation to Penélope Cruz, playing the pregnant Sister Rosa, in Pedro Almodóvar's *All About My Mother* (1999).

existed. It is in this peculiar and earthy world of hookers and ambisexuals that much of the rest of the movie plays out. While situations appear two dimensional and circus-like, the characters are very much multidimensional, another of Almodóvar's strange ironies. Almodóvar, by the way, had six submissions, two nominations—this and *Women on the Verge of a Nervous Breakdown* (1989)—and also *Volver* (2007), which made the January shortlist but not a nomination. The hour-and-forty-one-minute picture was viewed with mixed feelings through the first half, but its bizarre, colorful story grew to a B+, as befits a winner, by the end. A second viewing confirmed this. The film opened April 8, 1999, and was especially popular in America when it debuted March 31, 2000, garnering $8,264,530 in its first run. It included in the cast Marisa Paredes, Dora's mother in multi-Oscar winner *Life Is Beautiful* (1999). Also in the cast were Fernando Fernán-Gómez—*Mama Turns 100* (1980), *Belle Époque* (winner 1994) and *The Grand-father* (1999)—and Penélope Cruz from *Belle Époque*.

Alexei is a Russian. He also happens to be happily married to a French woman. He is a practicing physician who sees an opportunity to return home with his foreign wife and help rebuild the motherland immediately after World War II. What he doesn't realize is that Soviet dictator Josef Stalin—Paranoid Joe—is welcoming expats back so he can get rid of them. Alexei is spared, however, because of his needed profession. But he and his privileged wife are relegated to a substandard, overcrowded boarding-house, and his wife, used to the fineries of the West, doesn't like it, insisting on seeking a way to beat the Soviet system and escape. Such is the basis for **East/West** (*Est-Ouest*) from France, with production help from Russia, the Ukraine, Bulgaria and Spain. Although rooted in the way things were done at the time, the motion picture is fictitious, a melodramatic thriller-fantasy. "But the sumptuous romanticism of the story makes it bearable," reviewer A.O. Scott of the *New York Times* pointed out, adding that the film "is a historical pageant, full of grandeur and period detail, but it is also the por-trait of a marriage under extreme pressure, external and internal." The two-hour-and-one-minute movie scored a B+. It is tense and has its distressing moments, but all in all its cast is good. It was directed by Régis Wargnier, who also did *Indochine* (1993), a win in his only other submission. This film opened September 1, 1999, and later in the States May 5, 2000, where it earned a respectable $2,775,520. In the cast were Catherine Deneuve—who starred in *The Umbrellas of Cherbourg* (1965), *Tristana* (1971) and *The Last Metro* (1981)—and Oleg Menshikov, who appeared in *Burnt by the Sun* (win-ner 1995), along with cast-member Sergei Bodrov, Jr., in *Prisoner of the Mountains* (1997).

There is much to like about Sweden's **Under the Sun** (*Under solen*) but it falls headlong into an overemotional stewpot of scenes as incredible as those of any daytime melodrama. It's about Olof, a good-natured, soft-spoken, kind, virginal and illiterate middle-aged farmer in rural, southern Västra Götaland, who hires a maid and is quickly smitten by her blonde, voluptuous beauty. Enter Erik, a smooth James Dean wannabe, who also has designs on Ellen, but more as a conqueror than a lover. (He later would get his by hiring onto the ill-fated ship *Andrea Doria*, which sank with the loss of forty-six lives in 1956.) Needless to say, Olof and Ellen become lovers, but eventually Ellen leaves him for reasons we will not disclose here. Erik has to read him the note she's left behind but omits crucial information. In a fitting climax for a weepy melodrama, Ellen returns, reads the whole note to him and everyone lives happily ever after, except Erik of course. The two-hour-and-ten-minute motion picture was too melodramatic but well acted and deserved a B–. The film was directed by Colin Nutley, his third submission and only nomination. Among its cast were Rolf Lassgård, who was in *After the Wedding* (2007) and *A Man Called Ove* (2017), and Johan Widerberg, who played in *All Things Fair* (1996) and *A Man Called Ove*. The film picked up $266,519 in its first run in America starting August 3, 2001. It opened in Sweden December 25, 1998.

My acquaintance with Ioan Gruffudd was through the award-winning *Horatio Hornblower* television film series shown on the Arts & Entertainment Network (1998–2003). Tall, handsome and well-coiffed, Gruffudd grew up on Welsh television, speaking the Celtic language, so it isn't a stretch to see him in a full-length motion picture called **Solomon and Gaenor**, offered by the United Kingdom for the 2000 foreign Oscar. This is a love story (some critics called it more of a "lust story") in which an Orthodox Jewish boy woos a Gentile girl in 1911 coal-mining country to a tragic end. The picture explores innocent love, not-so-innocent love, adolescent foolhardiness, deliberate dishonesty, racial intolerance and, to a degree, working-class despair. It would be easy to compare this to the Romeo-Juliet theme but for the fact the star-crossed lovers of Shakespeare's invention are more a result of their fates, while Solomon's and Gaenor's are more happenstance and recklessness. This muted-color, hour-and-forty-five-minute film by Paul Morrison, in his only submission, received a C. It was recorded predominately in Welsh for the Academy nomination but was filmed a second time in Welsh, English and Yiddish for a wider audience. For the record, more than a dozen films have been submitted by Britain for BFF consideration, of which nine were in Welsh, two of them, including *Hedd Wyn* (1994), receiving nominations. The film opened in the U.K. April 30, 1999, and in New York City and Los Angeles August 25, 2000, with few other venues. It earned $301,754 in its limited U.S. run. Gruffudd was in two other multi-nominated Oscar pictures—*Titanic* (1998), with fourteen bids and eleven wins including Best Picture, and *Blackhawk Down*, with four nods and two wins—but no other BFF candidate.

"We're making a film about life, with non-actors," said Éric Valli, French director of the unusual documentary-like drama **Himalaya** (*Himalaya–l'Enfance d'un chef*), the first Nepalese submission and its only nominee to date for a Best Foreign Film statuette. It was Valli's only submission as well. Also known as *Caravan* or *Himalayan Caravan*, the motion picture was filmed in the restricted Dolpo region of the country and is said to have taken about three times as long as planned to shoot. Dolpo, in western Nepal, survives on salt trade from Tibet to more populous centers in the south. The story begins in a village where the septuagenarian elder, Tinle, and his family await the arrival of the caravan. When it comes with Tinle's group-leader son dead from an accidental fall, he vows to take over the convoy. His adversary is Karma, who replaced the son as trail boss and indeed professes to be his best friend who happened to find the body. But Tinle doesn't believe him. Karma, frustrated in his negotiations with the elder, leads the caravan on, with Tinle and his youngest grandson in hot pursuit. The cinematography and shots of load-ladened yaks deftly negotiating the high-cliff trails of this remote area are stunning. Critics did laud the beauty of the CinemaScope produc-

Thinle (Thilen Lhondup) awaits the arrival of the salt caravan with his grandson Tserin (Karma Wangel) in Éric Valli's *Himalaya* (1999), Nepal's first Oscar nomination.

tion but objected to the plot simplification, understated drama and lack of suspense. The movie opened in Switzerland August 20, 1999, and in the United States June 22, 2001, where it sold $2,481,690 worth of tickets. The hour-and-forty-eight-minute film garnered a C–.

Political Perspectives:
2001–2017

Z was a marvelous political adventure in 1970, *The Official Story* in 1986 and *38: Vienna before the Fall* that same year. It seems as though annually, Germany or the Netherlands or Italy—it doesn't matter—comes up with a film with a Holocaust theme. Indeed, practically every year since 1948 there has been some form of political drama presented for Oscar consideration.

Since the last century, a different kind of geopolitical film has emerged, one of more contemporary import. These films arrive from odd places and dwell on events that occurred in the recent past or are occurring today. These include Bosnia and Herzegovina's *No Man's Land*, Palestine's *Paradise Now*, Germany's *The Lives of Others* and *The Baader Meinhof Complex*, Israel's *Beaufort* and *Waltz with Bashir*, Canada's *Incendies*, Iran's *A Separation* and *The Salesman*, and Russia's *Leviathan*.

A few hard-to-watch films have surfaced during these last two decades, most notable, perhaps, being *Son of Saul* from Hungary, an in-your-face Holocaust drama that shows an out-of-focus vision of what was going on all around a Nazi death camp.

But there also have been some fun films—*Joyeux Noël, Pan's Labyrinth, Amélie, Wild Tales*—and tender, if sad, stories that stay with you: *Yesterday, Departures, The White Ribbon, Amour.*

Now that we've mentioned a fair number of them, let's take a closer look.

2001

B	*Everybody's Famous!*	Belgium
B	*Divided We Fall*	Czech Republic
B–	***Crouching Tiger***	**Taiwan**
C–	*The Taste of Others*	France
D	*Amores Perros*	Mexico

Had the Flemish Belgium's contribution to the 2001 ceremony, **Everybody's Famous!** (*Iedereen beroemd!*), been a TV reality show in America, it might have succeeded. Marva Vereecken—plump, 17 and deadpan, if not tone deaf—is the pride of her blue-collar father who fancies himself a songsmith—hers—and enters the girl in several talent contests to no avail. A teenage Honey Boo Boo she is not. Along comes a not-so-talented but highly popular vocalist, Debbie, whom Daddy kidnaps and holds for ransom to extort a record contract for Marva. Unexpectedly, news headlines propel the sales of the pop star's records off the charts and her manager, recognizing this development as a serendipitous goldmine, tells Mr. Vereecken to keep the pop singer—played by Thekla Reuten (*Twin Sisters* 2004)—a prisoner. Therein lies the comic thread of this innocuous piece of fluff that garnered a B. "Hey, it was great! And easy to follow," a personal note states. *Crouching Tiger* might have won this year—and many critics agreed with the results—but the survey placed *Everybody's Famous!* at the top of the 2001 chart. Directed by Dominique Deruddere in his only submission, the motion picture opened in Belgium April 12, 2000, and in New York June 29, 2001.

Described as a "dramedy," the Czech Republic submission, **Divided We Fall** (*Musíme si pomáhat*), is an hour-and-fifty-seven-minute, multilayered motion picture about ordinary citizens doing extraordinary things during Nazi-occupied Czechoslovakia. Josef is an antihero, seemingly a sympathizer on the surface, who with his wife Marie protects an escaped Jew. All around them neighbors—and particularly a Nazi postulant, Horst, who admiringly sports a Hitler mustache—poke around. The film was directed by Jan Hřebejk, 33, and written by Petr Jarchovský. As *New York Times* critic A.O. Scott put it: "Mr. Hřebejk and Mr. Jarchovský, working in the rich Czech tradition of absurdist humanism, construct a universe booby-trapped with impossible choices and ethical puzzles. 'Divided We Fall' ultimately resolves into a hopeful parable, but its unlikely glow of forgiveness is well earned." Like the previous film, this B effort appeared in the rankings above the winner. Hřebejk directed two other films that were submitted but not nominated. It opened March 16, 2000, and came to Los Angeles and New York City simultaneously June 8, 2001. It garnered $1,320,112 on the first U.S. run. Two cast members were in BFF contenders: Bolek Polívka appeared in *The Elementary School* (1992) and Jaroslav Dušek in *Želary* (2004).

The use of wires and gymnastics to affect superhuman mano-a-mano combat might put off the purist filmgoer. **Crouching Tiger, Hidden Dragon** (*Wo hu cang long*) has all of what the martial-arts genre demands and at a hefty price tag of $17 million—a pittance of what it brought in during its first run in the States, $128,067,808. But the film's allure for traditionalists is a cohesive storyline, strong characters and a love story that superseded choreographed trickery and CGI. Ang Lee of truly diverse, international, prize-winning motion pictures—*The Wedding Banquet* (1994), *Eat Drink Man Woman* (1995), *Sense and Sensibility* (1996), *Brokeback Mountain* (2006) and *The Life of Pi* (2013)—made this two-hour, swashbuckling entry from Taiwan, which not only won the 2001 BFF Oscar but also for Cinematography, Original Score and Art Direction-Set Decoration and was nominated in addition for Best Picture, Director, Editing, Screenplay, Costume Design and Original Song; only the year's Best Picture, *Gladiator*, had more nominations (twelve). The story revolves around two master kung fu artists, one a man (Chow Yun-fat) and the other a woman (Michelle Yeoh), and the unrequited love, admiration and loyalty they have for one another. The actors exude remarkable chemistry in the film. They seek a stolen sword but are blocked by the evil, and athletically talented, female warrior Jade Fox. A subplot involves a betrothed young woman, the hidden dragon, who is chasing her destiny to become a master warrior herself. The focus, however, is on Yeoh's strong role as the superior warrior (shades of Uma Thurman's in Quentin Tarantino's two-part *Kill Bill*), a marked departure from the Bruce Lee–like martial-arts films of the '70s, '80s and '90s, of which there are far too many to name. It warranted a controversial B– in the survey, an actual bump from the original verdict of C–, owing in part to the reconsidered cinematography, acting and cohesive script. Ang's résumé has been mentioned. One of the cast, Ziyi Zhang, appeared in *Hero* (2003).

The Taste of Others (*Le Goût des autres*) is about compatibility, or lack thereof; about "my taste vs. yours"; and about how tastes evolve, sometimes to harmful effect and sometimes not. The interesting thing about this French contender is the fact the screenwriters, Agnès Jaoui and Jean-Pierre Bacri, are also director and male lead respectively. Do they feel obliged to share something? Castella, played by Bacri (*Entre Nou* 1984), is going through a midlife crisis and, being somewhat henpecked, looks beyond his own marriage. He falls in love with a 40-something actress, from whom he's also begun taking English lessons, and changes into an art devotee. Jaoui, meanwhile, also plays a drug-dealing barmaid involved with Castella's bodyguard. This parallel relationship, which has its own set of disagreements, juxtaposes with the others in the consistent examination of how tastes differ from person to person and the diverse consequential results. The hour-and-fifty-two-minute romantic comedy received only a C–, in part because of its convoluted storyline. Debuting in France March 1, 2000, it also had a limited, albeit somewhat profitable ($635,282) run in the United States. Another cast member, Anne Alvaro, played as well in *The Diving Bell and the Butterfly* (2007), which had four Oscar nominations, but not in the foreign-language category. Jaoui had no other submission.

Husband and wife Jean-Jacques and Angelique Castella (Jean-Pierre Bacri and Christiane Millet) attend the theater in Agnès Jaoui's *The Taste of Others* (2000).

First of all, Mexican director Alejandro González Iñárritu, who struck gold with two consecutive Best Picture nominations in *Birdman* (a winner in 2015) and *The Revenant* (2016), is a force to be reckoned with. He also produced *Biutiful* (2011) and another non-foreign, multiple-Oscar contender, *Babel* (2007). Even so, his feature debut, **Amores Perros**, Mexico's nomination for 2001, with its difficult-to-watch dogfight sequences, will never be an award-winner among the PETA or ASPCA folks, even though a disclaimer at the very beginning states that "no animals were harmed in making this film." *Amores Perros* is a three-part, interconnected anthology picture with critical references to Quentin Tarantino's *Pulp Fiction* and *Reservoir Dogs*. The first part concerns a man's race to get his dying rottweiler, subject of an illegal dogfight, to a veterinarian and the subsequent car crash. The second involves a middle-aged man and his lover, a model, who is injured in that same crash and later loses her beloved Lhasa apso among the floor interstices of her new home, a movement described by some critics as a bit melodramatic in the manner of a feverish Mexican *telenovela*. The third segment gets down and dirty, featuring an assassin and his pack of dogs. Wesley Morris of the *San Francisco Chronicle* summed up his review this way: "There's a seething moral core in 'Amores Perros' that uses the canine savagery as an entry to human brutality. By the time the film has slipped into its glorious, redemptive final movement, there's no mistake: Bite for bite, the people are worse, but they can be saved." This movie is not for the faint of heart, especially animal people who may want to turn away a few times. The two-hour-and-thirty-four-minute, D film cost $2 million and opened June 16, 2000, and in the U.S. April 13, 2001, where it garnered $5,383,834. Two cast members need mentioning: Emilio Echevarría was in *Babel*, which was nominated for Best Picture and other Oscars, and Gael García Bernal starred in *The Crime of Padre Amaro* (2003) and *No* (2013) and also had a part in *Babel*. Most of Iñárritu's films have been well received by the Academy. Even films not on the Best Picture or BFF lists were cited, such as *21 Grams* (2004) in which Naomi Watts and Benicio Del Toro were nominated for acting roles.

2002

A	*Amélie*	France
A–	*Son of the Bride*	Argentina
B+	**No Man's Land**	**Bosnia**
C	*Elling*	Norway
C–	*Lagaan*	India

Director Jean-Pierre Jeunet said of the colossal success of his fanciful French film **Amélie** (*Le fabuleux destin d'Amélie Poulain*) that it was truly an international motion picture, despite its highly stylized Parisian setting. The true key to its success was the main character, played by actress Audrey Tautou, whose China-doll looks, big dark eyes and constant effervescence made the 2002 nomination endearing and popular. The lighthearted fantasy in brilliant, if somewhat supernatural, color centers on Tautou's Amélie Poulain, a shy café waitress who discovers immured in the wall of her flat an old box containing the long-ago treasures of a young boy. She makes it her life's goal to locate the man it belonged to and, along the way, make people she encounters happy. It's a whimsical romp, which received additional nods for Writing Directly to the Screen, Art Direction-Set Decoration, Cinematography and Sound. But it did not win in any category. Even so, it's not difficult to love this A film, chosen over the winner from Bosnia and Herzegovina as Best Foreign Language Film for the year. The two-hour-and-two-minute picture came out April 25, 2001, and cost about $10.92 million,

A delight for the senses, the French film *Amélie* (2001) features doe-eyed Audrey Tautou, here peering out of a photo booth on her quest to find the owner of a long-lost box of souvenirs.

a third what the American gate brought in, $33,201,661. Tautou's career exploded from there, but most films were mediocre American affairs (e.g. *The Da Vinci Code*, *Dirty Pretty Things* and *Coco Before Chanel*). *Amélie* was also Jeunet's only submission. One character, Jamel Debbouze, played in another BFF candidate, *Outside the Law* (2011).

An overachieving middle-aged restaurateur suffers a mild heart attack and sees the light of day in Argentina's nominee **Son of the Bride** (*El hijo de la novia*). This delightful dramedy has dark moments, but also scenes of hilarity that make it an A– film—shades of *Wild Tales* more than a decade later. Our title hero, Rafael Belvedere, has a mom with Alzheimer's, played by Norma Aleandro, whom he wants his dad, played by Héctor Alterio, to remarry. (One might recall these two together seventeen years earlier in Argentina's winning film *The Official Story*. For that matter, Ricardo Darín, who plays Rafael, was also Simón the bomber in the 2015 nominee *Wild Tales* and the novelist in the original *The Secret in Their Eyes*, winner in 2010, for which Campanella had his other nomination.) What makes this film work is the dialogue, which Eddie Cockrell of *Variety* noted "sparkles with inventive wit and is strewn with smart one-liners," the result of a screenplay by director Juan José Campanella and co-writer Fernando Castets. The cinematography isn't bad, either, with sweeping colorful views of Buenos Aires. According to Edward Guthmann of the *San Francisco Chronicle*, the picture "manages to be affectionate without drawing too deeply from a well of sugar and schmaltz." Aleandro also was in *The Truce* (1975) and received a Best Supporting Actress nomination for *Gaby: A True Story* (1988). *Son of the Bride* opened August 16, 2001, and for a limited, $624,153 run in the States starting March 22, 2002. It's three minutes over two hours long.

Using his skills in documentary filmmaking, Danis Tanović brings to the silver screen a biting satire about war titled **No Man's Land** (*Ničija zemlja*), this year's winner from Bosnia and Herzegovina (in partnership with a host of other nations). It was the war-beleaguered country's second-ever submission, and it won the Oscar. It's 1993, and two bitter enemies unexpectedly find themselves trapped in the same trench during the Bosnian war. What's more, a dead man is placed as a booby trap on a bounding landmine and then suddenly comes alive! What to do? There's no 911 here, only the United Nations Protective Force. One of several ironies of the picture is the way the adversaries learn to trust one another, despite their petty arguments over which side started the war, and through teamwork they attract two key neutrals: an officious U.N. observer and an acerbic female cable news reporter. Now, as the film plays out, the men feel trapped between the bureaucrats and the media with nowhere to turn. Tanović had not forgotten his special talent for producing realistic cinematic set pieces and sharp edits. Four of his features got submitted for Oscar consideration, this one the only nominee and another a shortlister. Nature, not commonly a leading element of war documentaries, finds its way into the script as well, with expansive shots of fluffy clouds and bucolic fields that hide the ghastly battle trenches. The winning picture warranted a B+, but it wasn't enough to supplant two other entries for the year. It opened in France September 19, 2001, in New York City December 7, 2001, and Los Angeles a week later. The hour-and-thirty-eight-minute film produced $1,059,830 in revenue in the United States alone. Among the cast was Katrin Cartlidge of *Before the Rain* (1995).

The Odd Couple meets *One Flew Over the Cuckoo's Nest* sans Nurse Ratched and the pill cups: That's **Elling**, Norway's nominee. Elling is a squeak of a mama's boy, afraid of his own shadow and more than just a little bit agoraphobic, who befriends Kjell Bjarne, a lumbering virgin who lusts after women but forgets to bathe and change his clothes. Both in their early 40s, they are paired up in a provincial psychiatric ward and then discharged together and sent to a home to make their way in the world. This presents quite a challenge, especially for Elling, but through odd adventures, a relationship with a neighbor who happens to be pregnant and alcoholic, and a healthy dose of nuanced comedy, they manage to get by. Based on a series of novels about the Elling character by Ingvar Ambjørnsen, the hour-and-twenty-nine-minute movie was directed by Petter Næss with a straightforward, unsentimental and gentle hand. He had one other film submitted but not selected. This one, a C movie, cost $1.93 million to produce and premiered March 16, 2001, and in New York City on a $313,436 run May 29, 2002.

The Hindi word *lagaan* can be translated as "assessment," and back in the jewel-in-the-crown days of the Raj in India, farmers had to pay an annual tax in grain, even in times of drought and starvation. **Lagaan: Once Upon a Time in India** is a so-called "Bollywood" motion picture that crossed over to international acclaim. A truly good-vs.-evil film, it's about the relationship between a young girl and an idealistic farmer in a small village back in 1893. Caught between the good of the poor inhabitants and the mean-spirited British soldiers stationed nearby is the old maharajah, a devout vegetarian who happens also to take his share of tribute (*lagaan*) each year. Meanwhile, the arrogant, racist, sadistic captain of the Brit contingent provides the villagers with an opportunity to beat the system in a "friendly" game of cricket, which of course the English had perfected long before the Indians mastered the dreadfully boring game. It's an insuperable situation, a David and Goliath story, replete with Bollywood music and dances that spring out of nowhere amid the melodramatic dialogue of the principals. The cinematography is great; the color is exuberant; the acting is typically over the top. And the flick made more than $12 million, more than doubling its lavish budget, so it had a spectacular following. The three-hour-and-forty-four-minute film at first received

Bollywood dancing and singing highlight the film *Lagaan: Once Upon a Time in India* (2001), starring Gracy Singh and Aamir Khan.

the lowest possible ranking, but upon review, the ranking was elevated to a C– because of redeeming production values, namely set design, makeup, costumes and choreography. Directed by Ashutosh Gowariker in his only submission, the motion picture opened June 15, 2001, and in America May 8, 2002.

2003

B	***Nowhere in Africa***	**Germany**
B–	*The Crime of Padre Amara*	Mexico
C+	*Zus & Zo*	Holland
C–	*The Man without a Past*	Finland
C–	*Hero*	China

Unlike Sydney Pollack's sweeping epic *Out of Africa*, which won seven of eleven nominated Oscars including Best Picture in 1986, **Nowhere in Africa** (*Nirgendwo in Afrika*) is a character-driven production about a Jewish family of three that escapes Third Reich Germany for the hardscrabble of rural East Africa and how they interact with the proud but guileless natives. Told from the perspective of a young girl, Regina, who arrives at 5 and immediately embraces the easy-going lifestyle of the local tribesmen, the German film, winner of the 2003 Best Foreign Language Film Oscar, is more of a memoir than a political drama. Significant to the storyline, the Scarlett O'Hara-like mother arrives in Kenya as a supercilious, upper-class snob and is utterly transformed by the time they are ready, and able, to return to Germany. Another character worth noting is the family's cook, a tall uninhibited Masai native who considers himself, not a servant to these white farm managers, but a true professional who, when asked by the woman to dig a well, makes it clear, "I'm a cook; cooks don't dig in the ground." He also refuses to go after water, since that is "women's work." Contrasting his early recalcitrant relationship with Regina's mother, he quickly becomes the young girl's best

In *Nowhere in Africa* (2001), young Regina (Lea Kurka) becomes best pals with the tall family cook Owuor, played by Sidede Onyulo.

friend and confidante. Despite its B ranking, this was the best foreign film of the year. The two-hour-and-twenty-one-minute motion picture, which opened December 27, 2001, was directed by Caroline Link, known also for her other submission, *Beyond Silence* (1998). She made it for $6.17 million and coincidentally gained that back and $3,485 more when it opened in the States. Starring was Juliane Köhler, Eva Braun in *Downfall* (2005); Merab Ninidze, who appears in Best Picture candidate *Bridge of Spies* (2016); and Matthias Habich, also *Downfall* as well as five-times-nominated *The Reader* (2009).

The controversial film ***The Crime of Padre Amara*** (*El crimen del Padre Amaro*) from Mexico is reminiscent of the winning Best Picture for 2016, *Spotlight*, wherein journalists effectively investigate reports Catholic priests in the Boston diocese consistently abused children. Both films are based on true events. In the case of Father Amara, his crime did not involve pedophilia; instead, he broke his vow of celibacy and knocked up a young woman named Amelia, played by 22-year-old Ana Claudia Talancón. What really rankled the movie's detractors, however, was the fact he paid for her illegal abortion—a strict no-no in the Church of Rome. Others, including some priests, disagreed and said the motion picture was insightful and important, shining a light on what was considered a serious problem in the church at the time. Directed by Carlos Carrera, who had three features submitted but only this one nominated, *The Crime of Padre Amara* (sometimes "Father" is used instead of "Padre" in the title) was based on an 1875 novel by Portuguese-Mexican writer Eça de Queiroz. Amara was played by Gael García Bernal who also starred in contenders *Amores Perros* (2001) and *No* (2013). *Amara*, a B− feature, runs two minutes shy of two hours and cost an estimated $1.8 million to make. It opened August 16, 2002, and again in the United States December 13, 2002, where it earned $5,709,626.

"This and That" sums it up. *Zus & Zo* was Holland's entry in this lackluster year for foreign film nominations. Three sisters, described at one point as "monsters," will do anything to keep the family hotel in their possession, and their little brother, Nino, a professed gay man, will do anything to fulfill the pledge of his father to inherit the hotel, located in Portugal, upon his wedding. Enter vivacious female Bo, who makes a marriage-of-convenience pact with him so he can obtain the hotel and ultimately sell it to earn enough money for a sex-change operation. This film has more intertwinings than a reptile zoo, much of it around sex, or lack of it, where the three sisters and the men in their lives are concerned. Seeing the film was late in coming, and then off a streaming service where it was presented, with English subtitles, from an adequate print. At times the film touches on madcap hilarity; most of the time it is rather silly and farcical. There's a catch to it—no, two—which one needs to watch to the very end, even beyond the credits, to appreciate. Paula van der Oest directed and wrote the hour-and-forty-six-minute, C+ film, which opened May 8, 2002, and in New York City February 7, 2003. She had three films submitted of which this was the only nominee, but one other, *Accused* (2015), was on the January shortlist.

It's hard to get into **The Man without a Past** (*Mies vailla menneisyyttä*), the second of Aki Kaurismäki's "Finland Trilogy." The characters are wooden; the dialogue stiff and deadpan; the movements blocky and perfunctory. This is supposed to be a comedy: "The funniest film Kaurismäki has ever made!" according to a testimonial on the DVD cover. A rugged-looking man is badly beaten by punks and left for dead. He's hospitalized, then released, and finds himself in a vagrant camp where he befriends others who, like him, are destitute. While fishing with one of his newfound friends, Anttila the security man asks, "Who are you?" Before he can answer, his friend replies, "He doesn't know. Found on the beach ... some sort of driftwood." The man woos Irma, a lonely, rock'n'roll-loving Salvation Army spinster, and gets involved with the charity's band. Eventually he learns who he is when his former wife recognizes a mugshot. He sees her but wishes her away, since she's been taken by another. The picture closely follows the director's trademark minimalism to such a degree that it leaves viewers scratching their heads. The dry humor is too arid, the action too spare and the cuts too abrupt. A note from the first viewing of the hour-and-thirty-seven-minute film stated, "This was a movie you watched for the novelty of it being Finnish, with unknown actors doing a credible job." Nevertheless, it merited only a C–. Kaurismäki was, if nothing else, hesitant about submitting films to the Academy. Of four pictures submitted for consideration, this one was nominated, another was passed over and two others were withdrawn by the director prior to screening. That's taking minimalism to an extreme. Producers paid $1.19 million for the film, which opened November 6, 2002, and for a limited time in America April 4, 2003, earning $921,547.

Said to be one of many legends about assassins sent to murder the king, **Hero** (*Ying Xiong*) stars Jet Li as the nameless killer who in 227 BCE attempts a hit on King Zheng of Qin, the unifier of China. It was directed by prolific filmmaker Zhang Yimou, who also made *Ju Dou* (1991) and *Raise the Red Lantern* (1992), as well as five other Chinese-submitted films that didn't make the cut. The story is told from different points of view, à la *Rashomon* (1952), and with Li in charge, you can bet on lots of miraculous swordplay and cutting-edge action from gracefully soaring and gliding martial-arts fighters. The

Jet Li, as "Nameless," shows off his swordsmanship in the Zhang Yimou *wuxia pian* martial-arts film *Hero* (2002).

picture is styled like China's popular low-budget *wuxia pian* martial-arts dramas so prevalent from the 1920s through the '70s. Even so, there's a fair amount of dreamy animation in *Hero* as well. The movie is visually spectacular—a trademark of Zhang's—albeit at times dark and foreboding, as swashbuckling Chinese combat films can be. The C– film cost an estimated $31 million to produce and made a paltry $84,961 when it opened in the United States August 27, 2004. It runs an hour and thirty-nine minutes. Also in the cast was Ziyi Zhang of *Crouching Tiger, Hidden Dragon* (2001).

2004

A	*Twilight Samurai*	Japan
B–	*Twin Sisters*	Netherlands
C+	***The Barbarian Invasions***	**Canada**
C	*Želary*	Czech Republic
D	*Evil*	Sweden

Unlike the popular *jidaigeki* films of Akira Kurosawa and others featuring super-samurai who can cut down ten sword fighters in one battle without suffering a wound, Yoji Yamada, one of the world's most prolific directors, set out to make a realistic period drama about a low-ranking warrior, his struggles and frugality, and do so "without any lies." ***Twilight Samurai*** (*Tasogare Seibei*) is that film, about Seibei, an indebted but still committed vassal who labors to raise his two young daughters after the death of his wife. He's forced into an uncompromising situation in which his lord orders him to kill Yogo, the clan's crazy captain of the guard. Seibei reluctantly takes the assignment and challenges the arrogant, brutish Yogo using what amounts to a fake bamboo sword. Even so, he succeeds in his mission and later becomes part of the movement that transformed the *Bushido* Code to more of a business culture at the beginning of the 1868 Meiji Restoration. *Twilight* in the title has two meanings: Seibei's coworkers consider him dull and rather vacuous; second, the story takes place in the "twilight" of Japan's still-revered feudal-authoritarian period. In giving this Japanese action film a robust A, it's worth noting that the author is somewhat biased, as demonstrated by high rankings for other *jidaigeki* fare—starting with *Rashomon* (1952)—whether nominated or not. So much for objectivity. Four of Yamada's films were submitted for consideration for ceremonies in 1987, 1989, 1997 and 2004, but only *Twilight Samurai* received a nomination. The two-hour-and-nine-minute film cost an estimated $5 million to make and opened November 2, 2002, and in New York City April 23, 2004.

Twin Sisters (*De Tweeling*) from the Netherlands is another film rooted in the devastating consequences of World War II's European Theater. It's an epic story about two sisters separated at six, Anna to reside with mean-spirited relatives in Germany and Lotte to live, first at a Swiss sanatorium to recover from tuberculosis and then with a kind, wealthy Dutch family. Anna toils, Cinderella-like, on a muddy pig farm; Lotte learns to play the piano. Part II: The war is on the cusp and the two girls meet again, but Lotte loves a Jewish lad and Anna a Nazi-loving blacksmith, which doesn't go well. Anna eventually marries a young German soldier, an SS officer, who is immediately sent to the front line in the Eifel region where he dies a "heroic" death. Part III: Many years have passed and the Bamberg sisters are now aged. They meet again at a Belgian health spa and are reconciled. As Deborah Young of *Variety* put it: "The most notable aspect of the film ... is its timely entry into the current debate about whether the German people were also victims of Nazism." As an older woman, Anna tells her sister: "I hardly knew anything about what was happening in Holland." Perhaps such a weighty thought was a heavy lift for the picture's creator, Ben Sombogaart, a director of television and children's films. Reviewer Peter Bradshaw ruthlessly wrote: "This tiring and cliché-ridden Second World War drama from Holland is such a quaintly period piece that it appears to have been developed in cold tea." Another critic, Richard Kuipers, opined that it would play well on the Hallmark Channel, with its weepy, soap-operatic quality. In other words, and as the same writer inferred, the two-hour-and-seventeen-minute film should never have been given any credit by the Academy. In any event, it received a B– in the survey. It opened December 12, 2002, and had a limited run in the U.S. beginning May 6, 2005. In the cast was Thekla Reuten as the young Lotte, who was also in *Everybody's Famous!* (2001).

"The history of mankind is a history of horrors," says Rémy, the cancer-ridden father and history professor who is central to the story of ***The Barbarian Invasions*** (*Les Invasions barbares*), Canada's winning satire in the 2004 Best Foreign Film competition. This Marxist-leaning Québécois nationalist speaks here of the slaughter of 200 million natives during the European conquest of the Americas, but he also could be speaking about what is happening at the time of his hospitalization, namely 9/11, or that of his own plight. His daughter is sailing on a yacht in the South Pacific, his long-suffering ex-wife is by his side but helpless, and his son, Sébastien, a rich trader who comes from London to Montreal to try to bribe union workers and health administrators to secure a private space for his father in an overcrowded hospital, is the water to his father's oil. Sébastien hates Rémy because of his early womanizing, but what he does for dear old dad is the stuff of filial love and respect: he uses his business prowess to inveigle the dying man's old and new academic friends and girlfriends to come to a lakeside cabin in Vermont to celebrate his life before he dies. The movie, directed by Denys Arcand who also was nominated for Best Original Screenplay, cost an estimated $3.8 million and premiered in France September 24, 2003. It opened in the United States March 5, 2004, and sold $3,432,342 worth of tickets. Arcand was also responsible for directing and writing *The Decline of the American Empire* (1987), *Jesus of Montreal*

A dying father (Rémy Girard) and his son (Stéphane Rousseau) reconcile after years of estrangement in Canada's *The Barbarian Invasions* (2003).

(1990) and a film that made the January shortlist, *Days of Darkness* (2008). Dorothée Berryman, a cast member, was also in *Decline....* While given positive reviews for its intelligent script and strong acting, the picture itself lacked quality in many filming categories and garnered a mere C+.

This year's entry by the Czech Republic, *Želary*, is, as critic A.O. Scott termed it, "another small-scale drama of life during World War II." It's beautifully filmed by Ondřej Trojan in his only submission and stars strawberry-blonde Anna Geislerová, who must marry John Wayne–like György Cserhalmi (never mind that he's 28 years her senior) to protect her assumed identity after she has narrowly escaped from a Nazi crackdown on Resistance fighters, of whom she is one. Now, as Hana, she travels by train and cart to the tiny village of *Želary* in rural Czechoslovakia where slowly but surely she transforms from a sophisticated nurse to a pleasant peasant and dutiful wife of the churlish Joza. We meet many of the interesting characters of *Želary* and participate in their deliberate, sometimes desperate way of life, and we feel for the villagers as they put up with Soviet military drunks and vicious SS men. It's a likable film, but it plods along and is a little confusing toward the end, rendering it only a C. The two-and-a-half-hour picture opened September 4, 2003, and was then in America for a limited time where it earned $329,723. Cserhalmi can be seen in BFF-nominated films *Hungarian Rhapsody* (1979), *Mephisto* (winner 1982) and *Hanussen* (1989). Also in the cast in a supporting role was the director's brother, Ivan Trojan, as well as Jaroslav Dušek (*Divided We Fall* (2001).

There's little redeeming value in the brutal Swedish submission *Evil* (*Ondskan*).

Basically, the well-named motion picture is about a bunch of thugs in an elite boys' school who go on a rampage for nearly two hours hazing underclassmen and punishing anyone who speaks out or gets in their way. It was made by Mikael Håfström, who is also known for his horror and slasher flicks both American and Swedish, and should there be any question, this was his only foreign-language submission to the Academy. The working-class hero of the picture, Erik, shows early signs of being "above" his "willowy, sneering aristocrats who flaunt their pedigrees and wealth as badges of their superiority," as Stephen Holden of the *New York Times* put it. But he eventually becomes pure evil himself and takes no prisoners. The hour-and-fifty-three-minute color movie is set in the 1950s but has a modern look and feel about it, not unlike *Rebel Without a Cause* but with more close-ups; it could have taken place at anytime, anywhere. It included Bjørn Granath—*Pelle the Conqueror* (1989) and *The Ox* (1992)—as the headmaster and among the thugs, Gustaf Skarsgård, who was in *Kon-Tiki* (2013) and, quite incidentally, played Floki in the *Vikings* TV series. Also in the cast was Filip Berg from *A Man Called Ove* (2017). *Evil* is evil and warranted the lowest grade of D in the survey. It was made for $2.29 million and debuted September 23, 2003, and then appeared in a limited, $15,280 run in the States starting March 10, 2006.

2005

B+	*As It Is in Heaven*	Sweden
B	***The Sea Inside***	**Spanish**
B	*Yesterday*	South Africa
B	*The Chorus*	France
C	*Downfall*	German

Lyrically named Daniel Dareus, a famous international musical conductor, suffers a heart attack and returns to his childhood home in the far north of Sweden in Kay Pollak's ***As It Is in Heaven*** (*Så som i himmelen*). Dareus, yearning to "create music that will open a person's heart" even in this remote area, involves himself with a church choir full of idiosyncratic, forlorn and neglected men and women and turns it into a class act. Pollak uses his talent to paint a picture rife with many fine character studies that include not only the choir members but their diverse spouses, the longtime preacher Stig and the lead actor himself, played by Michael Nyqvist best known for his lead role as Mikael Blomqvist in Stieg Larsson's *The Girl with the Dragon Tattoo* trilogy. *As It Is in Heaven* also offers extracurricular instruction in the art of singing, the protagonist, a true professional, offering his tiny choir conservatory-level training. All is well that ends well in this emotionally charged drama, enjoyable enough to extend a B+ and raise it above the year's winner. The two-hour-and-thirteen-minute motion picture was Pollak's second submission and only nomination. It cost $2.86 million and opened September 3, 2004, and then appeared briefly at the Seattle International Film Festival June 2, 2005.

Over the years, assisted suicide, or euthanasia, has become legal in the Pacific states, Colorado, Vermont, a county in New Mexico and by court order in Montana, but it's looked on as an abomination in many other states and parts of the world. A handful of European countries have permitted passive and active doctor-assisted euthanasia—Switzerland since the '40s—but in places like Catholic Spain, it's highly illegal. The 2005 winning foreign film, *The Sea Inside* (*Mar adentro*)—yes, from Spain—takes a dramatic look at both sides of the question. Rámon Sampedro, played with great charm and grace by Javier Bardem (Anton Chigurh from *No Country for Old Men*, really?), is a quadriplegic and has been imprisoned in his own body, in his room, for twenty-six years. Everyone around him—family, friends, a lawyer, a wannabe lover—adore him. But he wants to die; he's had enough. The movie plays through all the thematic possibilities a writer can muster until a solution is found. What's remarkable about this film is Bardem, the larger-than-life, manly Academy Award-winning supporting actor from *No Country for Old Men* (2008). As Stephen Holden of the *New York Times* wrote: "Mr. Bardem, acting above the neck (except in brief flashbacks and fantasies), creates a complicated male character, volatile and witty, with a poet's soul." The script is based on a true story. Sampedro died in January 1998 in a deliberate procedure that was taped and shown later on Spanish television. How he accomplished this should be left to the viewer to see. Although surprisingly fascinating and well done, the film merited only a B, relegating it to second place, despite the Academy's decision. The two-hour-and-five-minute motion picture cost $12.63 million to make by Alejandro Amenábar, his only submitted film, and debuted September 2, 2004. It did well in the United States when it opened March 4, 2005, raking in $2,086,345. Barden also appeared in *Before Night Falls* (2001) and *Biutiful* (2011), earning a Best Actor nomination for each; the multiple Oscar nominee *Skyfall* (2013); as well as Woody Allen's *Vicky Cristina Barcelona*, which won a Best Supporting Actress award for Penélope Cruz in 2008.

Known as an anti–Apartheid filmmaker, Darrell James Roodt cast Leleti Khumalo, 33, in the role of Yesterday, a Zulu mother dedicated to both her young daughter, Beauty, and her brutal, mine-laboring husband, a philanderer who has contracted AIDS and made his wife HIV-positive. She learns this after developing a serious cough that takes her many miles on foot to the closest medical clinic, where she is diagnosed and sent home with little more than a sympathetic pat on the head. She then travels to Johannesburg to confront her live-away husband about their plight. Unwilling to accept that he's given his wife the disease, he beats her. Nevertheless, when he finally goes home to die, his wife builds him a "clinic" out of scraps of metal and wood and cares for him. Understanding her own fate, she prays that at least she'll live long enough to see Beauty start school. This is *Yesterday*, the South African nomination for the 2005 prize, which deserved a B. It runs an hour and a half and opened September 3, 2004, thereafter appearing in various American film festivals, New York City November 17, 2005, and on television eleven days later. It was Roodt's second submission but only nomination. Khumalo appeared in two English-speaking multi-nominated films: *Hotel Rwanda* (2005) with three and *Invictus* (2010) with two.

In the beginning, *The Chorus* (*Les Choristes*) seems like another morality play about a school for wayward boys wherein bad things happen, sometimes because of the general bullying but also because of a draconian headmaster and system. This changes when a do-gooder professor arrives. It's post–World War II rural France and the new guy is a frustrated musician and composer who slowly, through love rather than the rod, converts the kids, young and older, into angelic singers as good as the Vienna Boys' Choir. (The voices of these rough-and-tumble kids were just a little too sweet, frankly.) In any event, the acting by Gérard Jugnot as the teacher was fine, if understated. This hour-and-thirty-seven-minute film rated a B, perhaps because of a lack of originality. It reminded one of the 1988 Louis Malle award-winning picture *Au Revoir les Enfants*, which happened to star one of this film's cast members, François Berléand, who also was in *Camille Claudel* (1990) and boasted 215 acting credits to his name. *The Chorus* was Christophe Barratier's only directorial submission and cost the producers $5.77 million, though it made $3,629,758 in the United States alone after it opened in Los Ange-

Yesterday (Leleti Khumalo) comforts her daughter Beauty (Lihle Mvelase) in the film *Yesterday* (2004), by Darrell Roodt.

les December 22, 2004. The movie, also with a Best Original Song nomination, debuted originally in Belgium March 17, 2004.

Remember the 1973 English film *The Last Ten Days* starring Alec Guinness, of all people, as Adolf Hitler? Well, **Downfall** (*Der Untergang*), complementing the same subject, was Germany's Oscar entry for this year, and it really fell on the Germans to tell the detailed, unembellished history of the final days in a Berlin bunker of the Führer, Eva Braun, their German shepherd Blondi, Joseph and Magda Goebbels and the Goebbels' six children. The screenplay is based on several sources, but one in particular, the memoir of Hitler's secretary, Traudl Junge. She witnessed the deterioration of the grotesque group in the dark, claustrophobic warren under the garden of the Reich Chancellery between Hitler's 56th birthday on April 20, 1945, and April 30 when the adults committed murder and suicide as the Russian army approached. Oliver Hirschbiegel, who claimed to observe the strictest authenticity in this his only nominee of two submitted films, showed the inner circle warts and all, an element considered somewhat controversial in that it attempted to humanize the "little band of monsters" perhaps too much. Hitler is played with aplomb

Joseph Goebbels (Ulrich Matthes) kills his wife Magda (Corinna Horfouch) in *Downfall: Hitler and the End of the Third Reich* **(2004), the dramatization of what transpired in the** *Führerbunker,* **April 30–May 1, 1945.**

by veteran actor Bruno Ganz and Eva Braun by Juliane Köhler, the wife in the 2003 BFF *Nowhere in Africa.* The two-hour-and-thirty-six-minute picture was filmed at a cost of $17 million in purposely tight quarters at Bavarian Studio, and to augment the realism, the actors used little or no makeup. The C picture opened September 8, 2004, and in the U.S. April 8, 2005, where it earned $5,501,940. Six actors had chops from other BFF nominees: Köller, of course; Ganz in Iceland's *Children of Nature* (1992) and *The Baader Meinhof Complex* (2009); Julia Jentsch, the lead in *Sophie Scholl: The Final Days* (2006); and Alexandra Maria Lara, also appearing in *The Baader Meinhof Complex,* as well as the American film *The Reader* (2009), which garnered five Oscar nominations including a win for Kate Winslet (Ganz was in that film, too, as well as another Oscar-nominated film from 1979, *The Boys from Brazil*); and finally, Matthias Habich, also in *Nowhere in Africa* (2003), and David Striesow of *The Counterfeiters* (2008).

2006

A–	*Sophie Scholl: The Final Days*	German
B+	***Tsotsi***	**South Africa**
B+	*Joyeux Noël*	France
C–	*Paradise Now*	Palestine
D	*Don't Tell*	Italian

Not far into the German film **Sophie Scholl: The Final Days** (*Sophie Scholl: Die letzten Tage*) the two protagonists distribute piles of anti–Nazi leaflets in the hallways of the University of Munich's main building. It's a heart-throbbing moment—dramatized in part by the soft pounding of drums in the background—because we know that Sophie and her brother Hans, if caught, will be summarily executed. After classes have let out, they almost make it to safety before a low-level toady, a janitor, fingers them on the crowded staircase and they are arrested by the Gestapo. Sophia Magdalena Scholl was a real person, and the story is a recounting of the last two days, in February 1943, of the 21-year-old student-activist who was a member of the White Rose nonviolent resistance group that dispensed propaganda against the Hitler regime. She is interrogated, shown to a barren cell, and just when it looks like she will be freed, orders come down to hold her. As close as she comes to freedom, the vicious arm of Nazi law finds flaws in her elaborate alibis and within two days she is dead. As noted by critics, this two-hour film, directed by Marc Rothemund in his only submission, is more a police procedural than a thriller, but even so, you're on the edge of your seat nearly all of the time. The script was taken, mostly verbatim, from interrogation and court records. The beautifully filmed entry garnered an A−, elevating it a step above the winning film. It opened February 24, 2005, and in New York City February 17, 2006, garnering $676,167 in a brief run. Among its cast were Julia Jentsch of *Downfall* (2005), as Sophie, and Alexander Held, with 165 acting credits, who also was in *Downfall* as well as *The Baader Meinhof Complex* (2009) and the American-made blockbuster *Schindler's List*, which had twelve nominations and seven wins including Best Picture in 1994.

Tsotsi is a simple story about murder, kidnapping, vengeance, an emotional change of heart and retribution. The 2006 winner from South Africa features a young *tsotsi* (gangbanger, in urban Afrikaans slang) who, while engaged in a carjacking in an upscale neighborhood of Soweto, discovers he also has kidnapped a 3-month-old baby boy. At a loss of what to do with the infant, he enlists at gunpoint the help of a nursing mother who later is able to convince him to give it up to its parents. Much of the film is devoted to the young street thug's transformation—recalling his early youth with a dying, therefore unresponsive, mother and a cruel father—from a life of violent crime to emotional pain, awareness and outright contrition. How the picture concludes has little bearing on the whole, made more obvious by the fact that the DVD viewed included two alternate endings. But one can guess what they are. This "best" movie competed extremely well against two other films and earned a B+. The film cost about $3 million to make and opened December 23, 2005, and again for a respectable $2,912,363 run in the United States beginning March 31, 2006. It's an hour and thirty-four minutes long.

Fraternizations occurred frequently during times of war, especially on special occasions such as Christmas, but were rarely publicized. Several are known to have taken place along the Western Front during World War I between the German soldiers and their adversaries from England, Scotland and France, and while *Joyeux Noël*, the French nominee for 2006, represents one of these strange gatherings, it's actually a compilation of several documented fraternizations that took place during Christmases between 1914 and 1916. These acts were seen as "worse than mutiny" by the higher-ups, but epitomized the "live and let live" notion of many of the troops who, after all, were conscripted to fight. The film itself, in color, is well done and in many cases heart-rending, especially as the two sides take a timeout on Christmas Day to bury their dead, many of the corpses having lain in the no-man's-land divide between the close-by trenches for days or weeks.

Directed by Christian Carion in his only submission, the hour-and-fifty-six-minute film, which merited a B+, cost an estimated $22 million to make and opened November 9, 2005. It appeared at the American Film Institute (AFI) film festival November 11, 2005, and for a limited—albeit a profitable $1,050,445—run in the U.S. starting March 3, 2006. Among the cast were Benno Fürmann of *In Darkness* (2012) and Diane Kruger, who appeared in Quentin Tarantino's *Inglourious Basterds* (2010), which vied for eight statuettes including Best Picture and won one for Best Supporting Actor in Austrian-German Christoph Waltz.

One of the most controversial films to garner Academy acceptance was the Palestinian product ***Paradise Now***, about the recruitment as suicide bombers of two young West Bank Arabs. The motion picture, five years in the making, concerns forty-eight hours in the lives of Said and Khaled, best friends from youth, who go through the detailed process of preparing for their mission, including video-taping their good-byes and glorifying Allah and their cause, before their clandestine entry into the Israeli state to carry out their nefarious deeds. Both believe two angels will snatch them up to paradise upon their successful martyrdoms. How they go about their prep work is straightforward, almost documentary, in the able hands of director and co-writer Hany Abu-Assad, a Levantine Arab himself, who had one other submission and nomination: *Omar* (2014). Three years before, Palestinians had submitted a film for Oscar consideration but it was rejected on the notion that Palestine was not a country. Rules then stated that only countries with viable governments could submit foreign films to the Academy, this despite the fact that in 1990, Puerto Rico, a *territory* of the United States, was allowed to offer *What Happened to Santiago.* The rules were relaxed for this picture in

Khaled (Ali Suliman, *left*) and Said (Kais Nashef) scramble to safety during a cat-and-mouse chase between the two suicide bombers in *Paradise Now* (2005).

2006, but groups opposed to its glorifying—or at best referring to—suicide bombings demanded the feature be disqualified, which it was not. (It also *won* a Golden Globe in the same category.) The hour-and-a-half movie at times is engaging, but it's for the most part mediocre. This C– movie opened September 7, 2005, in Belgium and November 18, 2005, in the States, earning there $1,452,402. One of the cast members, Lubna Azabal, stars in *Incendies* (2011).

"The darkest of dark horses," said one critic in describing the Oscar chances of **Don't Tell** (*La bestia nel cuore*) from Italy. The movie is about a conflicted woman with a sinister secret from her childhood that triggers nightmares. She wants them to go away before the child she's carrying is born. The protagonist, Sabina, travels to America to see if her brother can shed light on her troubled past and learns that he shares her experiences and pain. Meanwhile, an attractive blind woman is smitten by the straight Sabina, who goes out of her way to find a lesbian substitute for her friend. The film is slow and plodding with more emotional twists and turns than a daytime soap opera, which it best resembles, and warranted an unabashed D. The two-hour picture is the product of debut director Cristina Comencini, who wrote the novel it's based on with the better title: *The Beast in the Heart*. It cost $8.17 million to make and opened September 9, 2005, and in America March 17, 2006, in a limited run that yielded a mere $27,105.

2007

B	*The Lives of Others*	Germany
B	*Pan's Labyrinth*	Mexico
B	*Days of Glory*	Algeria
C–	*Water*	Canada
C–	*After the Wedding*	Danish

Much of the buzz for the 2007 BFF Oscar centered around Mexico's *Pan's Labyrinth*, and it was an especially well done film, garnering six Oscar nominations. But it wasn't the Spanish-language picture that took the big prize, but Germany's entry, **The Lives of Others** (*Das Leben der Anderen*). It's not difficult to appreciate the intricacies, the superb acting and the affecting script about the Staci of 1986 GDR (East Germany) and how it dealt not only with its victims and suspects, but with itself as well. Where many dramas of this kind end abruptly on a sad note, this film goes a step or two farther and shows what happened to the immediate participants (from both sides) after the Berlin Wall fell in 1989 and the secret police was reduced to a "Visitors Welcome" museum of documents and other records that gave away the Staci secrets. This German entry by Florian Henckel von Donnersmarck, in his only submitted film, deserved the Oscar it received, even though its B ranking tied it with *Pan's Labyrinth* and Algeria's contribution, *Days of Glory*. The two-hour-and-seventeen-minute film cost $2 million to make and premiered March 15, 2006. In America, where it opened March 30, 2007, it earned a spectacular $11,284,657 on its first run. Two members of the cast appeared in other BFF contenders: Ulrich Mühe was in *Schtonk!* (1993) and Martina Gedeck was in *The Baader Meinhof Complex* (2009).

The late critic Roger Ebert called ***Pan's Labyrinth***, the 2007 runner-up from Mexico, "a fairy tale for adults," and it does, indeed, have an R-17 rating. Oscillating between the brutal reality of Fascist Spain during World War II and classical mythology, *The Labyrinth of the Faun* (*El laberinto del fauno*), as its Spanish name translates, is about 11-year-old Ofelia, who enters a strange, dark but enchanting stone labyrinth representing the underworld. She's led in by a mantis-type human creature, just as Alice discovered her netherworld thanks to a sprightly, absentminded rabbit. Ofelia, in part, is escaping from the realities of her sadistic, militaristic stepfather. The creatures she encounters in the maze welcome her as a long-lost princess. She becomes constrained to make choices against authority through challenges and ordeals, the stated purpose of writer-director Guillermo del Toro, who had one other submission. His rich and magical perspectives and application of innovative makeup, costumes, CGI and animatronics created a visual spectacle unlike any other film, reflected in the $15.93 million price tag. This is a motion picture the Academy loved, voting top honors in Cinematography, Art Direction and Makeup and further nominating it for Original Screenplay and Musical Score. Its B grade demonstrates the truly subjective nature of such a ranking system. Even so, Ebert wrote that this hour-and-fifty-eight-minute picture "is one of the greatest of all fantasy films." Maybe he's right. The motion picture opened October 11, 2006, and then in the United States January 19, 2007, where it earned an outstanding $37,623,143. In the cast was Ariadna Gil, the lead in *Belle Époque* (1994).

Algeria boasts five nominations since its first in 1970, when *Z* won Best Foreign Language Film. Three of the nominated films were products of Rachid Bouchareb's direction. He's a Frenchman of Algerian descent, and ***Days of Glory*** (*Indigènes*)—his

The Pale Man, with eyes on his hands, is awakened when Ofelia consumes two grapes in Guillermo del Toro's fanciful *Pan's Labyrinth* (2006).

second of three nominees, the others being *Dust of Life* (1996) and *Outside the Law* (2011)—was a World War II film compared in quality and content to Steven Spielberg's multi-Oscar-winner *Saving Private Ryan* (1999) and Edward Zwick's *Glory* (1990). It's about a diverse group of *Indigènes*, North Africans who fought for France, believing for the most part that as colonial soldiers it was their duty. Exceptional battle scenes seen from dirt level are a mark of excellence and the outstanding screenplay paints an honest, sometimes controversial picture of how these patriotic troops were treated by their French leaders for whom they served with honor. A.O. Scott of the *New York Times* wrote: "It is a chronicle of courage and sacrifice, of danger and solidarity, of heroism and futility, told with power, grace and feeling and brought alive by first-rate acting. A damn good war movie." Yes, and well worth its B in a year of competitive entrants. The two-hour film cost $17.11 million and opened in France September 27, 2006, and for a limited time in America February 16, 2007. The cast included Roschdy Zem and Sami Bouajila, both in *Outside the Law*, and Mélanie Laurent who was in the Tarantino vehicle, *Inglourious Basterds* (2010), which also had several nominations including Best Picture. Altogether, Bouchareb had five submissions that made to the Academy.

Water, as the astrological sign, represents emotion, feelings, purification. And these can be the bases for action, or reaction, as illustrated in the Hindi-language motion picture appropriately named **Water**. It's the third of a film trilogy that began with "Fire" and "Earth" by progressive director Deepa Mehta, seen as controversial in her country to the extent she was forced to complete it, after a substantial delay, in Sri Lanka—hence the reason Canada was chosen as the submitting country. She did have another submission via India, but it wasn't nominated. *Water* is about an 8-year-old widow (that's right: *widow*) named Chuyia, who is sent to an ashram, or nunnery, in 1938 to live out the rest of her life, as was the custom. She befriends an older widow, Yalyani, who is being pimped out to help fund the spiritual center. The two become *reactive* rebels. Mehta's film is symbolic in another way: India in the late 1930s was starting to emerge from the traditional fundamentalism that had shaped society for centuries. *Purdah*, or child marriage, was not only acceptable but *expected* for young girls, and still is in some quarters. Mahatma Gandhi, who fought against *purdah*, is also credited with bringing India into the last century. In *Water*, Mehta explores the rapidly changing roles of women in contemporary Indian society with her trilogy, according to *A Short History of Film* by Dixon and Foster. The hour-and-fifty-seven-minute feature attempts to exemplify the battle between modern and medieval ways. It's an interesting film, but not spectacular. The acting is good, especially by the youngster, Sarala Kariyawasam, a Sri Lankan. The direction is credible and Mehta's humanistic, realistic approach has been compared to the early films of India's foremost director, Satyajit Ray. A C– film, it opened in Canada November 4, 2005, and in India March 9, 2007, after a $3,222,857 four-month run in America, starting May 26, 2006.

Usually films with "wedding" in the title are happy, fun, comedic romps. Not Denmark's **After the Wedding** (*Efter brylluppet*), which explores the deep human emotions of four principal characters. Lead actor Mads Mikkelsen (Jacob)—known for *A Royal Affair* (2013), *The Hunt* (2014) and TV's *Hannibal*—runs an orphanage in India and sometimes travels to his home country, Demark, to obtain funding from multimillionaire Rolf Lassgård (Jørgen)—also known for *Under the Sun* (2000) and *A Man*

Called Ove (2017). While there, Jacob is invited to attend the wedding of the philanthropist's daughter, played by Anna. Arriving late, he sits in back of the chapel, but the betrothed's mother, Rolf's wife Helene, notices him and realizes he's an old flame and that her daughter, the one getting married, is the product of a one-night stand she had shared with the man. Sounds a little coincidental, perhaps a reason the picture has been labeled a melodrama. Over the course of the two-hour film, however, the brooding Jacob is

Mads Mikkelsen appears as Jacob in a scene from Susanne Bier's *After the Wedding* (2006).

united with Anna, reconciles with Helene and chooses between life in Denmark and India, where he has left an 8-year-old boy he's raised since infancy. There's little good to say about this rather severe and complicated film by Susanne Bier, although it does have its moments. It received a C–. Bier had three submitted films and two nominations, including the 2011 winner *In a Better World*. This film debuted February 24, 2006, and in the States May 11, 2007, where as of July 6 of that year it had garnered $1,526,359 in ticket sales.

2008

A	*Mongol*	Kazakhstan
A–	**The Counterfeiters**	**Austria**
C	*Katyń*	Poland
C–	*12*	Russia
C–	*Beaufort*	Israel

A Marvel Entertainment film ***Mongol*** is not. But Kazakhstan's 2008 nominee for a foreign Oscar is definitely about a superhero—at least one in the making—for the subtitle of the film is "The Rise of Genghis Khan." It's the product of Russian filmmaker Sergei Bodrov, who wrote, produced and directed *Mongol* and contrived an action-packed, blood-soaked motion picture about Khan's early life. Given the name Temüjin (meaning "of iron") in northeastern Mongolia in 1162, the boy at 9 is taken by his father to find a bride and becomes smitten by a 10-year-old girl named Borte. When his father dies, he inherits a slew of enemies, and with the help of Borte, he sets out to eventually unite all the tribes that reside between today's China and Siberia. The movie, made by Russia, Germany and Kazakhstan but submitted by the latter, is not for everyone; those squeamish about gouts of blood, ferocious swordplay and fierce battle scenes should be forewarned. But it's a highly entertaining two hours and five minutes, with outstanding cinematography on the steppes of Inner Mongolia and the Central Asian republic

Genghis Khan made his mark in history by uniting the tribes of northeastern Asia into the Mongol Empire. *Mongol* **(2007) relates the story of the early life of Temüjin, who became the Great Khan.**

of Kazakhstan. It is also well acted and deserved an A, which propelled it past the winning entry. *Mongol* cost an estimated $20 million to make. It opened in Russia September 20, 2007, and in the United States July 4, 2008, where over a two-month first run it garnered $5,701,643. Two Bodrov features were submitted by Kazakhstan with this one nomination, and another called *Prisoner of the Mountains* (1997) also got a bid via Russia.

Adolf Burger waited twenty years to write his book *The Devil's Workshop*. **The Counterfeiters** (*Die Fälscher*), an Austrian submission, tells the story of a contingent of talented forgers sent to a Nazi concentration camp to produce £136 million worth of phony banknotes so authentic looking they avoided detection until the end of the war. The intention of Operation Bernard was not to use the bogus bills to bolster the Third Reich war effort as much as flooding Western economies with fake notes to create economic chaos. Director Stefan Ruzowitzky took Burger's book and later firsthand accounts and melded them into his Holocaust tale, stating that, in many cases, fact was stranger than fiction and had to be incorporated into the screenplay. The acting in this carefully scripted drama is exceptional and Ruzowitzky took special pains to make every character three-dimensional, each with his own quirks and talents. The center of the hour-and-thirty-eight-minute film is Salomon Sorowitsch, branded "the King of Counterfeiters," a ruthless crook more interested in staying alive than practicing his moral duty as a Jew. Burger, the character, is drawn as a sort of antithesis, searching for ways of sabotaging Operation Bernard, since he believes doing the devil's work to exist, enjoying extraordinary privileges unimaginable to other camp inmates, and feeling pride of accomplishment are simply beyond the pale. Even so, for the most part, this is another

World War II survival film, but one of the better ones. The film cost an estimated $5.53 million to make and was Ruzowitzky's second submission and only nominee. It opened in Germany March 22, 2007, and in America April 18, 2008, where over four months it earned $5,484,715 in its first run. This is a great picture, but only an A– nominee, which dropped it a notch below the film the survey selected for top honors. Among its cast were David Striesow, who played in *Downfall* (2005), and August Diehl, who was in Quentin Tarantino's *Inglourious Basterds* (2010), which garnered eight nominations including one for Best Picture.

Katyń is a devastating film, again centered on a series of incidents during World War II. Caught between two diabolical dictatorships, the Nazis on the West and Soviets on the East, citizens of Poland had nowhere to turn in 1940, just months after the invasion of their sovereign homeland. Thousands fled, but as the first scene of the film symbolically depicts, many were trapped on a bridge between the two brutal armies. In reality, more than 22,000 Polish policemen, troops and officers, many of them irregulars, as well as 8,000 members of the intelligentsia, were swept up and massacred in the forest called Katyń near Smolensk in Western Russia. But who did it? The Germans said the Russians; the Soviets claimed the Nazis. Over the years, each political authority in turn exhumed the bodies to prove the other side was to blame. When the USSR annexed Poland, it quashed any discussion about Katyń. Meanwhile, Andrzej Wajda, whose father was among the murder victims, decided to make this 2009 contender at the age of 82. Wajda took twelve years and $5.16 million to produce his epic, in part because of the lack of information kept secret until 1989 when Poland became free again, and also because he didn't know whether to concentrate on the crime or the lies that followed. He said he decided to go with both. The celebrated Polish director was responsible for two influential 1950s films, *Kanal* and *Ashes and Diamonds*, neither submitted for an Oscar. *Katyń*, which garnered a C, opened September 21, 2007, and in New York City for a three-month stay February 18, 2009. It runs a minute more than two hours. Wajda, one of the most prolific foreign directors, submitted nine films to the Academy of which four were nominated, including *The Promised Land* (1976), *The Maids of Wilko* (1980) and *Man of Iron* (1982). Maja Ostaszewska, who plays Anna, had small parts in *Schindler's List* (1994) with twelve nominations and seven wins, including Best Picture, and *The Pianist* (2003) with seven bids, including Best Picture, and three wins.

An admirer of Sidney Lumet's drama *Twelve Angry Men*, the 1957 black-and-white film based on Reginald Rose's screenplay as seen live on CBS's *Studio One* in 1954, might theorize the Russian remake of the movie under the title *12* left something to be desired. Lumet's version is considered by some, arguably, among the top ten films of all time. The plot is simple: Twelve jurors are deciding the fate of a man accused of murder, but one of them holds out; over time, and for various reasons, the other eleven panelists change their minds until the accused is exonerated. The Russian version is the same, but instead of a stifling, stuffy room, the scene is set in a wide-open and airy high school gymnasium, where director Nikita Mikhalkov uses space and camera angles to depict the deliberations. The $4 million picture runs long at two hours and thirty-nine minutes, but critics admire Mikhalkov's ability to keep it flowing. Even so, it only rates a C–. It opened September 20, 2007, and had a limited first run in the United States starting

March 4, 2009. Mikhalkov submitted five films, resulting in three nominations—this film, *Close to Eden* (1993) and *Burnt by the Sun* (winner 1995)—and one disqualification for tardiness. Cast member Roman Madyannov was also in *Leviathan* (2015).

Occasionally, a movie struggling for ultra-realism jumps the shark and drags on, like a wounded gastropod, to a wholly unsatisfactory conclusion. Such was Israel's **Beaufort**. It's about a contingent of Zionist soldiers charged with the responsibility of defending a remote outpost in southern Lebanon during the late-20th-century conflict with Hezbollah, despite the fact the bastion had long been deemed insignificant. Faithful to the cause, the troops hold Beaufort, around a 12th-century fort, through thick but mostly thin, which some would say also well describes the screenplay. Critics cite the many clichés of the film and liken it to an old-fashioned Aldo Ray, William Holden or John Wayne style of war film from the '50s. There are also some parallels to be drawn to superior films such as the 2002 winner *No Man's Land* from Bosnia and Herzegovina and an unsubmitted Israeli picture from 2009, *Lebanon*. *Beaufort*, a C– film, was Israel's seventh nominated film since *Sallah* in 1965 and the first of four selected within five years. The director, Joseph Cedar, had four submissions, including one other nominee, *Footnote* (2012). *Beaufort*, at two hours and eleven minutes, cost an estimated $2.5 million to make and opened March 1, 2007, and January 18, 2008, in the States. Critics criticized the Academy for nominating *Beaufort* over another film, *4 Months, 3 Weeks and 2 Days* from Romania, definitely a greater piece of work. So it goes.

2009

A	*Departures*	**Japan**
B	*Revanche*	Austria
B	*The Baader Meinhof Complex*	Germany
B	*Waltz with Bashir*	Israel
C	*The Class*	France

The Oscar winner in 2009, **Departures**, received mixed, even polarized, reviews. For example, Roger Ebert liked the Japanese film, called it "lovely" and "well-made," while A.O. Scott of the *New York Times* wrote that it was "overlong, predictable in its plotting and utterly banal in its blending of comic whimsy and melodramatic pathos." It's the story of a 30ish Japanese musician who falls on hard times and takes a job he thinks involves travel. It turns out to be an undertaker's position, based on the Japanese ritual of *nokanshi* (encoffinment) in which the corpse is carefully and respectfully bathed and dressed for cremation in view of the family. Daigo, the protagonist, has a loving wife, Mika, who recoils when she learns of his new profession, as do others in the community who know him. But he carries on, even when Mika leaves him. He learns the trade and becomes a master under the tutelage of the company owner. Reviewers cited as negatives the predictability and sentimentality of the film, while others noted the humanity in the picture and how death of a loved one brought out the best in family and friends observing the ritual. Even so, upon two reviews it was a no-brainer to give this two-hour-and-ten-minute film a solid A and concur with the Academy members who chose it as the year's Best Foreign Film. It was director Yojiro Takita's only sub-

In *Departures* (2008), Masahiro Motoki (*left*) and Ryoko Hirosue, playing husband and wife Daigo and Mika Kobayashi, quarrel over Daigo's occupation of ceremonially preparing bodies for cremation.

mission and opened September 13, 2008, following up with a run in America starting June 19, 2009, which resulted in a gate of $1,542,503. One of the cast members was Tsutomu Yamazaki, who appeared in *Kagemusha* (winner 1981).

Götz Spielmann, writer, director and producer of Austria's entry **Revanche,** said of shooting film in confined spaces that it was "simple, precise, elegant and natural." He might as well have been describing the movie itself. An ex-con-turned-handyman falls in love with a Ukrainian prostitute who, like him, works in a seedy brothel owned by a sleazy man who wants to raise her prospects to a higher-paying hotel room in exchange for sex. The couple wants *revanche*, which can mean either "revenge" or "a second chance," and to flee, but to do so he must first rob a bank for escape money. All goes well until a foot patrolman happens across the getaway car with the woman inside, waiting. Her beau arrives; he forces the cop onto the pavement and drives away, but during the escape, the policeman fires a series of shots at the fleeing car. End the setup. What transpires from here makes this film a top contender, because Spielmann takes the cast into a new realm of character-driven drama: Nothing too artsy—somewhat *noir*—but one is inextricably drawn to their emotions, which at various times and among other things include grief, respect, desperation, loneliness, discovery, connectedness, adultery, empathy and forgiveness. A minute over two hours long, *Revanche* received a well-justified B. It was Spielmann's third and only successful submission to the Academy and opened in Austria May 16, 2008. It also had a run in New York City starting May 1, 2009. Andreas Lust from the multi-nominated, including Best Picture, *Munich* (2006) was in it.

There is likely little fiction in Germany's submission for this year, **The Baader Meinhof Complex**, though it plays like an action-prison-court drama and entails, in almost comprehensive documentary style, how a ruthless group of young terrorists managed to wreak chaos from Stockholm to Mogadishu over a seven-year period and beyond. The film tells the story of the Red Army Faction, which attempted to bring West Germany to its knees in the 1970s, and although failing and resulting in the end for most participants, it left death and destruction in its nefarious path. While overly long at two and a half hours, the color movie by Uli Edel in his only submission has a good cast, not the least of whom is veteran actor Bruno Ganz (*Downfall* 2005) as the top policeman on the case, Horst Herold, who tries to get into the head of the many members of the ultraviolent gang. The B feature cost an estimated $29.44 million to make and opened September 25, 2008, and three days later in Los Angeles where it collected $476,270 in a brief run. Other actors worth noting were Martina Gedeck, who was in *Lives of Others* (2007), and Moritz Bleibtreu, in *Munich* (2006), nominated five times including Best Picture.

For a time, the author demurred on seeing **Waltz with Bashir** (*Vals Im Bashir*), the nominee from Israel, in part because it was an animated war film, which does not easily compute. It's about an incident that took place during the Lebanese Civil War in which Palestinian refugees were mass-murdered during the Sabra and Shatila Massacre of 1982. The action was carried out by a Christian faction shortly after their leader,

The only animated feature nominated to date, *Waltz with Bashir* (2008), is a dynamic portrayal, often in chromatic contrasts, of the Lebanese Civil War.

Bashir Gemayel, was assassinated. Director Ari Folman, with two submissions and one nomination, filmed the feature as a documentary, but except for explicit newsreel footage at the close of the movie, it was entirely, and uniquely, animated for an estimated $1.5 million. The feature takes us through the process of selective memory, post-traumatic-stress disorder, in which participants or observers of violent acts forget or abbreviate details of what they have seen to protect themselves from nightmares and hallucinations of war. A number of these soldiers are sought out and interviewed by Folman, himself a caricature in the film. The animation process was significant in that it allowed the viewer to see what the interviewee related, and was accomplished using techniques Folman and his staff perfected, including the use of real subjects to "act out" gestures and lip movements. These were applied by a computer application that broke them down into animated body parts and facial expressions, adding a sense of realism to otherwise simple, black-outlined figures. Color, often duo- or trichromatic, played an important part as well, as did the use of high contrast. The title comes from a scene during a violent street fight in Beirut in which a solder grabs an FN MAG 58 machine gun and waltzes to a Chopin tune into harm's way, dodging bullets while posters of the dead Bashir Gemayel look on, an attempt to illustrate the absurdity of war—for this is, after all, an antiwar film of the first order. It opened in Israel June 12, 2008, and later garnered $2,283,276 in the United States. It received a middling B in the survey. One wonders now why other animated foreign-language films have been passed over for BFF consideration—among them *The Triplets of Bellville* and *The Illusionist* by Sylvain Cholmet. *Persepolis* (2008) was submitted by France but didn't make the cut.

　　　A sort of *Blackboard Jungle* in a multicultural learning environment, **The Class** (*Entre les murs*) appears to be a documentary based on *Between the Walls*, the fictionalized autobiography of the teacher, François Bégaudeau, who indeed plays himself in France's Oscar contribution. Director Laurent Cantet, in his only submission, cast Bégaudeau and a handful of gifted middle-school students in diverse roles that he, and indeed the teacher-writer, envisioned as convincing and real, which to a degree they are. Nearly all of the motion picture takes place in the classroom in the poor, multiethnic 20th Arrondissement of eastern Paris. Michael Phillips of the *Chicago Tribune* said Cantet's "indirect dramatic approach," using a small crew and three handheld video cameras, presents a microcosm of life that might take place in classrooms anywhere in Western Europe, Canada or the United States. "Between these walls an unruly world of conflict, frustration and joy comes to life, whether the topic at hand is a part of speech or a troubled student's fate," he wrote. Seen by some as controversial given the growing immigrant problems in Europe, *The Class* has its moments, especially when focused on individual students, but warranted only a C. It lasts two hours and eight minutes and premiered September 24, 2008, and six months later earned $3,766,595 during a run in the States.

2010

A	*El Secreto de Sus Ojes*	**Argentina**
A–	*Un Prophète*	France

B+	*The White Ribbon*	Germany
B−	*The Milk of Sorrow*	Peru
B−	*Ajami*	Israel

The eyes have it. This second Argentine Best Foreign Language Film winner, **The Secret in Their Eyes** (*El Secreto de sus ojos*), not to be confused with the American remake, is part whodunit and part rekindled love, both over a timespan of roughly twenty-five years. Benjamin, played with verve by Ricardo Darín—*Son of the Bride* (2002) and *Wild Tales* (2015)—visits his old boss and former lover, Judge Irene Menéndez Hastings, played by Soledad Villamil. He has a proposal to reinvestigate a 1974 murder, having written a novel based on the case and believing those convicted of the crime were innocent. Writer-director Juan José Campanella closely focuses on eyes, since Benjamin's premise stems from what he can see in the eyes of a man who shows up frequently in the woman's photo album; his vision is always on her, he notes. The search is ongoing and elaborate; ratiocination is afoot in the complex investigation. When Benjamin is unable to locate the suspect, he goes to the dead woman's husband, thinking he might shed light on the affair. The widower admits to him that sometime after his wife's naked, blood-streaked body was found lying on the floor next to a disheveled bed, he found the murderer and shot him dead. That might spell the end of the search, but there's more to the story, and much of it includes the growing romance between Benjamin and Irene. *Secret ...* was a surprise winner at the 2010 Academy Awards with two highly regarded films right behind it. The two-hour-and-nine-minute drama deserved a rare A. Campanella also directed *Son of the Bride*, his only other submission. This film, costing $2 million, opened August 13, 2009, and appeared in America the first time May 21, 2010. Also starring was Pablo Rago from *The Official Story* (winner 1986). An American version appeared in 2015.

Power is at the root of the brutal prison film by Jacques Audiard called **Un Prophète** (*A Prophet*), the French runner-up. It's about a nominal criminal, 19-year-old Malik, an Arab thrust into the brutal jaws of prison where Cesar and his Corsican gang control every phase of life. In order to become accepted, he must undergo a violent initiation; failure could result in death. He looks to the warden for help, but this is Cesar's world—Corsican vs. Moslem—and he's forced to comply. He succeeds, but barely. Now, as Cesar's protégé, Malik learns to survive and at one point even carries out the Corsican's bidding. The name Prophet stems from a scene later in the film in which a wiser, more proficient Malik, to avoid a confrontation with an angry Arab out to assassinate a Corsican turncoat, correctly predicts a collision with a deer on the road. Because of his prescience he's given the appellation and becomes one of them, one of several twists in the multilayered story. The film, in color as dull as a prison wall, is well acted and riveting. It did not win but was a firm runner-up with an A− rating. The two-hour-and-thirty-five-minute movie was Audiard's only submission and cost his producers $16.7 million. It opened August 26, 2009, and in the U.S. March 26, 2010, earning $2,084,637 in three months. It also starred Niels Arestrup, who appeared in two multi-Oscar-nominated films, *The Diving Bell and the Butterfly* (2008) and *War Horse* (2012); neither was up for foreign-language film, but the latter was on the Best Picture list.

The puzzling German contender **The White Ribbon** (*Das weiße Band—Eine* *deutsche Kindergeschichte*) takes place just before World War I in a small, puritanical northern town in which strange accidents befall various villagers. No one is to blame; no one that we know of is accused; no one seems to be responsible. It's a whodunit without a just conclusion. It involves children, members of a choir who are abused by adults without culpability, and has been described as a parable about the rise of Nazism where the civil population grows more suspicious and

Leonard Proxauf, as Martin, is inconsolable, having been abused in Michael Haneke's drama *The White Ribbon* (2009).

fearful but ultimately accepts what comes along without involvement or complaint. The acting is superb, especially by a handful of youngsters. There's one poignant moment when young Gustaf, played by Thibault Sérié, learns about death from his sister, Anna, and is upset when told it's inevitable. Director Michael Haneke used the starkness of black and white to add an element of mystery to the story, even though it's said he filmed it originally in color. It garnered a B+. One of the more prolific international directors, Haneke submitted five films via his native Austria and one from Germany and received two nominations, including the winner for 2013, *Amour*. He also had one feature disqualified because it failed to satisfy a rule at the time that required the language of the script be that of the country of origin (Haneke's Austrian film *Caché* was in French). This one cost $16.2 million to make and opened September 17, 2009, coming to the United States March 5, 2010, where it sold $2,222,647 worth of tickets. It runs two hours and twenty-four minutes. By the way, narrating the story was Ernst Jacobi, who also starred in the 1980 winning film *The Tin Drum*.

The Milk of Sorrow (*La Teta Asustada*), Peru's first nomination for the foreign award, is a slow, languorous, allegorical drama about the consequences of the '80s civil war between the Maoist Shining Path guerrillas and the newly elected government. Many women in the affected areas outside the capital, Lima, were raped, some numerous times and mostly by controlling government soldiers, resulting in unwanted pregnancies and severe trauma. The hour-and-thirty-four-minute film, one of Claudia Llosa's two submissions, features the heart-wrenching story about a mother and her daughter. It opens with the dying mother, Perpetua, singing a haunting song in the Quechua language about her plight. According to folklore, a woman raped during pregnancy will pass the legacy down to the child through breastfeeding. So frightened is the daughter, Fausta, that she crams a potato into her vagina to protect her from sexual assault and refuses to remove it, though the twelve years of terror are now over. Augmenting the deliberate pace and subject matter was the cinematography illustrating the arid landscape of the Andean foothills and poorer pockets of suburban Lima. The picture was critically more popular outside of the South American country but enjoyed art-house praise in the United States and Europe. It received a B– ranking and opened in Spain February 13, 2009, and in New York City for one month starting August 27, 2010.

In a year with great nominees, along comes *Ajami*, an Israeli venture showing the seedier side of conflict in a shabby neighborhood of Jaffa, south of Tel Aviv. This is a multilayered film where plotlines are sometimes drawn from different perspectives, which can be annoying at times. What is important are the points of view of the two director-writers, Scandar Copti, an Israeli Arab, and Yaron Shani, an Israeli Jew. As *New York Times* critic A.O. Scott points out, "[T]he film is acutely insightful about the social divisions within Israel, but it examines them without scolding or sentimentality." The storyline centers on two Moslem boys who live in the slums of Ajami and stumble upon a package of drugs. Both need money and decide to sell it, one to finance his mother's marrowbone transplant surgery and the other to pay his way out of a blood feud brought on by an assassination gone bad. Copti and Shani peopled their only submission to date with interesting, diverse characters who keep the film vibrant and moving along through five separate stories, culminating in a surprising finish. This two-hour-and-four-minute motion picture merited a B–, but even at that it settled at the bottom of the pack in a strong field. It opened in Israel September 17, 2009, and in New York City February 3, 2010, where over more than six months it earned a mere $621,240.

2011

A–	*In a Better World*	**Denmark**
A–	*Incendies*	Canada
B+	*Outside the Law*	Algeria
B	*Biutiful*	Mexico
D	*Dogtooth*	Greece

A sizable number of female directors have brought foreign films to the big stage at Oscars. Among them is Susanne Bier of Denmark with *After the Wedding* (2007) and now the 2011 Oscar winner, *In a Better World* (*Hænven*). Critics were not very kind to this winning movie, dismissing it as "dull-witted," too ethical and a "crushing bore," according to David Edelstein of *New York* magazine. The drama is curiously appealing, if complicated, and deserved its award and an A– grade. Basically it's about two boys, one who's tormented at school and the other, his friend, who becomes his protector but is a kind of bully himself. The former's dad, a doctor, commutes between his medical clinic in Africa, where he tends to a tyrant so large and important he's called "Big Man," and Denmark where he wimps out in a confrontation with an intimidating auto mechanic. You get the picture. This is a movie of parables, sometimes involving brutal conflict. The film, a minute short of two hours long, opened August 26, 2010, and in the States April 1, 2011, where it took home $1,007,908 in ticket sales. In it was Trine Dyrholm from *A Royal Affair* (2013). Bier had a total of three submissions. Incidentally, nineteen women directors have been honored in this category, and only a few of them as multiple nominees; for that matter, only one female director has won the Best Picture

Award over the years—Kathryn Bigalow in 2010 for *The Hurt Locker*—although four have been nominated.

With many of the characteristics of a dark Greek tragedy, ***Incendies*** tells in flashbacks the convoluted mystery of a Middle Eastern Christian mother who dies of a stroke in her adopted home in Canada. In her will, she charges her twin adult children with the responsibility of going to an unnamed Arab country and seeking out and delivering letters to their long-lost father and older half-brother. After many twists and turns, the film finally arrives at a shocking conclusion. Written and directed by Denis Villeneuve and based on a modern play of poetic monologues, the picture was Canada's entry. It was filmed in color; included French, Arabic and a smattering of Canadian English; and contained all the elements of a Sophocles drama and then some. It was an A– film, aligning it with the winner. The mother was played by Lubna Azabal, also in *Paradise Now* (2006). Villeneuve submitted four films for consideration, this being his only nomination. It was made for an estimated $6.8 million and earned that and $57,096 more when it appeared in the United States. It runs two hours and eleven minutes.

Outside the Law (*Hors-la-loi*), the 2011 Algerian entry, takes place during the French-Algerian War. It's a solid, well-directed, superbly acted motion picture by Rachid Bouchareb, who also directed the 2007 Algerian nominee *Days of Glory* using many of the same actors. (He also did *Dust of Life* in 1996.) In this film, three brothers, who grew up in poverty after the French confiscated their hereditary land through the *Code de l'Indigénat*, harbor strong resentment that leads ultimately to their participation in the Front de Libération Nationale (FLN) during the late 1950s and early '60s. This is a

Messaoud (Roschdy Zem) is one of three Alergerians in France who want revenge during the French-Algerian War in Rachid Bouchareb's *Outside the Law* (2010).

political film—more so than a historical drama—as seen from the anti-colonialist point of view, and it was received controversially when first shown in France September 22, 2010. The title comes from a secret branch of the French intelligence service called La Main Rouge (the Red Hand), which existed to do whatever was required to stop the insurgency, whether through normal police channels or "outside the law." The picture also was criticized for stretching truths through artistic license, leaving some viewers to consider myths the film perpetuates as historical fact. This B+ drama cost Bouchareb $28.81 million to make and runs two hours and eighteen minutes. The cast includes Jamel Debbouze, who was in *Amélie* (2002), nominated for five Oscars including its BFF win, and *Days of Glory*, together with his costars here, Roschdy Zem and Sami Bouajila. Bouchareb's creative output gave the Academy five submissions in toto.

Alejandro González Iñárritu had the hot hand when it came to directing films in the second decade of this century; few could approach his record for wins and nominations. **Biutiful**, Mexico's candidate, received two nominations including one for Best Actor in star Javier Bardem, already a Supporting Oscar winner for *No Country for Old Men* (2008). Bardem plays Uxbal, a hard-luck guy in Barcelona, Spain, who takes care of his two children, Ana and Mateo, while eking out a living as a con artist, importing, housing and overseeing illegal Chinese workers fabricating fake Gucci bags to sell on the streets. His wife is bipolar and sleeps with his brother. If that weren't enough, he's recently discovered he's dying of prostate cancer and pees blood now and then. For Uxbal, life is *not* "biutiful," as young Mateo spells the English word. But he struggles on, taking the best care he can of his Chinese factory workers, his kids and Ekweme, his Senegalese nanny and lover. Iñárritu has been on a tear since he received seven nominations including Best Picture for *Babel* (2007). Since then, besides *Biutiful*, his film *Birdman (The Unexpected Virtue of Ignorance)* (2015) received nine nominations—four of them wins including Best Director and Best Picture—and *Revenant* (2016) with twelve nominations—three of them wins including Best Director, Best Original Screenplay and Cinematography. That's some fancy moviemaking. He's also responsible for BFF nominee *Amores Perros* (2001). *Biutiful*, worthy of a B, runs two hours and twenty-eight minutes and opened in France October 20, 2010, and two days later in Mexico. On February 4, 2011, it opened in the United States and took away $5,100,937. Barden, by the way, appeared as well in *The Sea Inside*, which won the foreign-language Oscar in 2005, and garnered a Best Actor nomination for *Before Night Falls* (2001).

At first, it's difficult to understand what is happening in **Dogtooth** (*Kynodontas*), the strange, surreal Greek contender. A father, mother, two teenage daughters and a son about 20 years old are confined to an estate, teaching and learning absurd words, myths and concepts. Only the father is allowed to leave. In one of the early scenes, Dad brings home an employee, a young female security guard who must travel blindfolded. She's there for the express purpose of proffering her body to the son for sexual release. In long set pieces, the children go through the motions of surviving this arcane environment, accentuated by the milky color in which director Yorgos Lanthimos, in his only submitted film, chose to shoot. They don't know any better, only that they must remain on the property until they lose a "dogtooth," or canine, which appears impossible unless something violent takes place. The film offers several bizarre twists that border on depravity, and as a critic noted, one might want to take a hot shower after watching it. How this "very strange and rather pornographic" film ever became an Oscar nominee is beyond reason, and it truly rates a low D when all is said and done. The hour-and-thirty-four-minute drama opened November 11, 2009, and in New York City June 25, 2010, where it was chiefly ignored during its short run.

2012

A–	*A Separation*	**Iran**
A–	*Monsieur Lazhar*	Canada
A–	*Footnote*	Israel
B–	*In Darkness*	Poland
C	*Bullhead*	Belgium

Emotions run strong in the 2012 Oscar winner ***A Separation*** (*Jodaeiye Nader az Simin*), enhanced by the knowledge this family-driven, docudrama by Asghar Farhadi takes place in modern theocratic Iran. No politics here, although the patriarchal, religion-centric society is always present. Basically, a man must choose between accompanying his wife abroad and caring for his aged father, who has advanced Alzheimer's. A judge forces them to separate to avoid conflict that would involve their 11-year-old daughter. Meanwhile, seeing as the man is employed, he hires a woman on hearsay to come and care for the father while he's at work. She is pregnant, and the work is intense, but also she has to commute two and a half hours each way by public transportation to get to the man's apartment. She also brings her curious young daughter with her and maintains her Islamic convictions, though they run contrary to a woman's taking care of the private aspects of a man's well-being. That's the set-up. What occurs brings all the characters, including the caretaker's out-of-work, hot-tempered husband, into sometimes violent confrontation bordering on manslaughter and he-said-she-said conflict that only a judge supposedly can unravel. A winner, it deserved an A–. The film cost an estimated $500,000 and opened in Iran March 16, 2011, then in America December 30, 2011, where in less than six months it garnered $7,098,492. Farhadi saw four of his Iranian films submitted for consideration, and besides this winning entry, *The Salesman* (winner 2017) got the nod. Two actors, Shahab Hosseini and Babak Karimi, appeared in both pictures.

In an interview, director of Canadian Oscar nominee ***Monsieur Lazhar***, Philippe Falardeau, said he had a dream that his characters spoke English instead of French, negating the feature as a legitimate Best Foreign Language Film. For all intents and purposes, the venue elementary school—which essentially could be anywhere—happens to be in Montreal, Quebec, and the participants there are reared to speak Québécois. Based on a one-man play, the film is about an Algerian seeking asylum in Canada after his wife and daughter are murdered by terrorists in an apartment fire back home. He has a tragic background. He applies for a substitute position after a sixth-grade teacher has hanged herself in her classroom, sending the school and her students into profound grief. The school pulls out all the stops to help the kids, with well-meaning psychologists on hand for counseling and attempts to mum all talk about the death. Bashir Lazhar, however, has other intentions. For the most part, the film is touching and endearing.

Simon, played by Émilien Néron, stands out in a classroom, guilt-ridden by the suicide death of a teacher who hugged him, in *Monsieur Lazhar* (2011).

The little girl, Alice, is outstanding, as is the young boy, Simon, who believes he caused his teacher's death when he claimed she had kissed him instead of proffering the actual, albeit forbidden, hug. The emotions—not only of the two 11-year-olds but of Lazhar, the students' parents and the principal who is caught between her own belief in the emigrant and her school board—are major strengths of the film. *Monsieur Lazhar* received a fervent A–, tying it with two others in competition, including the winner. Faladeau's only submitted film opened in Belgium March 7, 2012, and for a limited time in the States April 13, 2012, collecting $2,009,041. It runs an hour and thirty-four minutes.

The Israeli film ***Footnote*** (*He'arat Shulayim*) raises a tantalizingly moral question: When it comes to honor, what's more important, the country's largest prize for a lifetime of achievement or family? Father and son academes compete for the Israeli Prize. The father has lost out twenty times during his thirty years as a professor, but now he appears to have, finally, been named a recipient. Even so, their last names, being the same, are mixed up by an administrator in the minister's office and the wrong man, the father, is publicly announced as the winner. It turns out the man responsible for naming prize recipients has something academically against the father and believes his work over time has been haphazard and weak—a mere and literal footnote, found in someone else's book—but the son disputes this assessment and strikes a life-changing, Faustian deal with the man. In an uncomfortable scene that takes place in a broom-closet-sized room, seven people gather around a table barely large enough to fit there to tell the son it is he who has the prize, not his father. However, he angrily denounces the decision and even physically attacks the older decision maker. Up to this point, the film has levity, with a full-score orchestration to keep it light, even humorous. But it takes a turn after the son discovers the mistake. The music becomes morose, more weighty, and the dialogue practically dries up in the heavy, ponderous and juxtaposed scenes. The older man appears to freeze up during interviews and praise; the son can't seem to bring himself to tell him the truth and takes it out on his immediate family members and one young student. The hour-and-forty-seven-minute film is supposed to be humorous, and at times it is, in an awkward way, but the actors play it straight, with a certain amount of pathos. It fits more into the realm of farce: so many things left unsaid, the error, the misunderstanding. The father is grossly reticent (a form of autism is suggested) and blows off two interviews and a congratulatory colleague. Created by Joseph Cedar, who also made *Beaufort* (2008) and had two other submissions denied, *Footnote* premiered May 25, 2011, and later in New York City, March 9, 2012, where it gained $2,007,451 in receipts. The entry deserved an A– though it did not win.

At the end of ***In Darkness*** (*W ciemności*), Poland's submission for this year, a small band of Jews emerges from gloom and doom, squinty and bewildered by the sun after fourteen months of hiding from Nazis in the sewers of Lvov. It's a literal and thematic conclusion to a story that was filmed in claustrophobically tight quarters by handheld cameras. Even the topside scenes are gloomy and obscure, showing drifts of winter snow or shadowy, close and almost lightless ghetto hovels. This is not a film for the faint of heart, unless one is inured by the preponderance of European features and documentaries, many of them nominated over the years for Oscars, that tell of the horrible plight of Jews during the Holocaust. Despite its BFF bid, this movie—two hours and twenty-five minutes long—was not overwhelmingly accepted by film critics, and some of the reasons have already been mentioned: too dark, too close, too melodramatic, too Holocaustic. It was the product of Agnieszka Holland, who previously made *Angry Harvest* (1986) and a deserved foreign film candidate but without nomination, *Europa, Europa* (1992). Among the cast were Benno Fürmann of *Joyeux Noël* (2006) and Jerzy Walczak, who appeared in *Son of Saul* (winner 2016). It earned a B– in a year with several A– entries. It opened in New York City for a run of five months December 9, 2011, garnering $1,038,733.

Bullhead (*Rundskop*) is another dark, brooding movie, about extreme violence committed to a child and its effect on him. Made in Flanders, this Belgium nominee is haunting in its moody aspects, the film filtered to almost obfuscation in indoor scenes, as though the main character, who fills himself with illegal hormones sold on the black market to farmers for their cattle. He does so to build his body and offset a crime he endured when he was about 10. The music, too, is constant and ominous, like the man at any time is going to fly apart. It's also a crime drama, centered on the "hormone mafia" of Belgium. Sinister characters fill the screen, meeting around tables, at a race track, on a rural dike, in a muddy dock loaded with containers. Stephen Holden of the *New York Times* called it, an "overly complicated ... impressive but deeply flawed" first film by Michaël R. Roskam. Michael Turan of the *Los Angeles Times* wrote that it's "an intense, shattering film, a confident and accomplished, punch-in-the-gut debut ... that starts out like a thriller and turns into a disturbing tragedy in an unlikely and unexpected key." It was a C– motion picture, but the acting in parts deserved an A; therefore, it received a compromise C+. Matthias Schoenaerts stars. He was in *Daens* (1993) and the more recent mainstream film, *The Danish Girl* (2016), which garnered four nominations and a win for Best Supporting Actress (Alicia Vikander). It cost $2.67 million and debuted in Belgium February 2, 2011, and for a first, short appearance in the States starting February 17, 2012, in which it earned $42,070. It runs two hours and nine minutes.

2013

A–	*Amour*	**Austria**
B	*War Witch*	Canada
B–	*A Royal Affair*	Denmark
C	*No*	Chile
C–	*Kon-Tiki*	Norway

The 2013 Best Picture contender **Amour**, which won Best Foreign Film, is a superbly made Austrian film, with exceptional acting and direction from Michael Haneke. The drama rated an A– and deserved the foreign-language award, but not Best Picture, for which it was nominated. That went to *Argo*. *Amour* is about two retired music teachers in their 80s who epitomize the strong bond of love that comes with a long and fruitful marriage. She suffers a stroke and over time slowly declines, leaving her husband forced to cope with an untenable situation. Haneke paced the film notably slowly, but unlike many films that crawl along, one never feels impatient. It was, after all, about two aged people plodding along through life. Notable was his *in situ* filming style with a stationary shot that could last up to several minutes—there were no hand-held cameras moving helter-skelter, or none that caught the viewer's eye. It was filmed very playlike with few actors, more dialogue than action, and done so almost entirely in the couple's upper-floor French apartment, whose windows revealed through diaphanous curtains the mansard roofs and iron balconies so characteristic of Parisian side streets. The ending is a sad one, but not sentimentally so. Some reviewers have called it a tearjerker, but we are aware of what will happen because of the first scenes and we are prepared for it. *Amour* received five nominations in all: for Best Picture, Actress, Directing and Original Screenplay, as well as the win in this category. Haneke has had six films submitted to the committee since 1990, with two nominations including also *The White Ribbon* from Germany (2010), and one candidate, submitted by Austria, disqualified for using French instead of German; by the time *Amour* came around, the rule on this had changed. *Amour*, two hours and seven minutes long, opened in Germany September 20, 2012, and, for the first three days in America, December 19–21, 2012, it brought in $225,377. It cost the producers $8.9 million. Star Emmanuelle Riva was nominated for Best Actress. She's also known for *Kapò* (1961). Her acting partner, Jean-Louis Trintignant, starred in three Best Foreign Language Film candidates: *A Man and a Woman* (1967), with a total of four Oscar nods including two wins; *Z* (1970), with five nominations and two wins; *My Night at Maud's*, with two nominations including language (1970) and writing (1971); and add to that list *Is Paris Burning?*

Georges Laurent (Jean-Louis Trintignant) calms his wife Anne (Emmanuelle Riva) in a tender scene from the 2013 Best Picture nominee and Best Foreign Film *Amour*.

(1967), with two nominations but none in the foreign film group, and *Three Colors: Red* (1995), which garnered three Oscar bids but not for foreign language. One other actor in *Amour* deserves mention: Isabelle Huppert, with more than 130 acting credits among the finest female actors in the world, appeared in *Coup de Torchon* (1983) and *Entre Nous* (1984); she also got passed over for *Elle* (2017), which garnered a Best Actress Oscar nomination for her, as was the case with her win in that category at the Golden Globes. But ironically, while the film received a foreign-language win there, it wasn't even considered in the BFF January shortlist. Go figure!

Compelling, heartrending, yet glossed over to give it a PG rating, **War Witch** (*Rebelle*) is about Komona, a 12-year-old girl who's kidnapped by rebels in the Congo, trained to kill anyone including her parents on orders of Grand Tiger, but allowed to survive on true grit. Contemplative with limited dialogue, the Canadian-sponsored film in French and Lingala is set in the jungles of sub-Saharan Africa and transitions into a kind of love story. Komona, as she progresses to 13, finds a battle buddy a little older than she, an albino named "The Magician." They break from the rebels and find creative ways of eluding detection. Eventually, the boy asks the girl to marry him. She tells him her father cautioned her not to accept a marriage proposal unless the man gave her a rare white rooster. The two set off to find the rooster, and they do, in a colony of similar albinos. They are, at least in their eyes, now essentially married. It's a sweet partnership, but they become separated and she is recaptured by Great Tiger. She is impregnated at 14 and, heavy with child, manages to escape again, this time to return to her village for the express purpose of burying her mother and father. On the way, she has the child, a boy she names "Magician." The film, which deserved a strong B, was a product of Kim Nguyen in his only submission. It cost $3.5 million to make and opened in the Netherlands August 23, 2012, and in New York City for a three-week run starting March 1, 2013.

The Danes have long been effective in manufacturing great films. Proofs of this: *Babette's Feast* (1988), *Pelle the Conqueror* (1989) and *In a Better World* (2011), all BFF winners. In the Age of Enlightenment of the 18th century, Denmark alone prided itself on being unenlightened and feudal, according to that country's entry, **A Royal Affair** (*En kongelig affære*), directed by Nikolaj Arcel in his only submission. The "mad monarch" Christian VII took the sister of Britain's King George III as his wife, and from almost the first moment, they hated each other. Even so, they were able to conceive the future Frederick VI for posterity. This movie, so full of angst and melodrama, is a beautifully costumed, set-designed and filmed period piece around the love triangle that existed between the bully, mentally-disturbed king, his German private physician, and the woman who came to love the doctor and have his child. This didn't go over well with Christian, his dominating council, the king's nasty stepmother, or the hoi-polloi who were manipulated by the court into taking action. The cast includes Mads Mikkelsen, who was in *After the Wedding* (2007) and *The Hunt* (2014); Trine Dyrholm from *In a Better World* (2011); as well as up-and-coming star Alicia Vikander, who while not prominent in any other BFF nominee, still has chalked up a reputation acting in Academy Award nominees such as *Anna Karenina* (2013), *Ex Machina* (2016) and *The Danish Girl* (2016), for which she won Best Supporting Actress. *A Royal Affair*, garnering a B–, opened March 29, 2012, and in America November 9, 2012, where it earned $1,545,726 during a relatively limited run.

No is fiction but has a quasi-documentary feel to it, submitted by Chile. It is shot, often in low light or indoors, with vintage Sony video cameras and incorporates stock footage from the brutal dictatorship of General Augusto Pinochet (1974–1990). The point is that Pinochet, who earlier had overthrown the Marxist regime of Salvador

The liaison in *A Royal Affair* (2012) involves the mad Danish King Christian VII's wife Princess Caroline Matilda, played by Alicia Vikander, and his physician, Johann Friedrich Struensee, performed by Mads Mikkelsen.

Allende, bowed to international pressure to hold a referendum to decide whether he should stay in power for another eight years. To many, it was a sham contest. To others, it was an opportunity to get rid of him. Enter René Saavedra, played by Mexican actor Gael García Bernal, who like the *Mad Men* of television, works to sell products through advertising. The "Yes" and "No" sides to the referendum each would get fifteen minutes a day to promote their campaigns, and Saavedra, who appears more up to the difficult challenge than being anti–Pinochet, takes the No side. As a *New York Times* review by Manohla Dargis put it: "Rene helps the No activists wage war against one type of dictatorship, but an argument can be made that he represents another kind of tyranny, one in which freedom is reduced to freedom of consumer choice." The film is riddled with clichés and banal banter. One good scene shows police battling demonstrators with batons inside a confined office space. Among those beaten is Saavedra's estranged wife, a radical, but her husband, who witnesses the attack, seems apathetic, just as he appears to be toward the No campaign. It's a C movie. The hour-and-fifty-eight-minute drama was filmed by Pablo Larraín, who had three other submissions that did not make the cut and is also responsible for 2017 blockbuster and Best Picture contender *Jackie*. The film opened August 9, 2012, and again in the States on a limited run starting February 15, 2013, which brought in a remarkable $2,341,226. Bernal also appeared in *Amores Perros* (2001) and *The Crime of Padre Amara* (2003), as well as another Best Picture nominee, *Babel* (2007).

Norway's **Kon-Tiki** also does not measure up to the scale on which the true adventure, pitting men on a raft sailing the high seas for 101 days, was based. At the expense of sounding counterintuitive, since the famous Thor Heyerdahl story is indeed real (if his theory that Polynesia was populated by South Americans proved wrong), the film is wholly predictable from start to finish. What's more, the acting is stilted, the script banal, and it's easy to anticipate the sequence in which the writers prepared it—well stocked with whale pod sightings, gory shark attacks, massive thunderstorms and the obligatory gull that flies over the craft when land is near. This really is a technical movie and it should be praised as such. According to the DVD's "Extra," much, if not most, of the motion picture was filmed in CGI. Even the islands were painted in, as were layers showing postwar New York street scenes. The anatomical shark pulled up onto the raft by hand was kind of cool, as was the attention to detail to period clothing, products and props used in the film. But it was a C– nominee and a big disappointment from the community that helped shape Heyerdahl's legacy. Costing a whopping $16.6 million, the hour-and-fifty-eight-minute adventure was filmed by the directorial duo Joachim Rønning and Espen Sandberg, who together had one other unselected submission, and premiered August 24, 2012. After it came out in the United States April 26, 2013, it made $1,511,798. Cast member Gustaf Skarsgård was also in *Evil* (2004).

2014

B	*The Hunt*	Denmark
B	*The Missing Picture*	Cambodia
B–	*Omar*	Palestine

| B– | *The Broken Circle Breakdown* | Belgium |
| C | ***The Great Beauty*** | **Italy** |

Mads Mikkelsen, a tough guy in most recent films and Dr. Hannibal Lecter on television, becomes the hunted in the Danish contribution to the controversial 2014 Best Foreign Film competition, ***The Hunt*** (Jagten). The recently divorced kindergarten teacher's assistant is accused of pedophilia when a little girl, played brilliantly by 5-year-old Annika Wedderkopp, misinterprets a sexual comment passed on in jest by her brother and sets in motion a firestorm of indignation and sometimes violent reaction by the small town in which this bleak winter tale takes place. Captivating, well paced and socially instructive, the film, a B, is definitely worth watching and deserves to be among this year's seventy-six films vying for one of the five positions for Oscar. As a sidenote: The DVD Netflix sent had a brief alternate ending in direct opposition to the one portrayed in the released film, the latter frankly being the better of the two. The hour-and-fifty-five-minute drama, which cost $3.8 million to make, is the product of Thomas Vinterberg, who had one other film submitted without selection. It opened January 10, 2013, and during a limited run in the States between July 12 and September 27, 2013, earned $610,968. Mikkelsen has been in two other BFF movies: *After the Wedding* (2007) and *A Royal Affair* (2013).

The Cambodian documentary ***The Missing Picture*** (*L'Image manquante*) tells in poetic prose the story of how one boy witnesses the 1975 takeover of his country by the Khmer Rouge, who killed an estimated two million souls under the brutal dictator Pol Pot. Here is how the narrator described it:

The Hunt (2012), directed by Thomas Vinterberg, stars Mads Mikkelsen as a hunted, falsely accused child abuser in a close-knit Danish community.

> Sometimes, silence is a scream...
> A political film should unearth
> what it invented.
> And so I make this missing picture.
> I look at it.
> I cherish it.
> I hold it in my hand like a beloved face.
> This missing picture
> I now hand over to you,
> So that it never cease to seek us out.

The hour-and-thirty-two-minute motion picture is portrayed through stark black-and-white film records of the period, some assumed to have been resurrected from chemical nitrate destruction. But more important are the clay figures—hundreds of them—set in scale-model scenery to tell the story of the people, what they had to endure, how they survived or didn't, and what happened to them when Pol Pot was defeated. The quotation is that of narrator and filmmaker Rithy Panh, whose solitary voice throughout is sincere and moving but not doleful or pathetic. The film, not the usual sort of fair found in these awards, deserved a B. Panh had one other submission, but it was not selected. The movie debuted in Britain January 3, 2014, in Cambodia March 6, 2014, and in the United States March 19, 2014, but it was widely circulated among the international film festivals.

No one wins in **Omar,** a nominee from Palestine. For much of the first half, the film appears to dwell on the dichotomy of a controlling Israel over the new Palestinian Territories and the wall that serpentines along the border with the West Bank; indeed, the picture could be titled *The Wall*, since that twenty-six-foot concrete separation barrier, 440 miles long, serves as a reference point for the hour-and-thirty-six-minute drama. The movie by Hany Abu-Assad evokes other nominated Palestinian films, Scandar Copti and Yaron Shani's *Ajami* (2010) and Abu-Assad's *Paradise Now* (2006), that pit idealistic youth against the Israeli establishment. There is death, but it doesn't come as a suicide bombing; there is torture, which may or may not be realistic; there is pursuit, with over-the-top chase scenes through narrow byways of Nazareth and Nablus; and there is a love triangle. But there are no really good guys or bad guys; just people entwined on both sides through coercion, misinformation, misunderstanding, fear and naiveté. The last third of the film has more twists and turns than Nazareth's alleyways, but that allowed the product to escape from the clichés and mediocrities of its first two thirds. This B– runner-up cost $2.1 million to make and was one of only three submissions by Abu-Assad. It opened in France and Belgium October 16, 2013, and for a limited run in America February 21, 2014. In addition, it had a significant screening at the United Nations May 1, 2014.

"Will the Circle Be Unbroken?" Mother Maybelle Carter and her musical family expanded the bluegrass universe when they teamed with the Nitty Gritty Dirt Band in 1972 to record a two-record album with that title. It was quickly interpreted to mean continuance: of family, music, spirituality, life and Americana, even though the title song, "*Can* the Circle Be Unbroken," was composed by an Englishwoman in 1907. Meanwhile, we have Didier, a musician in Ghent, Belgium, who is in love with America and he loves quintessential American bluegrass music. He falls in love with a lovely tattoo artist, Elise, who becomes the center of his performing group, and they have a child they name Maybelle. Things could not be better—until the child, at 6, contracts cancer. The first half of this BFF nominee moves along smoothly, ambitiously, lovingly, until the title, *The Broken Circle Breakdown* (also *Alabama Monroe*), begins to manifest itself. Much of the second half borders on the melodramatic, causing the film to actually "break down" as it nears its conclusion, justifying its B– rating. Based on a play co-written by Johan Heldenbergh, who stars as Didier, and director Felix Van Groeningen, the hour-and-fifty-one-minute picture employs flashbacks in an unusual way: as the film progresses forward, the earlier scenes retreat farther back in time, reminiscent of a circle unwinding. It's quite effective. Groeningen's second submission and only nominee, *Breakdown …* opened in Belgium October 10, 2012, and during a run in New York City between November 1 and 15, 2013, it made $30,700. Among the cast with BFF chops were Johan Heldenbergh from *Antonia's Line* (winner 1996) and Jan Bijvoet from *Embrace of the Serpent* (2016).

There's a point in Paolo Sorrentino's ***The Great Beauty*** (*La grande bellezza*), which *won* the 2014 BFF award for Italy, where the protagonist, Jep Gambardella, is strolling along a canal, hands behind his back, as a small boat chugs by. The only person on board slow-turns to maintain a continuous bead on the unobtrusive, if well-dressed, man. It is the one time in this strange, almost Italian New Wave film when Jep, always the observer, is alone and being watched. Lengthy at two hours and twenty-two minutes (originally forty-eight minutes longer) and purposefully Felliniesque with circuslike characters and situations, the movie is as perplexing at times as *8½* (1963) and as sexy as *La Dolce Vita* (1962), to which it has been compared. But perhaps, it better resembles Alain Resnais' submitted but unchosen *Last Year at Marienbad* (1962) in its bewildering perplexity. That may be unfair, but to use comparisons to *8½*, there is more than a hint of Fellini's characters Guido Anselmi in Gambardella and Saraghina in Lorena, or is it Ramona? When the film begins with Louis-Ferdinand Céline's epigraph to *Journey to the End of the Night,** you know you're in for a strange ride. On a positive note, one thing Sorrentino and his cinematographer, Luca Bigazzi, did exceptionally well was compose a picture; *The Great Beauty* of this film was in its composition: murmuring birds, shots up luxury stairwells, literally colossal views of Rome and its many antiquities, and a bizarre rooftop scene that takes a page from Jerome Robbins' "Dance at the Gym" sequence in *West Side Story*, slowing down and obscuring the action for effect. In a year of controversial choices, the Academy might not have gotten this one right. There were better films nominated—indeed, there were better films *not* nominated, beginning with *Wadjda* from Saudi Arabia—so it gets a C and we move on. Sorrentino's only submission opened March 14, 2014, and cost $12.14 million. In a limited run in the United States leading to November 5, 2013, it collected a sizable $2,835,886.

---

*"Travel is very useful and it exercises the imagination. All the rest is disappointment and fatigue. Our own journey is entirely imaginary. That is its strength. It goes from life to death. People, animals, cities, things, all are imagined. It's a novel, simply a fictitious narrative."

2015

A	*Wild Tales*	Argentina
A–	*Leviathan*	Russia
A–	***Ida***	**Poland**
B	*Tangerines*	Estonia
C+	*Timbuktu*	Mauritania

In the opening credits of **Wild Tales** (*Relatos salvajes*), Argentina's 2015 contribution, director Damián Szifron is represented by a fox. No other animal will do, since the six separate stories he presented in his portmanteau masterpiece—all centered around revenge and retribution—were cunning, sly and clever, if occasionally predictable. Indeed, while most multistory feature films struggle to maintain balance and attention, this one works, in part, because all of the elements—acting, direction, cinematography, writing, sound and definitely music—mesh beautifully. To describe any of the six, roughly 20-minute set pieces would be a vast disservice to the viewer, since they build to unforgettable climaxes. However, note the way Szifron used his camera, beginning with a ground-level view of a young model crossing the floor of an expansive airline terminal, or a straight down image of a young bride, brilliantly played by Érica Rivas, standing at the edge of a hotel roof-garden restaurant, the camera tacitly suggesting a possible suicide attempt. Or, in the tale of the demolition expert, how his downfall begins with the successful and celebrated implosion of a line of tall grain silos in Buenos Aires. All of the *Wild Tales* have a strong black-comedic tone, and we feel that no matter how Quentin Tarantino or Rod Serling they may be, we can't help empathizing with the characters and vicariously enjoying their—as one friend put it—"delicious" retributions. It was worthy of a solid A, which placed it ahead of the winning film *Ida*. This macabre classic, Szifron's only submission, cost $3.3 million to make and pulled $3,079,012 from the States alone during a limited appearance between February 20 and April 26, 2015. It premiered in Argentina August 21, 2014, and runs two hours and two minutes. One cast member had previous experience in nominated foreign films: Ricardo Darín appeared in *Son of the Bride* (2002) and *The Secret in Their Eyes* (winner 2010).

Leviathan has several meanings, and in one of the four known films with that title, entered from Russia and chosen as a 2015 nominee, a few definitions apply: There's the sea monster account from scripture, for one, and what Webster called "a totalitarian state having a vast bureaucracy" for another. **Leviathan** is too big of a film for a simple accounting and, according to some reviewers, too complex in analyzing today's post–Soviet society for non–Russians to wholly appreciate. Andrey Zvyagintsev, the director, pulled off a coup of sorts. His two-hour-and-twenty-minute movie—a second submission but first nomination—was practically half-financed by the bureaucratic government of Vladimir Putin and given international recognition through numerous film festivals and awards, and yet it strikes hard at the corrupt, deadly and unwieldy regime that, for a long time, refused to allow it to be shown at home. Quoted in *Film Comment* magazine, Russian critic Anton Dolin said, "'Leviathan' is not merely a film; it's a statement." A few notes on the production: The film was masterfully pieced together, starting with opening scenes of sea and desolate landscapes that lead past capsized fishing boats, half-sunk and rotting, and large, empty fish-processing plants left unpainted and deteriorating. It's about a derelict town far in the north, about one man's struggle with the government represented by a corrupt, murderous drunk of a mayor trying to wrest control of the man's simple, hand-hewn home high on a barren bluff overlooking the harbor. There's a reason this falsely repentant official wants the land and is supported by the court of three women judges, one of whom cites laws and regulations chapter and verse like a salesman spewing caveats during a car commercial. There's violence; there's mystery involving death; there's an adolescent with an over-the-top bad attitude; there are important symbols of a decaying church used by youth as a place to smoke and consume forbidden alcohol; and there is plenty of drinking—another annoyance Russians possess while trying to allay the world's perception of their country's advancing decrepitude. Indeed, the acting could not be better, with a multitude of realistic scenes involving drunkenness the likes of which few have ever seen, given that most actors truly have trouble *acting* drunk when not actually under the influence. The film, albeit depressing and difficult at times, is a definite must-see, and it generated an A− when viewed on the big screen. Like *Wild Tales*, *Leviathan* also placed ahead of *Ida*, the winning Polish film. It debuted February 5, 2015, and in New York City December 25, 2015. One cast member, Roman Madyanov, was in a previous nominee: *12* (2008).

The Oscar winner for 2015, **Ida,** is a simple story with a complicated theme. Two women, blood relatives but opposites in every sense of the word, join in a road trip to find the graves of the film's namesake's murdered parents. Ida, a 19-year-old Catholic novitiate on the verge of taking her vows, learns from her aunt that she is Jewish. It is 1961, and the aunt is a no-nonsense, officious communist judge as well as a serious alcoholic and possible depressive. Despite their differences, they grow closer together as their journey continues, until a surprising turn of events changes everything. Director Pawel Pawlikowski, known for his seat-of-his-pants direction (and unstoppable Academy acceptance speech), wrote a rare full script for the hour-and-twenty-two-minute,

Ida (2013) stars Agata Trzebuchowska in the title role as a novice nun who goes by the name of Anna and is informed by her dissolute aunt that she's really a Jew.

black-and-white film and at times seemed to be paying homage to an earlier Polish director, Roman Polanski, whose *Knife in the Water* was a well-received 1963 Best Foreign Language Film nominee that made the young director an international star. Most of the shots in *Ida* were static; the cinematography involved exquisite panoramas of desolate, wintry Polish countryside on a screen as wide as 3:4-aspect allows. Often the subjects are only partly seen at the base of the panel, the top of their faces barely present, giving an eerie sense of mystery to the scene. It's a good movie, worthy of an A–, but not as good, according to the survey, as the two previously mentioned films. *Ida* was Pawlikowski's only submitted film and it premiered October 25, 2013. When it had its run in the United States in 2014, it garnered $3,826,455, no doubt in part because of its Oscar win.

Estonia's first-ever nominated submission for an Oscar was hardly Estonian at all, but most effective as an antiwar film, pitting the madness of raw conflict against the honor that draws combatants into it. *Tangerines* (*Mandariinid*) takes place in a muddy backwater of the remote Abkhazia region where Chechen mercenaries were fighting against Georgians in a 1992 civil war that had chased all but a few Estonian expatriates back home. Ivo is a tall, slender "Grandpa" who remains behind to help his compatriot neighbor, Margus, bring in a bumper crop of tangerines before the two warring sides, including Russians supporting Georgians, show up. But the war has already arrived, and in a brief skirmish just outside Margus' modest home, all are killed except one Georgian and one Chechen, who are hurt. The rest of the hour-and-twenty-seven-minute movie is about this pair of wounded soldiers, like two glowering boxers, convalescing together under Ivo's roof. It's also about how the Estonian, the good grandfather that he is, keeps them from killing each other. Over time, as each heals, they come to accept their fate and understand, with Ivo's guidance, how stupid war is. At one point in the picture, while they are feasting on *shashlik*, Ivo suggests they drink to the death, since the two combatants are likely to kill each other anyway, whether there or on the battlefield. Margus says, "I can't drink to death," and questions his friend's proposal. "It's their very mother. They are the children of death," Ivo states. "It's silly to make you sit at the same table." War is indifferent, Ivo implies. This is a solid, well-edited B film directed by Georgian Zaza Urushadze, who had one other film submitted without nomination from Georgia. Costing a mere $851,610, the picture was made in Russian and Estonian with English subtitles and earned a paltry $112,818 in the United States between April 17 and June 19, 2015; it opened in Georgia October 17, 2013, and in Estonia two weeks later. This was an unusual year in that two countries, Estonia and Mauritania (the next film up), were represented for the first time. This happened only once before, in 1995, when Cuba and Macedonia together received Oscar bids.

In the opening of *Timbuktu*, a gazelle dashes across a starkly beautiful sandscape, somehow evading multiple bullets fired from a Toyota truck full of Moslem extremists. "Tire it out first," shouts one of the men. It's a strong metaphor for this blunt, yet enigmatic, movie by Abderrahmane Sissako, who made it in his adopted country, Mauritania, for that country's (and Sissako's) first-ever BFF submission. It's fiercely anti-jihadist, drawing on true events in which Al-Qaeda-supported Tuareg and Libyan invaders seized most of northern Mali in 2012. But it shows a quiet resistance—at times brutally put down—from a diverse collection of brave women, one of them a touch mad. This takes place in the ancient university city, which despite the title oddly does not figure strongly into the motion picture. Seen at a local theater April 16, 2015, the nominee's cinematography was remarkable, but the acting from semi-professionals left much to be desired. There were a few graphic death scenes, but considering what we know about extremists' behavior in forcing their brand of Islam on a dissenting people, the film was notably absent of wanton mayhem and violence during its hour and thirty-seven minutes. A C+ movie, it opened in France December 10, 2014, and in New York City the following January 28 for a run that garnered $1,067,000.

2016

A–	*Son of Saul*	**Hungary**
B	*Mustang*	France
B	*Theeb*	Jordan
B	*A War*	Denmark
C+	*Embrace of the Serpent*	Colombia

Devastating is the best way to describe the 2016 winning film, **Son of Saul** (*Saul fia*), offered for consideration by Hungary. It opens with a medium, out-of-focus shot into a wooded area where men are laboring. In quickstep, a man comes toward the camera until his face, from the neck up, is fully in view. He is somber but alert, a middle-aged Jew who is part of an Auschwitz work detail of *sonderkommando*s, prisoners forced to help Nazis herd captives into the gas chambers, remove and burn their bodies, and clean up the dismal scene left behind. The handheld camera, in one long take riveted on the man's stoic face, follows him into the dingy death chambers where he goes straight to work on the newest trainload of Final Solution victims and discovers a teenage boy who somehow survives the hydrogen cyanide. Even so, the authorities immediately act to put him down like a rabid dog. It takes us awhile to learn that the boy is a son Saul fathered out of wedlock—or so he says—and most of the film is about his improbable efforts to find a rabbi, either among his own doomed group or the latest death-camp arrivals, to assist him in sanctifying and burying the child. As much as 80 percent of the film is focused on the man's face, but the screen ratio, albeit narrower than usual, provided enough disturbing peripheral scenes of blurred-but-distinguishable dead and alive naked bodies and fierce, gun-wielding Nazis to curdle one's blood. Saul, by the way, is played by Géza Röhrig, himself a converted Hasidic Jew, whose resolute face tells much about the man: his hopeless circumstance and his determination to take care of his son's body and perhaps survive himself. The director and co-writer is László Nemes whose debut feature film—with its use of Steadicam, close facial shots, diabolical off-screen sounds (dogs barking, gunshots, screams) and utter control—was highly sensory, innovative and a departure from normal shooting techniques. It merited an A–. The film was viewed in an eighty-seat theater just days after it won the Oscar. Sadly, there were only seven other people in the audience; as the credits rolled and everybody trudged toward the exit, one could easily see how moved each man or woman was. The hour-and-forty-seven-minute Hungarian winner cost $1.3 million to make and raised $1,776,814 in the United States alone during a limited run between December 18, 2015, and May 13, 2016. It originally premiered June 11, 2015. Among the players were two men who appeared in other BFF nominees: Sándor Zsótér acted in *Hanussen* (1989) and Jerzy Walczak of Poland had a part in *In Darkness* (2012).

If the 1994 winning film *Belle Époque* was a celebration of young girls finding freedom through sexuality, ***Mustang*** is its antithesis. This French submission, directed by Turkish-born Deniz Gamze Ergüven, is about five orphan sisters—all highly engaging and roughly ranging in age from 12-year-old Lale to 16-year-old Sonay—caught by a nosy orthodox neighbor lady who witnesses them marking the final day of school by frolicking in the surf with schoolboys. To her, they are sinners in the strict moral code rooted in Islam. The girls' grandmother and uncle, who are rearing them in a remote Black Sea village of northern Turkey, lock them up at home for the summer. They forbid the youngsters anything the tribal religious society would consider immoral, sensual, sexual or even fundamentally feminine. They escape their incarceration to attend a soccer match, but when they return, they're locked up again, this time with the windows and doors barred. Meanwhile, the babushka-like neighbors decide to teach them how to be wives in an effort to marry them off, and men of various ages and types are paraded through the house as marital candidates. Critic Christy Lemire explained that the Turkish-language film, acted for the most part by amateurs, "is patently designed to show how conservative morality, literally and figuratively, … imprisons women, equating natural development with sinful urges." Indiewire called the movie "a controversial 5-headed monster of femininity." *Mustang* also has been compared with Sofia Coppola's *The Virgin Suicides*, in part because the two pictures were debuts for the female directors, but this writer, bent on keeping it real with AMPAS nominations, couldn't help recalling the Penélope Cruz vehicle *Belle Époque*, although it served an opposing purpose. *Mustang*, at an hour and thirty-seven minutes long, rated a B for effort, acting and cinematography. It cost $1.79 million to make and opened in France June 17, 2015; it earned $835,318 during a limited run in America between November 20, 2015, and April 8, 2016.

Jordan's stunning desert region Wadi Rum, a World Heritage Site, has been filmed numerous times over the years: *Lawrence of Arabia* and more recently *The Martian* come to mind. Now the 2016 candidate, ***Theeb***, uses as its setting the wadi's red-earthed Valley of the Moon Protected Area. Described by debut director Naji Abu Nowar as a "Bedouin Western," the hour-and-forty-minute Jordanian motion picture takes place during the Arab Revolt 100 years ago. Thirteen-year-old Theeb, or Wolf, is the youngest of three orphaned brothers in a family of Bedouin pilgrim guides, an endangered species in 1916 when a fragile railway line ran between Damascus and the Islamic holy city of Medina. The controlling Ottoman Turks guarded the railroad, while the Arabs, operating under the auspices of the British military, tried to destroy it. The ever-curious Theeb and one of his brothers, Hussein, guide a British army officer to a water well only to be set upon by Ottoman marauders. Theeb and Hussein survive the attack but the latter is shot and killed the next day, leaving the nomadic boy on his own in the vast desert. Along comes Hassan, a gravely wounded mercenary, whose wound Theeb treats. The two team up on an arduous trek to an Ottoman station, little Wolf serving as the man's caregiver. It's at the remote station that the boy learns who Hassan really is, and Bedouin justice must be meted out. Acting, direction, cinematography, editing and, to some degree, music make this candidate a superior first film. It deserved a B. *Theeb* opened in the United Arab Emirates May 19, 2015, and for a limited, $282,152 run in the United States from November 6, 2015, to April 8, 2016.

Denmark allocated 20,000 peacekeeping soldiers to the war in Afghanistan, the most that country has committed to a conflict since World War II, according to Tobias Lindholm, director of the nominated docudrama *A War* (*Krigen*), his only submission. The picture—with as simple a story as its title—opens with a squad of battle-ready Danes tracking through unfriendly territory in Helmand Province when a young soldier is killed by an improvised explosive device (IED). Later, the same squad encounters a group of civilians in a nest of Taliban fighters and serious fighting erupts. Claus

"Theeb," which means "wolf," is a young Bedouin pilgrim guide during the Great Arab Revolt of World War II. Played by Jacir Eid Al-Hwietat, Theeb undergoes many trials within the vast expansive of Wadi Rum of Jordan (2013).

Pedersen, the leader, makes a fateful decision that costs the lives of eleven civilians. At the core of this heart-wrenching motion picture is how a combatant must react in a moment of total chaos while hamstrung by international rules and regulations that define circumstances, conditions, degree and manner of dealing with hostile situations. As Lindholm states, concerning soldiers' actions in the field, the Rules of Engagement make it "harder to do their job." In trying to explain how tough decisions are made, one of the squad members, Nagib Bisma, says, "You can't imagine what it's like out there." Pedersen's actions are called into question and he's brought back home to face charges. Interspersed between the raw scenes of war are vignettes of Pedersen's family, his harried wife, Maria, their daughter, Figne, and two younger children; the older boy, Julius, acts out at school, finding it difficult to understand and cope with the absence of his father. One startling moment in the film is when 7-year-old Figne is being tucked into bed by her father and asks, "Dad? Is it true you killed children?" The court setting fills the last third of the film and shows another kind of battle. Most of the picture felt like a documentary. This changed during the home-life scenes, perhaps because of their intimacy. One complaint was the use of a Steadicam in the courtroom where a fixed perspective would do just as well and without the distracting wobble. The hour-and-fifty-five-minute movie garnered a B. The picture opened September 10, 2015, and in the United States beginning February 12, 2016.

A spiritual journey of time and the river and a haunting study of the effects of colonialism in Amazonia serve to sum up ***Embrace of the Serpent*** (*El abrazo de la serpiente*) by Colombian writer-director Ciro Guerra in his third attempt at a nomination over eleven years. This entry tells the tale of conflict between aboriginal tribes and white intruders—in this case not soldiers or rubber barons but explorers and scientists. Using indigenous performers predominately speaking in their own native dialects or Spanish (there were actually nine languages spoken in the movie) and filmed on location along the border of Colombia and Brazil, the often mesmerizing, black-and-white movie relates loose interpretations of two separate events: the first the early 1900s when German ethnologist Theodor Koch-Grünberg explored the Yapura and Negro rivers with a back-breaking load of books and tools, and the second in the 1940s when botanist Richard Evans Schutes traveled there ostensibly in search of the elusive, sacred (and fictional) hallucinogenic yakruna plant. The link between them is a loin-clothed local guide and shaman named Karamakate—young, strong and levelheaded in his early days, but old, lonely and forgetful later on. The elder Karamakate is played by 71-year-old Tafillama Antonio Bolívar Salvador, whose own tribe is nearly extinct; notably, he was invited to share the Oscar celebration in Hollywood, quite a contrast to his own native habitat. Much of the two-hour-and-five-minute feature involved water—the river, reflective and gurgling or roaring, ever flowing toward the sea—or thick, almost impenetrable jungle. The opening credits played over the close-up view of a large anaconda giving birth to numerous young, seen as a symbol of fertility, original sin and, yes, colonialism. Film review compiler Rotten Tomatoes described the motion picture as "rich visually … a feast of the senses for film fans seeking a dose of bracing originality." Expecting a rather boring picture, one was surprised at the quality of photography, specifically involving the scenic splendor of the river, and the fundamental acting of the inhabitants, as well as neatly constructed parallel storylines—not the finest but tenable. The C+ movie premiered May 25, 2015, and received a limited run in the States starting February 17, 2016. Among the cast was Jan Bijvoet who appeared in the Belgian candidate *The Broken Circle Breakdown* (2014).

2017

B+	***The Salesman***	**Iran**
B+	*Land of Mine*	Denmark
B	*Toni Erdmann*	Germany
B	*A Man Called Ove*	Sweden
B–	*Tanna*	Australia

Best Foreign Film winner in 2017 ***The Salesman*** (*Forušande*) is classified by the International Movie Database (IMDb) as a thriller, and with an obvious homage to

Alfred Hitchcock (including reference to a shower-attack scene), one can see why. But it's much more than that. This is 21st-century Iran, after all, and while director and writer Asghar Farhadi has given us a glimpse into everyday middle-class life in Tehran, there are certain mores, cultural peculiarities and religious overtones apparent throughout. The title refers not only to the play the central couple, Emad and Rana Etesami, are performing at a small theater—Arthur Miller's *Death of a Salesman*—but also to the perpetrator of the attack, which being essential to the "mystery" of the film, we will leave there. More to the point, Farhadi examines his characters' marital and societal roles and the fact Emad, despite being a man of "culture" in a zealously faith-based, patriarchal world, slowly sinks to the level of primal vengeance as he searches for the man who assaulted his wife. Film critic Godfrey Cheshire III wrote that *The Salesman* is "a psychological and moral drama about how one man's anger and damaged self-image drive him to the brink of destroying the very thing he ostensibly most wants to protect: his marriage." The two-hour-and-five-minute feature—a B+ movie—opened August 31, 2016, and came to the States January 27, 2017, where it grossed $2,207,494 in less than two months. Farhadi refused to come to the United States for the Oscar ceremony because of a threatened travel ban on people from certain predominately Moslem countries, including Iran. Some felt this political hot potato might have influenced the judges and that the apparent leading foreign-language contenders, *Toni Erdmann* and *A Man Called Ove*, were being snubbed. Say what you will, it is the opinion of the survey that of all of the nominated films, *The Salesman* was the best of the lot and deserved the honor. It was Farhadi's second BFF win and fourth submission; he received the statuette in 2012 for *The Separation*, which also starred Shahab Hosseini (Emad). Babak Karimi was also in both films.

We are told in a written epilog at the end of Denmark's **Land of Mine** (*Under sandet*) that more explosive devices were concealed along that country's North Sea coastline during World War II than in any other Western nation: between one and two million. In May 1945, immediately following the war, young captive Germans, many still in their teens, were sent to the pristine-white, windswept beaches and forced to crawl on their bellies to locate and defuse the landmines. Martin Zandvliet's straightforward tale encapsulates an episode in this little-known event, which many label a war crime in violation of prisoner-of-war human rights as spelled out in the 1929 Geneva Convention. The motion picture evokes another disturbing BFF candidate involving young Germans at the close of the war: *The Bridge* (1960). In the beginning of *Land of Mine*, we are shown how the victorious and vengeful Danish military men held a total disregard for human life or emotions toward the young POWs. A sergeant, who already has beaten one German prisoner to within an inch of his life, is placed in charge of a cadre of twelve boys, one of whom wears an SS uniform. He trains them, drives them, starves them and locks them up at night like cattle. But predictably, as he—along with the filmgoer—gets to know their personalities, he softens. A.O. Scott, writing in the *New York Times*, says, "Mr. Zandvliet is less interested in the stark battle between good and evil than in the shifting ground of power and responsibility, and the way that every person carries the potential for decency and depravity." There is plenty of both in what *Variety* labeled a "bold, innovative, challenging" film. Zandvliet's first submission runs an hour and forty minutes of mostly German dialogue and stars an able ensemble of

Joel Basman (*left*) and Louis Hofmann perform in *Land of Mine* (2015), a runner-up in the 2017 Oscar race in which captured German boy-soldiers are forced to clear mines along the Danish coast.

young, fresh talent. Among the cast were two minor players who had parts in *A Royal Affair* (2013): Laura Bro and Mikkel Boe Følsgaard. Like *The Salesman*, this picture, which opened December 3, 2015, and in New York City February 12, 2017, also received a B+.

It is difficult to classify the German film **Toni Erdmann**. Is it farce? Is it black comedy? Is it slapstick? Basically, it's a character study about a Neanderthal-looking ex-hippy who strives to reconnect with his estranged daughter, Ines Conradi, a 30-something, unmarried career woman. She'd spent two years in faraway Shanghai and now a year as a business consultant in Bucharest where she leads a team of naïve, obsequious and sexist male coworkers as outsourcing fixers in the oil industry. Meanwhile, her father, Winfried, drops everything, leaves his ailing mother and travels to the Romanian capital to ingratiate himself with his overworked daughter, with surprising results. Along the way, he dons a pair of joke teeth and a ratty wig, takes on the alter ego "Toni Erdmann" and passes himself off to the pompous businessmen, government bigwigs and their wives as a life coach. The picture at two hours and forty-two minutes was way too long—there were a number of scenes that could be shortened or cut out altogether without ruining the effect—and at times outright silly. But that's the point, right? To create this—if not black, at least shady—comedy, director and screenwriter Maren Ade, in her first submission to the Academy, drew heavily on the talents of the two dialogue-heavy leads: Peter Simonischek, the jokester father who's made it his mission to convince his daughter through humor that she's wasting her life, and Sandra Hüller, the over-stressed, strawberry-blonde Ines. Ade also, it is said, loosely based the Toni Erdmann character on her own father. The B picture opened July 14, 2016, and in the States December 25, 2016.

To Ove Lindahl, everyone except his late departed, beloved Sonja is an idiot. The "whiteshirts" have caused him and his neighbors nothing but grief, and he's willing, and for the most part able, to accept their challenges with a take-no-prisoners defiance. In fact, attitude is a leading theme in this lovely character study from Sweden, *A Man Called Ove* (*En man som heter Ove*). The lumbering, cantankerous, 59-year-old, self-appointed, neighborhood warden is, indeed, gruff, brash and audacious, but also tenderhearted and willing to protect and defend the vulnerable at whatever cost. Ove's life, we learn through flashbacks, has endured multiple losses owing to tragic accidents, a taciturn father, schoolyard bullies, and a chance encounter with the love of his life. All have made him who he really is—a man with a literally "big heart," one as dedicated to rectifying wrongs as living up to being the assertive oaf we see him as. If there is anything wrong with this picture, it's predictability; one can guess what will happen at every twist and turn. But the story is delightful, if sentimental. It garnered a commendable B. It was director Hannes Holm's first submission, but three of his cast had BFF antecedents: star Rolf Lassgård was previously seen in *Under the Sun* (2000) and Denmark's *After the Wedding* (2007); Filip Berg was in *Evil* (2004); and Johan Widerberg, son of multiple-award-winning director Bo Widerberg, was in his father's 1996 nominee, *All Things Fair*. Released Christmas Day, 2015, and September 30, 2016, in the United States where the hour-and-fifty-six-minute film grossed nearly $3.5 million in the first three months, *Ove* cost €4 million ($4.86 million) to make, according to TrustNordisk. com.

Love hath no bounds, even in remote Oceania where half-naked natives marry off their daughters to adversarial neighbors just to keep a precarious peace in a truly tribal society. *Tanna* is unique among Best Foreign Film aspirants and is the first feature filmed in Vanuatu, a string of islands about 500 miles west of Fiji and 200 miles northeast of New Caledonia. Aussie directors Martin Butler and Bentley Dean lived nearly a year among the Yakel tribe on Tanna, one of the southern islands of the chain, where they learned of a 1987 tale of forbidden love between a young woman, Wawa, and the chief's son, Dain. Armed with a camera and one native sound man, they conscripted the island's indigenous people to tell their simple story using as backdrops the lush island jungle, rustic dwellings, a camera-ready bay of blue-green water, an actively spitting volcano and the bleak landscape of black sands, which greatly enhanced the drama and spectacle of the hour-and-forty-minute motion picture. The true tale centers on Wawa, who has fallen in love with Dain. But when the opposing tribe blames a shaman for a crop failure and murders him, the two villages come together and propose an exchange of girls in arranged marriages to avoid war. When Wawa becomes the chosen one from her village, she and her lover run away, causing a serious breach in the peace proposal. Their unforgivable action carries the drama to new heights. *Tanna* rated a B–. It opened March 10, 2016, in the Netherlands and had a short run in New York City starting September 16, 2016. It was the tenth foreign-language submission by Australia and its only nomination, although in 2010 the film *Samson and Delilah* made the January shortlist. It was the only submission by the two directors.

Index

Numbers in *bold italics* indicate pages with illustrations